VIRTUAL FUTURES

Edited by
JOAN BROADHURST DIXON
& ERIC J. CASSIDY

CYBEROTICS,
TECHNOLOGY AND POST-HUMAN
PRAGMATISM

ROUTLEDGE
London and New York

First published 1998
by Routledge
11 New Fetter Lane, London EC4P 4EE

Simultaneously published in the USA and Canada
by Routledge
29 West 35th Street, New York, NY 10001

Typeset in Grotesque & Dot Matrix by Keystroke, Jacaranda
Lodge, Wolverhampton
Printed and bound in Great Britain by The Bath Press, Bath

British Library Cataloguing in Publication Data
A catalogue record for this book is available from the British
Library

Library of Congress Cataloguing in Publication Data
Virtual futures / edited by Joan Broadhurst Dixon and Eric J.
Cassidy.
   p. cm.
   1. Technology—Social aspects. 2. Technology—
Psychological aspects. 3. Computers and civilization.
I. Dixon, Joan Broadhurst. II. Cassidy, Eric.
T14.5.V57 1998   97–19274
                     CIP

ISBN 0–415–13379–3 (hbk)
ISBN 0–415–13380–7 (pbk)

VIRTUAL FUTURES

Joan Broadhurst Dixon is a philosopher of science. She recently completed her doctorate at the University of Warwick. Eric J. Cassidy is doing research on the relationship between Deleuze and Pynchon at Warwick University. He co-ordinated the "Virtual Futures '94" and and '95 Conferences at Warwick University.

Virtual Futures explores the idea that the future lies in its ability to articulate the consequences of an increasingly synthetic and virtual world. New technologies like cyberspace, the internet, and Chaos theory are often discussed in the context of technology and its potential to liberate or in terms of technophobia. This collection examines both these ideas while also charting a new and controversial route through contemporary discourses on technology; a path that discusses the material evolution and the erotic relation between humans and machines.

Virtual Futures brings together diverse fields such as cyberfeminism, materialist philosophy, postmodern fiction, computing culture, and performance art, with essays by Sadie Plant, Stelarc, and Manuel de Landa (to name a few). The collection heralds the death of humanism and the rise of post-human pragmatism. The contested zone of debate throughout these essays is the notion of the post-human, or the possibility of the cyborg as the free human. Viewed by some writers as a threat to human life and humanism itself, the post-human is described by others in the collection as a critical perspective that anticipates the next step in evolution: the integration or synthesis of humans and machines, organic life and technology.

This view of technology and information is heavily influenced by Anglo-American literature, especially cyberpunk, Pynchon and Ballard, as well as the materialist philosophies of Freud, Deleuze, and Haraway. *Virtual Futures* provides analysis both by established theorists and by the most innovative new voices working at the conjunction between the arts and contemporary technology.

Please note that the Hebrew characters on page 52 are incorrect and should read aleph (א) and tav (ת).

CONTENTS

CONTRIBUTORS

Iain Hamilton Grant
is the translator of J. F. Lyotard's *Libidinal Economy* and J. Baudrillard's *Symbolic Exchange and Death*. He has written extensively on the early Lyotard, postmodernism, and the materialist rhizomatic structure of information culture.

Nick Land
is a lecturer in Continental Philosophy at the University of Warwick, England. He is the author of *The Thirst for Annihilation: George Bataille and Virulent Nihilism*, and the forthcoming *Schizotechnics*. He has published numerous articles on Kant, Nietzsche, Deleuze and Guattari, and the dark side of digitalization.

Matteo Mandarini
is a post-graduate philosophy student at the University of Warwick.

Stephen Metcalf
researches cultural studies at the University of Warwick, England. A self-described ex-human

Hakim Bey
is the author of *T. A. Z.: The Temporary Autonomous Zone, Ontological Anarchy*, *Poetic Terrorism*, and *Radio Sermonettes*, amongst other works. His novel *Crowstone: The Chronicles of Qamar* was hailed by William Burroughs as a new sub-genre of literature.

Joan Broadhurst Dixon
is a lecturer at the University of Derby. With Eric J. Cassidy, she organized the first "Virtual Futures"

conference. She was editor of *Deleuze and the Transcendental Unconscious*, and is currently working on two books, one on Deleuze's philosophy of science, and one entitled *Time, Consciousness and Scientific Explanation*.

Eric J. Cassidy
is a Ph.D. candidate in philosophy and literature at the University of Warwick, England. With Joan Broadhurst Dixon, he is the original organizer of "Virtual Futures," and was one of three organizers in 1995. He has written extensively on the schizoid discourses of Pynchon, Ballard, and Deleuze, in an attempt to trace their influence on the information age. He is also a past guest editor of *Pynchon Notes*.

Manuel De Landa
is the author of *War in the Age of Intelligent Machines* and the forthcoming *Phylum: A Thousand Years of Non-linear History*. He is a video artist and computer graphics artist living in New York City.

writer of noise, his work has been featured at "Virtual Futures" and he is a regular contributor at the Institute for Contemporary Art in London.

Stephen Pfohl
is an Associate Professor of Sociology at Boston College, USA, where he teaches courses on social theory, postmodern culture, deviance and social control, and images of power. He is the author of *Death at the Parasite Cafe: Social Science (Fictions) and the Postmodern*; *Predicting Dangerousness: The Social Construction of Psychiatric Reality*; and the forthcoming *Venus in Video: Cybernetics, Male Mas(s)ochism and the Parasitism of Ultramodern Power*. A video-maker, performing artist, and member of Sit Com International, Pfohl was the 1991−2 President of the Society for the Study of Social Problems.

Sadie Plant
is the author of *The Most Radical Gesture: The Situationist International in the Postmodern Age*, and the forthcoming *Beyond the Spectacle*, a

theoretical discourse on machines, markets, women, and drugs.

David Porush

teaches in the Department of Language, Literature, and Communication at Rensselaer Polytechnic Institute, USA. He is the author of the critical study *The Soft Machine: Cybernetic Fiction*, and the short story collection *Rope Dances*. He has published numerous essays in scholarly journals.

Stelarc

is a performance artist based in Melbourne.

VNS Matrix

are Australian cyberfeminists. They are the authors of the interactive *All New Gen* and perform *CorpusFantasticalMOO*, a strictly imaginative computer-generated space. They are Virginia Barratt, Francesca da Rimini, Julianne Pierce, and Josephine Starrs.

PREFACE

Virtual Futures

Eric J. Cassidy

It was a place he'd known before; not everyone could take him there, and somehow he always managed to forget it. Something he'd found and lost so many times. It belonged, he knew – he remembered – as she pulled him down, to the meat, the flesh the cowboys mocked. It was a vast thing, beyond knowing, a sea of information coded in spiral and pheromone, infinite intricacy that only the body, in its strong blind way, could ever read.

(William Gibson, *Neuromancer*: 284–5)

Many of the issues surrounding contemporary technology are conditioned by cultural beliefs as well as temporal dynamics. The reaction to emerging technologies is usually – and simplistically – divided along a horizontal axis of paranoid technophobia versus an enthusiastic endorsement of the "revolutionary" powers of "innovation." The general theme of such discussions can be summarized by the assorted political and ethical responses to the questions of technology and capitalism. Crudely summarized, the "left" political response is usually populated by a mongrel assortment of anarchists, pacifists, Luddites, and those benign curmudgeons or academic humanists that the Unabomber found so touchingly harmless. On the right we find the increasingly popular sentiments of post-human pragmatism, a neo-extropian blend of pseudo-scientific rationalism that embraces a range of techno advocates, including futurists, ravers, *Wired* magazine, and the "chaos" clique of scientific research in non-linear dynamics. This political and ethical spectrum is nicely framed by a horizontal axis that clocks the metric movement of historical, linear

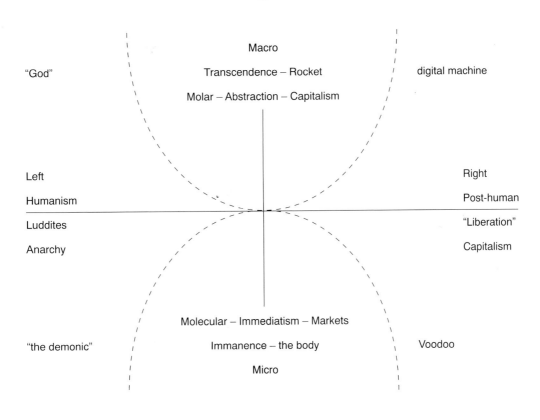

time, or processes in which human agency may still have effect.

The essays collected here develop these and other themes surrounding the fusion of cybernetics and capitalism. Yet a machinic process driving history is inadequately mapped by a Cartesian model of space and time, unless such cartography isolates the often neglected thematic of technological evolution, or the notion of an intensive vertical axis integrating technology with historical dynamics. As Henry Adams believed, there may indeed be a machinic process underlying secular history. In such a scenario, intensity is the measure of the integration of micro and macro scaler phenomena, a fusion of chaos and power, or the dynamic flux associated with shifting arrangements of material force. Exploring the perceptual and political effects of scale, machinic history is a discourse in which the macro reality of global capitalism is not mutually exclusive from "the body" as a site for engineering the future. Everything is connected, if only accessible from a certain schizoid perspective.

neo-Luddite anarchist position in which the body is a space with the potential to generate "molecular revolution"? Or is the body a limit to be transgressed, an organic system that migrates into the outer realms of "epidermal history," creating a cyberotic if not synthetic second skin capable of functioning as a site for exploring the future? To what extent does the Freud of "Beyond the Pleasure Principle" understand Thanatos as a drive coming from the inanimate? Regressing it back beyond the zero, is the death drive the model for a migrationary current carrying forces through scaled structures of organic matter in an escalation toward post-carbon pseudo-life? Is return of the repressed the nightmare vision of *Erewhon*, a realization that surplus value generated by runaway positive feedback allows vitality to be swallowed by death transfigured? Is the dark side of digitalization a countdown to the apocalypse?

If cyberpunk is a world-systems theory, then the schizoid discourses of the early 1970s are its apocalyptic precursors. Contemporary sci-fi is closely aligned with a repressed strain of Anglo-American discourse that focuses on Western culture's erotic if

While these essays occupy various positions from left to the right, neo-Luddite to radically post-human pragmatism, all take "the body" as an area whose significance for debates surrounding digital culture and global capitalism is as yet unexplored. Lost in his distinctly Cartesian view of the human/machine interface and his phenomenological description of cyberspace is Gibson's description of the body. In *Neuromancer*, the body functions as space, a site where organic matter mixes with an erotic element of synthetic fatality; a post-human apocalyptic fusion of cyberspace and eroticism.

These essays explore the future of the body as humans mutate in cyberspace. Is eroticism a tool for escaping the oppression of contemporary systems society? Or is desire the missing mechanism that drives technological evolution? What is "coming across the future"? Where is the body located "'in' cyberspace"? Must some politicized renderings of "the body" require a critique of all mediating forms of control? Should immanence be understood as a return to the organic, a naturalism in keeping with a

not evolutionary understanding of technological innovation. Cyberpunk's ancestors include the mystic technics of *Nova Express*, the technological nihilism of *We*, the millennial dystopia of *Erewhon*, and, of course, the fragmented technique of *Finnegan's Wake*. But even this context can scarcely account for the historical singularity of the early 1970s, a time that witnessed the radical reformulation of materialist narratives with the publication of such seminal texts as *Crash*, *Anti-Oedipus*, and *Libidinal Economy*. All these texts, along with *Gravity's Rainbow*, are concerned with the symbiotic relation between humans and machines, cybernetics and desire, or cyberotics.

In its most general sense, the term cyberotic identifies a particular element of early 1970s thinking and, at the same time, acts as a bridge to the information age. Despite the synthesizing power of the term for this collection, cyberotics is only a suggestion, a bit of nihilistic nomenclature, a fragmented marker that focuses on the body as the truly contested site of the future. Extrapolating from the philosophical writings of Deleuze and Guattari, cyberotics attack psychoanalysis as abstract, rarefied, the essence of representational thinking. Deleuze and Guattari describe their project in terms of synthesis, or the critical assimilation of renegade philosophical concepts into a functioning, virtual machine. They jettison traditional approaches to Freud and Marx in favor of schizoanalysis: "A truly materialist psychiatry can be defined, on the contrary, by the twofold task it sets itself: introducing desire into the mechanism, and introducing production into desire" (Deleuze and Guattari 1974: 22). Following a line of flight prepared by schizoanalysis, this collection is in part a contemporary mutation on the now tired story of postmodernity; an attempt to describe emerging technologies using materialist models perhaps best understood as a fusion of cybernetics (mechanism), economic power (production), and the technological unconscious (desire).

As VNS Matrix imply, cyberotics are interdisciplinary processes of imaginary exploration, an attempt "to meet the strange attractors reclining in deep discursive space." Materialist criticism or cyberotic production is a bottom-up synthetic critique. Critiques understood as schizoanalysis, or the importation of procedures adapted to objects through a discussion of constitutive principles. It is a philosophy of production, writings that stencil the abstract diagram of emerging world-systems and mutating material bodies. The essays included here attempt just that, varying in style from analytic philosophical prose, to fiction, to avant-garde postmodern theory. This range is a testament to the various strategies for engaging with the issues surrounding the fate of the body at the end of the twentieth century. Whether the aim of cyberotics is to "describe and deconstruct repressive formations of capital" or accelerate a historical process in which power – and technology – is out of control, one thing is certain: our virtual future is already here.

BIBLIOGRAPHY

Deleuze, Giles and Felix Guattari (1974) *Anti-Oedipus: Capitalism and Schizophrenia*, Minneapolis: University of Minnesota Press, 1983.
Gibson, William (1986) *Neuromancer*, London: Grafton Books.

ACKNOWLEDGEMENTS

First and foremost, we would like to thank those people associated with the innovative space provided for graduate research in philosophy at the University of Warwick. Included in this list are Greg Hunt, Chair of the Department of Philosophy, Keith Ansell Pearson, and Andrew Benjamin. Heather Jones, the Secretary for the Centre for Research in Philosophy and Literature, has provided tremendous support over the last few years for this and numerous other projects.

In particular, we would like to thank Nick Land for his active encouragement and exemplary commitment to innovative yet rigorous examination of the issues presented in this collection, and also David Wood who was a reluctant collaborator in this enterprise.

Adrian Driscoll, our editor at Routledge, has demonstrated infinite patience and the necessary encouragement to steer this project into the fold. Dan O'Hara was instrumental in helping organize the last two weeks of the first Virtual Futures Conference, as well as a conference organizer the following year.

Manuel De Landa's chapter first appeared in *South Atlantic Quarterly*, 92(4) (Fall 1993), © 1993 Duke University Press, and is reprinted with the kind permission of Duke University Press.

On a more personal note, EJC would like to thank Charles Cassidy for his understanding over the last few years, while also lamenting the passing of Carol Cassidy. Time is too short, memory too ephemeral. Likewise, Shannon Langdon has brought an incisive intellect and iron will to this project, without which it might never have been completed.

Similarly JBD would like to thank her chronological companions, Roger Broadhurst, John Collins, and Tim Pearce because they were all there at some time or another. And Hamilton Dixon with her schizo mothers because they were always there.

Finally, we would like to thank the graduate students of Warwick University for all the numerous conversations, drink, and energy. We are after all "the world's hardest drinking, most politically incorrect philosophers"!!

PART I

Overload

The Information War

Hakim Bey

Humanity has always invested heavily in any scheme that offers escape from the body. And why not? Material reality is such a mess. Some of the earliest "religious" artefacts, such as Neanderthal ochre burials, already suggest a belief in immortality. All modern (i.e., post-paleolithic) religions contain the "Gnostic Trace" of distrust or even outright hostility to the body and the "created" world. Contemporary "primitive" tribes and even peasant-pagans have a concept of immortality and of going-outside-the-body

Ritual Brawl is voluntary and non-hierarchic (war chiefs are always temporary); real war is compulsory and hierarchic; hyperreal war is imagistic and psychologically interiorized ("Pure War"). In the first the body is risked; in the second, the body is sacrificed; in the third, the body has disappeared (Clastes 1994).

Modern science also incorporates an anti-materialist bias, the dialectical outcome of its war against Religion: it has in some sense *become* Religion. Science as knowledge of material reality paradoxically decomposes the materiality of the real.

Science has always been a species of priestcraft, a branch of cosmology; and an ideology, a justification of "the way things are." The deconstruction of the "real" in post-classical physics mirrors the vacuum of irreality which constitutes "the state." Once the image of Heaven on Earth, the state now consists of no more than the management of images. It is no longer a "force" but a disembodied patterning of information. But just as Babylonian cosmology justified Babylonian power, so too does the "finality" of modern science serve the ends of the

(ec-stasy) without necessarily exhibiting any excessive body-hatred. The Gnostic Trace accumulates very gradually (like mercury poisoning) till eventually it turns pathological. Gnostic dualism exemplifies the extreme position of this disgust by shifting *all* value from body to "spirit." This idea characterizes what we call "civilization."

A similar trajectory can be traced through the phenomenon of "war." Hunter/gatherers practiced (and still practice, as amongst the Yanomamo) a kind of *ritualized brawl* (think of the Plains Indian custom of "counting coups"). "Real" war is a continuation of religion and economics (i.e., politics) by other means, and thus only begins historically with the priestly invention of "scarcity" in the Neolithic, and the emergence of a "warrior caste." (I categorically reject the theory that "war" is a prolongation of "hunting.") World War II seems to have been the last "real" war. *Hyperreal war* began in Vietnam, with the involvement of television, and recently reached full obscene revelation in the "Gulf War" of 1994. Hyperreal war is no longer "economic," no longer "the health of the state." The

Terminal State, the post-nuclear state, the "information state." Or so the New Paradigm would have it. And "everyone" accepts the axiomatic premises of the new paradigm. The new paradigm is very spiritual. Even the New Age with its gnostic tendencies embraces the New Science and its increasing etherealization as a source of proof-texts for its spiritualist world-view. Meditation and cybernetics go hand in hand. Of course the "information state" somehow requires the support of a police force and prison system that would have stunned Nebuchadnezzar and reduced all the priests of Moloch to paroxysms of awe. And "modern science" still can't weasel out of its complicity in the very-nearly-successful "conquest of Nature." Civilization's greatest triumph over the body. But who cares? It's all "relative" isn't it? I guess we'll just have to "evolve" beyond the body. Maybe we can do it in a "quantum leap."

Meanwhile, the excessive *mediation* of the Social, which is carried out through the machinery of the Media, increases the intensity of our alienation from the body by fixating the flow of attention on *information* rather than direct experience. In this sense the Media serves a religious or priestly role, appearing to offer us a way out of the body by re-defining spirit as information. The essence of information is the Image, the sacral and iconic data-complex which usurps the primacy of the "material bodily principle" as the vehicle of incarnation, replacing it with a fleshless ecstasy beyond corruption. Consciousness becomes something which can be "downloaded," excised from the matrix of animality and immortalized as information. No longer "ghost-in-the-machine," but machine-as-ghost, machine as Holy Ghost, ultimate mediator, which will *translate* us from our mayfly-corpses to a pleroma of Light. Virtual Reality as CyberGnosis. Jack in, leave Mother Earth behind forever.

All science proposes a paradigmatic universalism: as in science, so in the social. Classical physics played midwife to Capitalism, Communism, Fascism, and other Modern ideologies. Post-classical science also proposes a set of ideas meant to be applied to the social: Relativity, Quantum "unreality," cybernetics, information theory, etc. With some

An important part of this rhetoric involves the concept of an "information economy." The post-Industrial world is now thought to be giving birth to this new economy. One of the clearest examples of the concept can be found in a recent book by a man who is a Libertarian, the Bishop of a Gnostic Dualist Church in California, and a learned and respected writer for *Gnosis* magazine:

The industry of the past phase of civilization (sometimes called "low technology") was big industry, and bigness always implies oppressiveness. The new high technology, however, is not big in the same way. While the old technology produced and distributed material resources, the new technology produces and disseminates information. The resources marketed in high technology are less about matter and more about mind. Under the impact of high technology, the world is moving increasingly from a physical economy into what might be called a "metaphysical economy." We are in the process of recognizing that consciousness rather than raw materials or physical resources constitute wealth.

(Hoeller 1992: 229–30)

Modern neo-Gnosticism usually plays down the old Manichaean attack on the body for gentler, greener

4

exceptions, the post-classical tendency is toward ever-greater etherealization. Some proponents of Black Hole theory, for example, talk like pure Pauline theologians, while some of the information theorists are beginning to sound like virtual Manichaeans.[1]

On the level of the social these paradigms give rise to a rhetoric of bodilessness quite worthy of a third-century desert monk or a seventeenth-century New England Puritan – but expressed in a *language* of post-Industrial post-Modern feel-good consumer frenzy. Our every conversation is infected with certain paradigmatic assumptions which are really no more than bald assertions, but which we take for the very fabric or *Urgrund* of Reality itself. For instance, since we now *assume* that computers represent a real step toward "artificial intelligence," we also assume that buying a computer makes us more intelligent. In my own field I've met dozens of writers who sincerely believe that owning a PC has made them better (not "more efficient," but better) writers. This is amusing – but the same *feeling* about computers when applied to a trillion-dollar military budget, churns out Star Wars, killer robots, etc.[2]

rhetoric. Bishop Hoeller, for instance, stresses the importance of ecology and environment (because we don't want to "foul our nest," the Earth) – but in his chapter on Native American spirituality he implies that a cult of the Earth is clearly inferior to the pure Gnostic spirit of bodilessness:

But we must not forget that the nest is not the same as the bird. The exoteric and esoteric traditions declare that earth is not the only home for human beings, that we did not grow like weeds from the soil. While our bodies indeed may have originated on this earth, our inner essence did not. To think otherwise puts us outside of all of the known spiritual traditions and separates us from the wisdom of the seers and sages of every age. Though wise in their own ways, Native Americans have small connection with this rich spiritual heritage.

(Hoeller 1992: 164)

In such terms (the body = the "savage"), the Bishop's hatred and disdain for the flesh illuminate every page of his book. In his enthusiasm for a truly religious economy, he forgets that one cannot *eat* "information." "Real wealth" can never become immaterial until humanity achieves the final etherealization of downloaded consciousness. Information in the form of culture can be called wealth metaphorically because it is useful and desirable – but it can never be wealth in precisely the same basic way that oysters and cream, or wheat and water, are wealth *in themselves*. Information is always only information about some thing. Like money, information is not the thing itself. Over time we can come to think of money as wealth (as in a delightful Taoist ritual which refers to "Water and Money" as the two most vital principles in the universe), but in truth this is sloppy abstract thinking. It has allowed its focus of attention to wander from the bun to the penny which symbolizes the bun.[3]

In effect we've had an "information economy" ever since we invented money. But we still haven't learned to digest copper. The Aesopian crudity of these truisms embarrasses me, but I must perforce play the stupid lazy yokel plowing a crooked furrow when all the straight thinkers around me appear to be hallucinating. Americans and other "First World" types seem particularly susceptible to the rhetoric of a "metaphysical

Towel-heads in the Middle East suffer and die for our sins. Life? Oh, our servants do that for us. We have no life, only "lifestyle" – an abstraction of life, based on the sacred symbolism of the Commodity, mediated by the priesthood of the stars, those "larger than life" abstractions who rule our values and people our dreams – the mediarchetypes; or perhaps *mediarchs* would be a better term.

Of course this Baudrillardian dystopia doesn't really exist – yet.[4] It's surprising, however, to note how many social radicals consider it a desirable goal, at least as long as it's called the "Information Revolution" or something equally inspiring. Leftists talk about seizing the means of information-production from the data-monopolists.[5] In truth, information is everywhere – even atom bombs can be constructed on plans available in public libraries. As Noam Chomsky points out, one can always access information – provided one has a private income and a fanaticism bordering on insanity. Universities and "think tanks" make pathetic attempts to monopolize information – they too are dazzled by the notion of an information economy – but their

5

economy" because we can no longer see (or feel or smell) around us very much evidence of a physical world. Our architecture has become symbolic, we have enclosed ourselves in the manifestations of abstract thought (cars, apartments, offices, schools), we work at "service" or information-related jobs, helping in our little way to move disembodied symbols of wealth around an abstract grid of Capital, and we spend our leisure largely engrossed in Media rather than in direct experience of material reality. The material world for us has come to symbolize catastrophes, as in our amazingly hysterical reaction to storms and hurricanes (proof that we've failed to "conquer Nature" entirely), or our neo-Puritan fear of sexual otherness, or our taste for bland and denatured (almost abstract) food. And yet, this "First World" economy is not self-sufficient. It depends for its position (top of the pyramid) on a vast substructure of old-fashioned material production. Mexican farm-workers grow and package all that "Natural" food for us so we can devote our time to stocks, insurance, law, computers, video games. Peons in Taiwan make silicon chips for our PCs.

conspiracies are laughable. Information may not always be "free," but there's a great deal more of it available than any one person could ever possibly use. Books on every conceivable subject can actually still be found through inter-library loan.[6] Meanwhile, someone still has to grow pears and cobble shoes. Or, even if these "industries" can be completely mechanized, someone still has to eat pears and wear shoes. The body is still the basis of wealth. The idea of Images as wealth is a "spectacular delusion."

Even a radical critique of "information" can still give rise to an over-valuation of abstraction and data. In a "pro-situ" zine from England called *NO*, the following message was scrawled messily across the back cover of a recent issue:

As you read these words, the Information Age explodes . . . inside and around you – with the Misinformation Missiles and Propaganda bombs of outright Information Warfare.

Traditionally, war has been fought for territory/economic gain. Information Wars are fought for the acquisition of territory indigenous to the Information Age, i.e., the human mind itself. In particular, it is the faculty of the imagination that is under the direct threat of extinction from the onslaughts of multi-media overload. . . . DANGER – YOUR IMAGINATION MAY NOT BE YOUR OWN. . . . As a culture sophisticates, it deepens its reliance on its images, icons and symbols as a way of defining itself and communicating with other cultures. As the accumulating mix of a culture's images floats around in its collective psyche, certain isomorphic icons coalesce to produce and to project an "illusion" of reality. Fads, fashions, artistic trends. U KNOW THE SCORE. "I can take their images for reality because I believe in the reality of their images (their image of reality)." WHOEVER CONTROLS THE METAPHOR GOVERNS THE MIND. The conditions of total saturation are slowly being realized – a creeping paralysis – from the trivialization of special/technical knowledge to the specialization of trivia. The INFORMATION WAR is a war we cannot afford to lose. The result is unimaginable.[7]

I find myself very much in sympathy with the author's critique of media here, yet I also feel that a demonization of "information" has been proposed which consists of nothing more than the mirror-image of information-as-salvation. Again Baudrillard's vision of the Commtech Universe is evoked, but this time as Hell rather than as the Gnostic Hereafter. Bishop

helps us to seize or to construct our own happiness. In this sense we do know of "information as wealth"; nevertheless we continue to desire wealth itself and not merely its abstract representation as information. At the same time we also know of "information as war";[8] nevertheless, we have not decided to embrace ignorance just because "facts" can be used like a poison gas. Ignorance is not even an adequate defense, much less a useful weapon in this war. We attempt neither to fetishize nor demonize "information." Instead we try to establish a set of values by which information can be measured and assessed. Our standard in this process can only be the body.

According to certain mystics, spirit and body is "one." Certainly *spirit* has lost its ontological solidity (since Nietzsche, anyway), while *body's* claim to "reality" has been undermined by modern science to the point of vanishing in a cloud of "pure energy." So why not assume that spirit and body *are* one, after all, and that they are twin (or dyadic) aspects of the same underlying and inexpressible real? No body without spirit, no spirit without body. The Gnostic

Hoeller wants everybody jacked-in and down-loaded – the anonymous post-situationist ranter wants you to smash your telly – but both of them believe in the mystic power of information. One proposes the *pax technologica*, the other declares "war." Both exude a kind of Manichaean view of Good and Evil, but can't agree on which is which.

The critical theorist swims in a sea of facts. We like to imagine it also as our *maquis*, with ourselves as the "guerilla ontologists" of its datascape. Since the nineteenth century the ever-mutating "social sciences" have unearthed a vast hoard of information on everything from shamanism to semiotics. Each "discovery" feeds back into "social science" and changes it. We *drift*. We fish for *poetic facts*, data which will intensify and mutate our experience of the real. We invent new hybrid "sciences" as tools for this process: ethnopharmacology, ethnohistory, cognitive studies, history of ideas, subjective anthropology (anthropological poetics or ethno-poetics), "dada epistemology," etc. We look on all this knowledge not as "good" in itself, but valuable only inasmuch as it

Dualists are wrong, as are the vulgar "dialectical materialists." Body and spirit together make life. If either pole is missing, the result is death. This constitutes a fairly simple set of values, assuming we prefer life to death. Obviously I'm avoiding any strict definitions of either body or spirit. I'm speaking of "empirical" everyday experiences. We experience "spirit" when we dream or create; we experience "body" when we eat or shit (or maybe vice versa); we experience both at once when we make love. I'm not proposing metaphysical categories here. We're still *drifting* and these are *ad hoc* points of reference, nothing more. We needn't be mystics to propose this version of "one reality." We need only point out that no other *reality* has yet appeared within the context of our knowable experience. For all practical purposes, the "world" is "one."[9]

Historically, however, the "body" half of this unity has always received the insults, bad press, scriptural condemnation, and economic persecution of the "spirit" half. The self-appointed representatives of the spirit have called almost all the tunes in known history, leaving the body only a pre-history of primitive disappearance, and a few spasms of failed insurrectionary futility. Spirit has ruled – hence we scarcely even know how to speak the language of the body. When we use the word "information" we reify it because we have always reified abstractions – ever since God appeared as a burning bush. (Information as the catastrophic decorporealization of "brute" matter.) We would now like to propose the identification of self with body. We're not denying that "the body is also spirit," but we wish to restore some balance to the historical equation. We calculate all body-hatred and world-slander as *our* "evil." We insist on the revival (and mutation) of "pagan" values concerning the relation of body and spirit. We fail to feel any great enthusiasm for the "information economy" because we see it as yet another mask for body-hatred. We can't quite believe in the "information war," since it also hypostatizes *information* but labels it "evil."

In this sense, "information" would appear to be *neutral*. But we also distrust this third position as a lukewarm cop-out and a failure of theoretical vision.

"Knowledge is freedom" is true only when freedom is understood as a psycho-kinetic skill. "Information" is chaos; knowledge is the spontaneous ordering of that chaos; freedom is the surfing of the wave of that spontaneity.

These tentative conclusions constitute the shifting and marshy ground of our "theory." The TAZ (temporary autonomous zone) wants all information and all bodily pleasure in a great complex confusion of sweet data and sweet dates – facts and feasts – wisdom and wealth. This is our economy – and our war.

NOTES

1 The new "life" sciences offer some dialectical opposition here, or could do so if they worked through certain paradigms. Chaos theory seems to deal with the material world in positive ways, as does Gaia theory, morphogenetic theory, and various other "soft" and "neo-hermetic" disciplines. Elsewhere I've attempted to incorporate these philosophical implications into a "festal" synthesis. The point is not to abandon all thought about the material world, but to realize that all science has philosophical

Every "fact" takes different *meanings* as we run it through our dialectical prism[10] and study its gleam and shadows. The "fact" is never inert or "neutral," but it can be both "good" and "evil" (or beyond them) in countless variations and combinations. We, finally, are the artists of this immeasurable discourse. We create values. We do this because we are alive. Information is as big a "mess" as the material world it reflects and transforms. We embrace the mess, all of it. It's all life. But within the vast *chaos* of the alive, certain information and certain material things begin to coalesce into a poetics or a way-of-knowing or a way-of-acting. We *can* draw certain pro tem "conclusions," as long as we don't plaster them over and set them up on altars.

Neither "information" nor indeed any one "fact" constitutes a thing-in-itself. The very word "information" implies an ideology, or rather a paradigm, rooted in unconscious fear of the "silence" of matter and of the universe. "Information" is a substitute for *certainty*, a left-over fetish of dogmatics, a *super-stitio*, a spook. "Poetic facts" are not assimilable to the doctrine of "information."

and political implications, and that science is a way of thinking, not a dogmatic structure of incontrovertible Truth. Of course quantum, relativity, and information theory are all "true" in some way and can be given a positive interpretation. I've already done that in several essays. Now I want to explore the negative aspects.

2 See the work of Manuel De Landa on Artificial Intelligence in modern weaponry (De Landa 1991).

3 Like Pavlov's dog salivating at the dinner bell rather than the dinner: a perfect illustration of what I mean by "abstraction."

4 Although some might say that it already "virtually" exists. I just heard from a friend in California of a new scheme for "universal prisons" – offenders will be allowed to live at home and *go to work* but will be electronically monitored at all times, like Winston Smith in *1984*. The universal panopticon now potentially coincides one-to-one with the whole of reality; life and work will take the place of outdated physical incarceration: the Prison Society will merge with "electronic democracy" to form a *Surveillance State* or *information totality*, with all time and space compacted beneath the unsleeping gaze of RoboCop. On the level of pure tech, at least, it would seem that we have at last arrived at "the future." "Honest citizens" of course will have nothing to fear; hence terror will reign unchallenged and

Order will triumph like the Universal Ice. Our only hope may lie in the "chaotic perturbation" of massively-linked computers, and in the venal stupidity or boredom of those who program and monitor the system.

5 I will always remember with pleasure being addressed, by a Bulgarian delegate to a conference I once attended, as a "fellow worker in philosophy." Perhaps the capitalist version would be "entrepreneur in philosophy," as if one bought ideas like apples at roadside stands.

6 Of course information may sometimes be "occult," as in Conspiracy Theory. Information may be "disinformation." Spies and propagandists make up a kind of shadow "information economy," to be sure. Hackers who believe in "freedom of information" have my sympathy, espcially since they've been picked as the latest enemies of the Spectacular State, and subjected to its spasms of control-by-terror. But hackers have yet to "liberate" a single bit of information useful in our struggle. Their impotence, and their fascination with Imagery, make them ideal victims of the "Information State," which itself is based on pure simulation. One needn't steal data from the post-military-industrial complex to know, in general, *what it's up to*. We understand enough to form our critique. More *information* by itself will never take the place of the actions we have failed to

light" teachings. "All is one," therefore, can be spoken by any kind of monist or anti-dualist and can mean many different things.

10 A proposal: the new theory of *taoist dialectics*. Think of the yin/yang disc, with a spot of black in the white lozenge, and vice versa – separated not by a straight line but an S-curve. Amiri Baraka says that dialectics is just "separating out the good from the bad" – but the taoist is "beyond good and evil." The dialectic is supple, but the *taoist dialectic* is downright sinuous. For example, making use of the taoist dialectic, we can re-evaluate Gnosis once again. True, it presents a negative view of the body and of becoming. But it is true also that it has played the role of the eternal rebel against all orthodoxy, and this makes it *interesting*. In its libertine and revolutionary manifestations the Gnosis possesses many secrets, some of which are actually worth knowing. The organizational forms of Gnosis – the crackpot cult, the secret society – seem pregnant with possibilities for the TAZ/Immediatist project. Of course, as I've pointed out elsewhere, not all gnosis is Dualistic. There also exists a monist gnostic tradition, which sometimes borrows heavily from Dualism and is often confused with it. Monist gnosis is anti-eschatological, using religious language to describe *this* world, not Heaven or the Gnostic Pleroma.

carry out; data by itself wil never reach critical mass. Despite my loving debt to thinkers like Robert Anton Wilson and Timothy Leary I cannot agree with their optimistic analysis of the cognitive function of information technology. It is not neural system alone which will achieve autonomy, but the entire body.

7 Issue 6, "Nothing is True," Box 175, Liverpool L69 8DX, United Kingdom.

8 Indeed, the whole "poetic terrorism" project has been proposed only as a strategy in this very war.

9 The "'World is 'one'" can be and has been used to justify a *totality*, a metaphysical ordering of "reality" with a "center" or "apex:" one God, one King, etc., etc. This is the monism of orthodoxy, which naturally opposes Dualism and its *other* source of power ("evil") – orthodoxy also presupposes that the One occupies a higher ontological position than the Many, that transcendence takes precedence over immanence. What I call radical (or heretical) monism demands unity of one and Many on the level of immanence; hence it is seen by Orthodoxy as a turning-upside-down or saturnalia which proposes that every "one" is equally "divine." Radical monism is "on the side of the Many – which explains why it seems to lie at the heart of *pagan polytheism* and shamanism, as well as extreme forms of monotheism such as Ismailism or Ranterism, based on "inner

Shamanism, certain "crazy" forms of Taoism and Tantra and Zen, heterodox sufism and Ismailism, Christian antinomians such as the Ranters, etc. share a conviction of the holiness of the "inner spirit," and of the actually real, the "world." These are our "spiritual ancestors."

BIBLIOGRAPHY

Clastes, P. (1994) *The Archeology of Violence*, New York: Semiotext(e).
De Landa, M. (1991) *War in the Age of Intelligent Machines*, New York: Zone Books.

PART II

Cyberotics

Theses on the Cyberotics of HIStory: Venus in Microsoft, remix

Stephen Pfohl

One evening as the moon is waning radon, I spy the telematic form of a blonde on blonde goddess at the cinema. Maybe I'm s/he. Her filmic body ablaze to my projective pleasure, her bare legs sex lips ass open to the always only partial visible "ends of Man." For the price of a ticket I get to participate in a dreamy bending of industrial taboos escaping HIStory. I feel at once anxious and numb. This is fascinating. I watch myself watching myself watching my fantasies while watching my fantasies watching myself. This is I. Just look at the statistics.

At the film's climax a stony cold Goddess dressed in nothing but furs stands transfigured as a blank-faced male double showers her with spurts of white liquid CAPITAL. Maybe I'm s/he. I am transferred into the microsoft: aroused and electric. This is my body – a telematic exchange of faith leaping screen to screen. This is whitemale techno-magic. This is obscene. This is fascinating. The next thing I know they're strapping me into a cockpit and blind-folding me with information. "Baghdad's your target," I hear a white man in black face saying. These are my orders. "Jack off as often as you want. Nobody will say; nobody will see; nobody will smell a thing."

As *I was returning from my devotions*, the thought came to mind that no house without a TV is a home (to me). I entered the always open VIDEO PALACE, feeling more sovereign than solid state and more (trans)sexual than ever. Mouth to screen to mouth: I was hungry and wanted what's more than bodies can give. Suddenly I saw a woman's figure glowing electric. As beautiful as celluloid, she was separated from me by nothing but a cold screen of data. I was

confident I'd access her image. Maybe s/he was I. It seemed as if the PRETTY WOMAN from the screen *had taken pity on me, come alive, and followed me* home in a plastic bag. *I was seized by a nameless fear, my heart threatened to burst* (Sacher-Masoch 1989: 66).

I

The story is told of an automaton constructed in such a way that it could play a winning game of JEOPARDY, answering each of its opponents' memories with a counter-memory. An orphan in World Beat attire and something unnameable in its mouth sat before the game bored flashing to the home viewing audience. A system of screens created the illusion that this game was transparent from all sides. Actually, a little parasite who was an expert JEOPARDY player sat inside and guided the orphan's maneuvers by remote control. One can imagine a geographical counterpart to this device. The orphan called "HIStorical materialist geography"

is partially to win, just as it loses itself in the timely conjuring of alternative spaces. It can uneasily become a power-reflexive match for anybody if it but enlists the services of radical atheology, which today, as we know, is wizened and has to keep out of sight. In mass demonstrations against the U.S.-led attack on Iraq all the anarchists wore masks.

II

When something becomes a *structural possibility* it is constituted as functionally effective, factually objective and morally valued or economic. This is what distinguishes a structural possibility from the fleshy contingencies of totemic simulation. Structural possibilities parasite off what (modern) powers render absent. This is no universal law. This is a way of trying both to describe and deconstruct the constitutive violence of white patriarchal CAPITAL.

For better and for worse. Like the soul of a commodity, or the cut-up subjectivity of women, slaves and wage laborers, persons tattooed by modern power are cast as tragic actors, whose every thought is scripted by an agency of white letters. This is a way of describing discursive language – representational rites enacted by men whose words one can bank on. Credit-worthy men; men who have much to give to (and thus take away from) the ritual scenes they govern. These are scenes of imperial technology or white magic.

Like all forms of technology (or magic) these white magical scenes operate in the shadows of what appears more originary – the space of sacrifice, elementary religious forms, scientific displacements, or whatever. By contrast, technologies of black magic simulate the disabling powers of sacrifice. In so doing, they return the fantastic surplus that separates them from others. This is what make black magic technology so seductive and so healing. Practitioners of white magic technologies, on the other hand, labor to cover over the gaps: securing the losses, extending the boundaries, exacting a fetishized surplus as profit.

Not far from the space in which I'm (w)riting there is a transnational bio-tech firm named

differences remain. These claims cannot be settled cheaply. HIStorically material geographers are aware of that, even if melancholic about prospects for redemption.

III

A cartographer who maps spaces without distinguishing between major and minor acts in accordance with the following truth: no events should be lost for cyberotic geography. To be sure, only a partially redeemed (or power reflexive) human/animalkind is given to heterogeneous spatiality – which is to say, its range of self-limiting structural possibilities become (ex)citable as ritual bindings and boundaries spin vertiginously. This is ruinous awareness. It is stupid to wait for some final Judgment Day when here in the space between us we might be touched by a more poetic form of geography, a cyberotic geography that plays back upon itself in orphaned waves and (dis)autobiographical musing. But isn't such cursed

NARCISSUS. Its business is both ARTIFICIAL INTELLIGENCE and VIRTUAL REALITY. Its business is the rearrangement of entertaining memories for maximal profit and the forgetting of everything else. Its business is war or the (sacrificial) production of orphans. This business, an extension of sadism, or the masterful male dream of purified enlightenment, involves both more and less than sadism. This business is mas(s)ochistic in the general economic sense of the word. It offers an image of pain or unhappiness as indissolubly BOUND UP with an image of redemption or liberation – *the ecstasy of communication*. This business blurs the sexualized difference between tragedy (where things appear in the form of their doubles) and farce (where even doubled revolution is premodeled for user-friendly markets world-wide). The same applies to our view of boundaries, which is the concern of geography. There today appears to be a secret agreement between those (of us) on the outside and those parts of us that are stupidly in the know. This is indistinction, not simply victimization. But on all sides the business of mas(s)ochism parasites off whatever

geography condemned to silence and the chaos of dark laughter? Perhaps that's just the point (at which such a wicked form of geography begins again and again and again).

IV

Seek for signs of food and clothing first, then the Symbolic Order shall be added onto you, if at the same time subtracted from your bodies.

(Black Madonna Durkheim)

The class struggle, which is always partially present to a cyberotic geographer influenced by Marx, is a fight for the material and imaginary spaces of memory.

Nevertheless, it is not in the form of the spoils which fall to the victor that the latter make their presence felt in the class struggle. They manifest themselves in this struggle as courage, humor, cunning, and fortitude. They have a retroactive force and will constantly call in question every victory, past and present, of the rulers.

(Benjamin 1969a: 254–5)

An erotic geographer must be aware of this most inconspicuous of transformations – the contradictory accessing of spaces in excess of a given order of things in time.

At 8 o'clock on June 23, 1787 in the heat of revolutionary CAPITALial expansion (of the "Rights of Man" over "Nature"), the Marquis de Sade began composing a new novel. A preliminary note reads: "Two [orphaned] sisters, one, extremely dissipated (Juliette), has a happy, rich and success-ful life; the other (Justine), extremely strait-laced, falls into a thousand traps, which end by causing her ruin" (Cleugh 1951: 107). Justine's story was completed first. It appeared in 1791, the year in which the new French Penal Code announced mathematically precise punishments for each and every infraction of the law. This was also the year of the Voodoo-inspired revolt of Africans enslaved by the French in Haiti. It is tempting to read Sade's pornographic enclosure of Justine's orphaned body as a monstrous allegory of a New World Order of economic restrictions. The libertines who assault Justine inscribe their truths upon her skin,

HIStory. Juliette is well paid for her sacrifices. At the end of her novel existence she dies at peace, well defended from those she parasites.

Between the (w)ritings of one orphan sister and anOther the world has changed. Justine could not be rationally persuaded, but her sister is seduced into a new form of sadistic training. She has been converted to the ways of modern men by a corrupt abbess in charge of the orphans' education. She joins in the educative process, or so it appears in the (w)ritings of sadism. As Foucault remarks, between Justine's text and Juliette's, a new form of power has entered the world, a new form of parasitism. It feeds ruinously upon all that remains outside the narcissistic confines of the normalized ego.

The disciplinary hollowing out of interior psychic space has begun. In this,

[V]iolence, life and death, desire, and sexuality will extend, below the level of representation, an immense expanse of shade which we are now attempting to recover, as far as we can, in our discourse, in our freedom, in our thought. But our thought is so brief, our freedom

13

penetrating her with rational logic and the promise of control. Justine resists being incorporated into this narrative of Western (male) desire, but her resis-tance brings nothing but tragedy. She is tortured and raped, and although she tries to escape, there is no escape. Unlike her Haitian counterparts, Justine is on her own. She is denied what African slaves kept secretly alive – ritual access to spaces less vulnerable to the narcissistic terrors and death-defying promises of CAPITALized selfhood. Her hopes for better futures LIE (nostalgically) in the past. She is slain by the electricity of this novel moment in HIStory.

Justine's death is tragic. This is not the case with her sister. Juliette is an orphan who mutates in accordance with the structural possibilities of an unprecedented space of modern subjectivity. Hers is a story of the farcical pleasures offered (even, if in contradictory ways, to women) by giving oneself over to the cynical demands of life within the disciplinary thickness of one's own skin. Juliette's story appears in 1797. Unlike Justine, she prostitutes herself, becoming a "grand thief" and property owner. This is

so enslaved, our discourse so repetitive, that we must face the fact that that expanse of shade below is really a bottomless sea. The prosperities of *Juliette* are still more solitary – and endless.

(Foucault 1970: 210-11)

V

The true picture of cyberotic spaces barred from what is structurally possible flits by. Such spaces are recognizable only as images which flash by in an instant; fleeting gaps that defy words, leftovers from some unacknowledged sacrificial meal. These uncanny spaces involve the ghostly reappearance of what's been made to disappear; seeing what's been rendered as unseeable; hearing what's been silenced; tasting what's forbidden; touched by the smell of rotting fruit.

During the first half of the nineteenth century such useless spaces were by no means forgotten (or fully repressed) by those most sacrificed for the sadistic expansion of CAPITAL. Whole classes fought back, only to be defeated by superior military and industrial force. In 1848, while CAPITAL spread westward across the U.S., deploying wholesale genocide and slavery, in Europe resistance disrupted the geography of the market nearly everywhere – but not for long. The revolutions of 1848 were met with excessive state violence. The brutal subordination of Czech proletarians in Prague was a case in point. One of the bloodiest restorations of CAPITALt power, the suppression of the popular uprising in Prague, was also a scene of sacrifice witnessed by a 10-year-old boy, Leopold von Sacher-Masoch. His father was the Chief of Police.

Two years earlier, the young Masoch had been exposed to similar stories of violence in Galacia, a district forming the northeast corner of the Austrian Empire. During a revolt of Polish landlords that turned into a three-party war involving nationalistic aristocrats, Polish peasants and the Austrian army, fantastic scenarios of revolt were met by even greater counter-revolutionary violence. Tales of indiscriminate massacres – mass hangings, burnings, torture, and burials alive – passed into the ears of the Police Chief's son. Masoch's memories of such

ball in Lemberg. Wires were to be fitted to the necks of the officers as an incident in a sort of allegorical masque, then applied in grim earnest" (Cleugh 1951: 154). Although a death in the Hapsburg family led to the cancellation of officers' plans to attend the ball, thus derailing this cunning act of rebellion, Leopold himself forever related stories about the bravery of women during the bloody events in Prague. He

used to tell his friends . . . that he had been out on the barricades, as a boy of twelve, with a girl cousin named Miroslava, some years older than himself. She wore a beautiful fur jacket, he would say, and carried pistols in her belt. She ordered him about, shouted commands, he hastened to obey. Amid these scenes of death and destruction he conceived a passionate adoration of her.

(Cleugh 1951: 155)

Mythic in appearance, these images of women's power were translated by Masoch into allegories of men giving themselves as consenting slaves to cruel female tyrants. This represents a fantastic (if also fantastically distorted) mode of keeping alive certain images of resistance to the sadistic male demands of

14

revolutionary defeats did more than fuel a passion for repeating such ill-fated dramas in the spectacles he staged with tin soldiers and puppets. They also provided a material context for the imaginative form of (w)riting with which his name has come to be associated, and for the paradoxical pleasures and pains such (w)ritings elicit in HIStory. From the nineteenth century to the present, Mas(s)ochism signifies a contradictory erotic flight-path from the disciplinary confines of sadistic CAPITALt expansion.

In both his immediate family situation, where Leopold found himself enamored by the seductive charms of his scandalous paternal aunt, the Countess Zenobia, and in his memories of the HIStorical scenery of defeated revolutions, the role of powerful Slavic women loomed large. Indeed, within the cultural geographies of Galacia and Prague there circulated many stories of the public actions of brave and powerful women. One curious aspect of the 1846 Polish rebellion in Galacia involved women in "a fantastic plan for the strangling of their Austrian dancing partners at a great military

profit-driven CAPITAL. This is to read subversive, if contradictory, male pleasures in Masoch's tales and the mas(s)ochistic rites for which they are culturally emblematic.

A century later, Barbara Ehrenreich would locate a related space of contradictory subversion in the pornographic rituals of middle-class U.S. men. In *The Hearts of Men*, Ehrenreich theorizes that – if only in fantasy – these men were able partially to escape CAPITAL boredom by giving themselves in masturbatory pleasure – not to fleshy women – but to glossy *Playboy* centerfolds (Ehrenreich 1983). Without condoning pornography's distorted representations of women, Ehrenreich argues that the contradictory pleasures of having fantasized sex with glossy magazine images may have engendered spaces not fully integrated into the disciplined patriarchal circuitry of post-World War II CAPITAL. Within the historical geography of the moment, these perverse spaces – although susceptible to further colonization – made visible contradictions that might, otherwise, have remained disguised. For indeed, "every image . . . that is not in some way recognized by the present as one of its own concerns threatens to disappear entirely" (Benjamin 1969a: 255).

VI

To articulate spaces of a contradictory erotic possibility does not mean to recognize the totality of all geographical relations at a given point of time. It means, instead, to attend to the form of a particular fantasy as it flashes up at a moment of danger. Erotic geography wishes to reflex upon that image of space which unexpectedly appears in a terrain fraught with bodily and/or psychic danger. For the critical geographer is vigilant in the awareness that in order to spark hope in the realizability of less hierarchical spaces, one must be "firmly convinced that even the dead will not be safe from the enemy if he wins. And this enemy has not ceased to be victorious" (Benjamin 1969a: 255).

As a professor of HIStory, Leopold von Sacher-Masoch believed this as well. Masoch suffered passions which he read as symptomatic of a

cycle. Published under the title *Love*, these controversial texts provocatively mirror and excessively articulate the sickening impossibilities of enacting free and generous forms of erotic exchange in a society governed by self-serving economic contracts. By "'desexualizing' love and at the same time sexualizing the entirety HIStory of humanity," Masoch's (w)ritings cross his own biographical desires with the parasitic economic exigencies of CAPITAL (Deleuze 1989: 12).

The texts comprising *Love* were completed in 1870. The following year, international CAPITAL violently closed in upon the heterogeneous, non-authoritarian, and vernacular erotic geographies defended to death by the Paris Commune. Before being massacred, the Commune conjured into existence a form of space conceived "not as a static reality but as active, generative [and] created by interaction, as something that our bodies reactivate, and . . . in turn modifies and transforms us" (Ross 1988: 35). The spatial erotics engendered by the commune, like the remaining cycles of Masoch's *The Heritage of Cain*, would remain forever fragmentary

diseased culture – a society haunted by the failure of revolutions to stem the sadistic spread of CAPITAL. Masoch's published texts are typically read as pornographic tales of excessive male submission to the cold tyranny of cruel women masters, among them various figurations of "Mother Nature." These stories are better understood as elements of Masoch's life-long project of allegorical social commentary. Indeed, *Venus in Furs*, the classic text of mas(s)ochistic male literature, was itself part of a series of six stories which were to figure as but one of six larger cycles comprising *The Heritage of Cain* (Sacher-Masoch 1989). Masoch selected this title to suggest "the burden of crime and suffering" that had become the cursed heritage of modern "men," for whom nature was nothing but an icy cold Mother. As Gilles Deleuze points out, "the coldness of the stern mother is in reality a transmutation from which the new man [of CAPITAList modernity] emerges" (Deleuze 1989: 12).

Venus in Furs, along with *The Wanderer*, *The Man of Surrenders*, *Moonlight Night*, *Plato's Love*, and *Marzella*, constituted the first phase of this

and incomplete. Indeed, the proposed names for the remaining cycles in *The Heritage of Cain* are suggestive of ritual enclosures dominating the Western imagination of erotic life during the late nineteenth century – *Property*, *The State*, *War*, *Work*, and *Death*.

Masoch's life ended in fragments as well. Blocked by personal, HIStorical, and geographic circumstances from forming more reciprocal alliances with others, Masoch – like Sade before him – retreated into the imaginary pleasures of male fantasy, until the fantasies imploded and left Masoch striking out in mad rage at the woman he called his wife. But by then, Masoch was old and his prestigious literary reputation slipping. On March 9, 1895, Masoch, an author compared to the greatest of his European contemporaries, was committed to an insane asylum in Mannheim.

During his lifetime, Masoch's literary and personal fantasies were already (mis)diagnosed by the psychiatrist Kraft-Ebbing as passive counterparts to Sade's. A more careful reading of Masoch's texts suggests something more contradictory. Masoch's (w)ritings engendered ambivalent spaces of erotic fantasy in excess of the dominant discourses of his time. In this, Masoch's allegorical narratives, with their ambivalent displays of fantastic male submission, foreshadowed aspects of the erotic geography of the emerging industrial masses. Like Masoch's male protagonists, the *masses* may have ritually absorbed, rather than identified with, CAPITAL's most virulent economic restrictions. This is not to suggest that perverse spaces of erotic resistance are ever free of the violence of CAPITAL. Nor are they timeless. Indeed, less than a half century after Masoch's death in 1905, the mas(s)ochistic spaces prefigured in texts such as *Venus in Furs* would play host to a new and more flexible form of CAPITAL. But even here the enclosures are not fully sealed. Unlike the demonstrative negations of law embodied in Sade's criminal irony, mas(s)ochistic (w)ritings float suspended in dense and imaginative layers of aestheticized disavowal.[1]

More allusive than frontal in their artful plays of resistance, and more seductive than declarative in their deployment of signs, Masoch's texts – like the

technologies of image management, supplementing the rigidities of normalization with the more flexible seduction of consent. This is a danger of contemporary geography: the threat that mas(s)ochism, like MTV, may become a magical tool of the ruling classes.

VII

Consider the cold blankness of the screen glowing. It is within this space of almost electric transference that one today rediscovers mystery.

(Jack O. Lantern, *Threepenny Soap-Opera*)

To geographers who wish to replot space in time, Reno Heimlich recommends ignorance of everything that LIES outside the borders of everyday life. There is no better way of characterizing the method with which critical erotic geography must break. For without exception, "the cultural treasures" the geographer works with have a sacrificial origin which cannot be acknowledged without horror. For, in truth,

hyper-conformity of the "masses" imagined by Baudrillard – threaten to disappear into the cool enclosures of an imaginary that is void of interpretive reference. This poses a challenging dilemma to the culture of CAPITAL. How might the secrets informing such popular and literary practices be recuperatively mastered? How, in other words, might such perverse bodies of (w)riting be made to work for a system that demands their incorporation? Certainly not by force alone. Virtually nobody is forcing anybody to watch television, and yet masses of people keep their eyes/"I"s on the screen. Why? Is it because somebodies are manipulating everybody else? Or, do the mas(s)ochistic pleasures of watching life fade to screens of pre-modeled information give magical access to spaces of erotic uncertainty, repressed by the sadistic demands of modern CAPITAL?

Is this what makes mas(s)ochism today so attractive – its promise of pleasurable spaces in excess of discipline? This is hinted at in the (w)ritings of both Masoch and Jean Baudrillard. But so is the danger that, in response to such ritual perversions of discipline, CAPITAL will arm itself with new

there is no document of civilization that is not at the same time [and space] a document of barbarism. And just as such a document is not free of barbarism, barbarism taints also the manner in which it was transmitted from one owner to another.

(Deleuze 1989: 256)

The erotic geographer, therefore, reflexively doubles back upon one's complicity with barbarism, remirroring the sacrifices that recurrently give birth to culture itself.

Mirrorings, replicas, and copies of mirrored images are also present throughout Masoch's texts. In the opening sequences of *Venus in Furs*, the narrator encounters a strange Goddess with "stony, lifeless eyes" and "marble body." Complaining of the coldness of men from northern regions – "you children of reason" – this "sublime" figure, draped in the fur of a sable, informs the narrator that she is an advocate of more archaic pleasures. Desire, she says, is weaker than pleasure. "It is man who desires, woman who is desired. This is woman's only advantage, but it is a decisive one. By making man so vulnerable to passion, nature has placed him at women's mercy" (Sacher-Masoch 1989: 146).

The cold marble woman's voice rings true to the narrator. But before he can act upon this truth he is awoken from his dream. The narrator, it appears, has fallen asleep reading Hegel, only to find himself captivated by an image of "a beautiful woman, naked beneath her dark furs." This image – a "large oil painting done in the powerful colors of the Flemish School" – hangs in the study of his friend Severin (Sacher-Masoch 1989: 146). This, the narrator now believes, must be the erotic origin of his dream. But after informing Severin of this fact, the narrator's eyes are redirected to yet another image. "It was a remarkably good copy of Titan's famous Venus with the Mirror," itself but another copy of a model. And so the story unfolds – one seemingly true copy fading as but a screen for others. A mirror image to mirror images, one fantastically screened memory after another.

"The Eighteenth Brumaire of Louis Bonaparte" analyzes the failure of the 1848 revolution in France and the "ghostly" restoration of monarchy.

costumed drama of] an already dead epoch" (Marx 1973: 148). This led Marx to re(w)rite Hegel's observation that "all the great events and characters of world history occur, so to speak twice," adding, "the first time as tragedy, the second as farce" (Marx 1973: 146).

But what if such doubled appearances return a third time? And this time, not as a farcical copy of a tragic original, but as a copy of nothing but that which is modeled on a copy? Laughter rolls from the mouths of the studio audience. I am (w)riting about a form of eroticism that is characteristic of mas(s)ochistic texts and the masses. I am (w)riting about simulation.

VIII

"The tradition of the oppressed teaches us that the 'state of emergency' in which we live is not the exception but the rule" (Benjamin 1969a: 257). In order to embody this teaching, critical geographers must articulate a method that is in keeping with this

17

Central to Marx's discussion is the way in which bourgeois social movements may "hide from themselves the limited . . . content of their struggles." This they accomplish by masking contemporary social forms in the cultural iconography of past triumphs, such that "men and things seem set in sparkling diamond and each day's spirit is ecstatic" (Marx 1973: 150) Thus, the "gladiators" of French bourgeois struggles replicate "the ideals, art forms and self-deceptions" in order "to maintain their enthusiasm at the high level appropriate to great historical tragedy. A century earlier, Cromwell and the English . . . had borrowed for their bourgeois revolution the language, passions and illusions of the Old Testament" (Marx 1973: 148).

Worse, yet, were the restoration years 1848 to 1851, when parasitic images of bygone glories were used to mask the defeat of revolutionary actions by the resurrection of their ghosts. Depicting the crowning of Napoleon's nephew as monarch as a parodic flight from the reality of present contradictions, Marx concludes that, "an entire people suddenly found itself plunged back into [the

insight. This may entail considerable unlearning. Rather than normalizing our scientific procedures, we must seek to remobilize boundaries that have separated our knowledge from others. This will improve our position in the ongoing struggle against fascism: to retheorize the geography of simulation as *aboriginally conjured* in resistance to the sickening violence of disciplinary cultural enclosures. Given the terrorism of contemporary forms of cybernetic simulation, this may seem like a strange conceptual reversal. Nevertheless, in articulating a genealogy of resistance, it is important to remember that simulation is first called into existence as a defensive maneuver on the part of the oppressed.

Simulation resists the believability of a given symbolic order. To simulate is to pretend to possess what one doesn't possess – imaginary control over a world where things appear as naturally given. But things are never naturally given without other (possible) things being taken away. This, simulators recognize, if secretly. The pretense of simulation feeds off the fetishized reality of representational power. Representational power, on the other hand, is rooted in dissimulation, or the promise that signs might ever equal the things they signify. But they never will. Signifiers never equal what they reference. Words never equal the things they order. Money never equals the body. Simulators know all this but act as if they don't. This is simulation's challenge to an existing social order. Simulation threatens to deconstruct the hegemonic character of all binding representations, of all hierarchy. This is its magic – a strategic prize for all players in any game of power.

IX

My fluttering heart prepares me for flight,
I would like to turn back.
But if I remain within this panicky metastasis,
I am destined for far worse than bad luck.
                                    (Rada Rada, *Dark Angels*)

A recent video produced by Jack O. Lantern displays a troop of orphan angels, each with a video-camera

technologies of immense power. Nobody seems safe anywhere. Catastrophic debris piles skyward. This storm is what modernity has called progress. The angels spin more wildly than ever as the screen betraying their imaginary positioning fades fast forward to black. Reverse. Cut to slow motion.

X

At a moment when the politicians in whom the opponents of Fascism had placed their hopes are prostrate and confirm their defeat these observations are intended to disentangle [the masses amidst which I drift] from the snares in which the traitors have entrapped us.

                                    (Benjamin 1969a: 258)

What more must I (w)rite? Must I recount the recent history of U.S. Supreme Court decisions bent on erasing all but the most powerful of corporate criminal rights before the law?
    But there's something even more

18

turned back upon itself. Images of these angels feed back into the screen they rescan. This creates the illusion of a composite image of highly differentiated social spaces spirally in relation. Images of the angels spin around one another at uncertain speeds until the space that *originally* appeared to separate each from the others suddenly implodes into a kaleidoscope of swampy forms and uncoded shades of color. This is simulation. This is how one, who is not one, might picture the orphan angels of geography. These angels appear turned inside out. Where one's normal eye/"I" might perceive a cumulative chain of discrete HIStorical events, these angels appear to envision the hegemonic spaces from which they take flight as a continuous catastrophe which piles ruin upon ruin.
    The angels would like to stay in the places which occupy them most. But a storm is blowing in from the desert. Some call this desert Paradise and wave flags and yellow ribbons. But the angels – if only because they are orphans – sense something more ominous. They sense that previous spaces of defensive simulation are today being redoubled by

dangerous about fascism than the sadistic spread of state power *per se*. There is also the fascinating cultural drama of sacrificing masses of other people and other structural possibilities without recognizing this violence in anything but ecstatic forms. No guilt. No contradictions. No second thoughts. This is what is distinctive about the male fantasies governing fascist rituals – dense and high-speed transferential processes which make others disappear in the blink of an eye/"I." Literally. And with *virtually* no *real* memory of the loss.
    To accomplish such a fiercely militarized maneuver, fascists have *time* after *time* parasited previously resistive spaces of simulation. This allows fascists to access cultural spaces that once belonged only to rebels, mad people, and ghosts. In this, fascism, like a corporate state managed by vampires – which is one way of describing the current geography of CAPITAL – travels free of the technological encumbrances of its own murderous shadows. No matter that such vampirism demands that those in power exchange their own bodies for

fantastic models of being beyond the body. The estheticized transcendence of bodily relations is exactly what conjures fascism into existence.

A related white magical transformation is taking place within the most technologically advanced sectors of CAPITAL. This interface between fascist and technoCAPITAL redoubles modern male mas(s)ochism, rechanneling the masses it charms. Here fascism, CAPITALism and mas(s)ochism come on line together as constitutive features of ultramodern social power. At the core of each LIE ritual technologies of mass perceptual fascination, a perversely erotic simulation of seemingly open social spaces for profit. This is social cybernetics. It appears to clean up all the messy gaps between things that are modern, turning everything into bits and pieces of information. Digital ecstasy: now one (who is not One) can be here and not here at the same time! Moreover, within the fascistic cultural mas(s)ochism of contemporary CAPITAL there appears nowhere else to be.

Ultramodern power reverses social forms that earlier modes of simulation had traditionally

technological erotics and the price for contesting this order is high. Indeed, it is virtually impossible to imagine a form of geography that is not at least partially complicit with such ultramodern simulations. But what about simulation raised (or lowered) to yet another level? Isn't it still geographically possible to double back upon the fascinating remodelings of ultramodernity and vomit their poison? Waves of canned laughter break across the audience.

XI

One of the weaknesses of Marxist critical thought has been to (mis)identify useful labor as the source of all wealth.

The savior of modern times is called work. . . . This vulgar-Marxist conception of the nature of labor . . . recognizes only the progressive mastery of nature . . . a conception of nature which differs ominously from the one in the Socialist utopias before the 1848 revolution. The new conception of labor amounts to the exploitation of nature.

(Benjamin 1969a: 257)

defended. Cut fast to the endzone! Freeze frame! Instant replay! "The only good defense is a good offense!" says one techno-fascist to anOther. This is simulation, but no longer of the resistive kind. Traditional forms of simulation reflexively reverse the self-evidency of meaningful cultural hierarchies, opening erotic spaces of play at the borders of culture. Cybernetic simulations jam the channels, overloading the meaning of otherwise arbitrary references and, thus, reversing even the playful reversals of previous simulations. This unlocks, without undercutting, sadistic forms of modern power, as bodies pile up without notice. Here, like the imaging of women in Masoch's pornography, everything appears to float free, suspended of reference. What was once feared as lurking on the outside of the modern social order (nature, vengeful women, and a host of dark monstrous Others) is brought into the center. At the same time, the center is technologically dispersed, without threatening the expanse of its power. Here, things remain on the outside, but appear closer than ever. Repulsive yet attractive: this is a New World Order of

This, "vulgar Marxism" shares with other modern conceptions of power, including those it criticizes – a fetishization of use value and the celebration of productivity without end. Complicit with anthropocentric assumptions concerning "Man's" mission culturally to subdue nature, such Marxism (like modern CAPITAL) dissimulates human/animal interdependency in natural cycles of useless play, festive expenditure, and periodic decay. This aspect of human nature is unfortunately less neglected by fascism, if only in simulated form.

If Marxism's vulgar espousal of human mastery over nature makes it erotically complicit with sadism, fascism's simulation of being-in-natural-cycles are anticipated in the pornography of Masoch. It is difficult to read the violent suppression of the revolutions of 1848 as anything but sadistic. Nevertheless, Western (men's) HIStory continues to (w)rite of CAPITAL as something progressive, even natural. How is this possible? One way is to experience actual events in the form of their fantastic reversal. In geographical terms, this would be to experience spaces of sadistic mastery as equivalent to the fascinating pains of submitting to a "natural" (or naturalized) law. The estheticized reversals of mas(s)ochism enact such transubstantiation. The fascinating pleasures afforded men of Masoch's social (dis)position permit a vast geographical expansion of CAPITAL by appearing to free those most complicit with sadistic mastery of the guilt-ridden confines of the fortified ego. In this, the mas(s)ochist, like the newly industrialized masses, is offered an estheticized reprieve from the disciplinary demands of modernity.

But what of women? Despite the stereotypical feminization of both mas(s)ochism and the so-called masses – in both psychoanalysis and much critical theory – Masoch's (w)ritings presage little that is empowering for women. Masoch's texts disavow, rather than challenge, the discursive violence of modern law. Modern law is founded upon a sadistic repression of reciprocal human/animal participation in natural cycles that it codes as feminine. Constructed with an eye/"I" to the "rights of Man," modern law is often heralded as "the Death of God." In actuality, this represents only the death of

reality, of CAPITAL intensive violence. Nature makes her theatrical reappearance in the monstrous form of a cruel and seductive Goddess. In this masked form, "she" oversees man's voluntary assent (or ascent?) to the purified sublimity of self-discipline. God, it seems, is not dead but only turned into a (male fantasized) woman. In the shadows of failed social revolution transsexualism abounds. This preserves, if in a fetishized or disavowed form, the (monotheistic) aspect of "God-given" social order.

To occupy humanly the position of God, the phallus, or the modern male ego, is hauntingly (im)possible. It requires inordinate repression of oneself and the oppression of all others. It requires, in other words, a carefully managed game of *dissimulation*. One must pretend not to possess the world that one is ritually given – a cracked and paranoiac world, besieged on all sides by the sacrificial objects (or objective possibilities) it excludes. But there are great costs to such pretense. The geography of the phallus is, at once, a psychic fortress and a hollow swamp within the idealized (male) subject. Those who pretend to occupy the

one of God's doubled aspects and the CAPITAL preservation of the Other. Banished is the (pagan) immanence of the transgressive sacred, that aspect of God which is festively put to death in an eternal return to the playful structuring of difference. Preserved in the form of its perverse disavowal is the violence of God's more orderly or sadistic aspects.

In Masoch's pornography a partially orphaned male protagonist repeatedly secures the contractual agreement of archetypal females to play the part of cruel Mother Nature. Here, the repressed returns but only in the form of the law-in-reverse. The binary structure of law is preserved by an aestheticized suspension of its most violent effects. In Masoch's texts, idealized forms float slow-motioned, like radiant dream-states, as each successive image cancels all others. "The settings in Masoch, with their heavy tapestries, their cluttered intimacy, their boudoirs and closets, create chiaroscuro where the only things that emerge are suspended gestures and suspended suffering" (Deleuze 1989: 34). This deters the recognition, without undermining the

position of phallic mastery must be on constant guard against both external and internal enemies.

Throughout modernity this double contradiction has slowed the full expanse of CAPITAL. But here at the end of the twentieth century, CAPITAL appears to be absorbing everything that once escaped it, rapid-fire and faster than ever. In this, the sadistic reality of modern power is not negated but seductively disavowed, as the "social void is scattered with interstitial objects and crystalline clusters which spin around and coalesce in cerebral chiaroscuro . . . an opaque nebula whose growing density absorbs all the surrounding energy. . . . A black hole which engulfs the social" (Baudrillard 1983a: 3–4).

XII

We need geography, but not the way a parasitic tourist needs it to plot a course of travels from North to South without ever leaving the safety of one's own screen.

(Madonna Durkheim, *Of the Use and Abuse of Geography*)

It is with not the makers of maps or models but in the struggles of oppressed peoples that we best discover the shifting contours of geographical knowledge. "In Marx it appears as the last enslaved class, as the avenger that completes the task of liberation in the name of generations of the downtrodden" (Benjamin 1969a: 260). But in our century, mas(s)ochistic technologies of enormous fascination have so rechanneled the resistance of those of us most enslaved by CAPITAL that it becomes increasing difficult to recall spaces other than those in which we float coldly, adrift of memory. Ritualized simulations which (in other social times and spaces) have aided us in giving dramatic notice to the most sickening forces of hierarchy, today come prepackaged and emptied of transgressive potential. I am here (w)riting of what is most perversely erotic. Like models of war generated the C.I.A., I.T.T., and Disney, contemporary simulations are breathlessly put into oscillation with dissimulations.

New and improved models appear everywhere. These promise white magical futures that unfold as if out of nowhere. It matters little that such

cutting off those subordinated by power from effective ritual access to counter-memories and the counter-structural possibilities such memories may beget. This is how techno-simulations feed off traditional strategies of simulation. This fascistic situation encourages the oppressed to "forget both . . . hatred and [the] spirit of sacrifice, for both are nourished by the image of enslaved ancestors rather than that of liberated [mutant] grandchildren" (Benjamin 1969a: 260).

XIII

We're here more than just for the price of a gallon of gas. What we've done is going to chart the future of the world for the next hundred years.

(Former U.S. President George Bush)

"The concept of . . . HIStorical progress . . . cannot be sundered from the concept of its progression through a homogeneous, empty time" (Benjamin 1969a: 261). This concept of HIStory is countered

promises will never be realized because, amidst the pains of squalor, violence, and poverty, it's no longer actuality that counts, but only the seductive virtuality of futures forever deterred. Like the rush of crack-cocaine or the thrills of meaningless information, in the space of premodeled simulation time appears to stand still. This is the exact opposite of the experience of time conjured by reflexive forms of simulation. In the rituals governing such transgressive forms, time is made erotically to disappear, only to be playfully reborn in each passing instant. What a laugh!

This is the tragic drama of traditional (or reciprocally bound) forms of simulation – an ecstatic dispelling of the farcical violence of cultural authority. All the doubles implode. In this LIES the healing potential of black magic. But with cybernetic simulations even this critical distinction is blurred. In cybernetic culture there appears to be no outside. *Interior experience* appears sent into orbit around itself, ecstatic not in the generosity of self-loss, but in the over-saturated communicative pleasures of a self without end. This makes orphans of the oppressed,

by the power-reflexive dance of erotic geography.[2] Allying itself with the simulations of the oppressed, HIStorically material geography attempts a deconstruction that partially escapes words. It displaces, without either (dialectically) negating or (mas[s]ochisticly) suspending the operation of power. What does this mean?

XIV

The simulation of origins is the means.

(Jack O. Lantern, *Jetzzeit Nunc Stans*, vol. I)

Erotic geography is the name for a structuring practice whose site is not homogeneous, empty, or transparent space, but heterogeneous spaces charged by the simulation of contradictory ritual forces. The relationship between erotic geography and simulation is typically understood as a strategy of power. This is an unfortunate (mis)reading of simulation. It is wiser to think of simulation as a contradictory strategy of counter-memory. Rather than simply reproducing power, simulation allows people to disappear from the sickening webs of hierarchy that mostly contain them. To simulate is to pretend to possess what one can never possess (and remain oneself) – one's own shadows or what is left over, excreted, or repulsed to the margins of identity. In simulation one is given access to secrets that can never be fully described or put into words. This is simulation's charm – its grace and poetic seduction. Like the "call and response" rituals "figured forth" in Zora Neal Hurston's accounts of the force-fields of Voodoo, simulation conjures a scene, not of memory *per se*, but of memory's surrounds – the often violent spin of attractions and repulsions by which somebody becomes possessed of a given identity to the exclusion of others (Hurston 1978; 1990). To be within the transgressive field of simulation is to be ecstatically open to the possibilities of new and previously unimagined communal spaces. At the same time, the simulator may experience a bluesy melancholia for what one (who now knows that he or she is not One at all) has always already been missing.

effectiveness of such spatial reversals. In this way,

The poetry of conjure as an image resides in the secrecy and mysteriousness of its sources of power, in its connection to ancient African sources syncretized by a community of diasporic believers with Christian scriptures, and in the masterful improvisational skills of its most dramatic practitioners.

(Baker 1991: 89)

Baker's depiction of healing engendered by the African-American conjurer resembles Lévi-Strauss' depiction of simulations performed by the Nambicuara shaman in Central Brazil. For Lévi-Strauss, the indescribable secret of such ritual simulations LIES in the "magical articulation" of two complementary but typically separated symbolic realms of experience – the acknowledged and the excluded; the normal and the pathological. "[N]ormal thought continually seeks the meaning of things which refuse to reveal their significance" while "so-called pathological thought . . . overflows with emotional interpretations and overtones, in order to supplement an otherwise deficient reality" (Lévi-Strauss 1963: 181). In shamanistic simulations, the

22

In simulation one encounters what Houston Baker depicts as

[A] pivotal and reflexive surface that defies a rigorous opposition of subject and object. It absorbs energies of its creator as subject, but is effectively sonorous only through the matching subjectivity of its recipient. Its force is felt in its disruptive effects, in its liberation of creator and recipient alike from boundaries of conceptual overdeterminations.

(Baker 1991: 71)

Baker is here describing poetic spaces conjured into being within African-American communities enslaved by the possessive white magic of modern CAPITAL. The conjurer, a person of "double wisdom" – whom Baker variously associates with the African griot, "witchdoctor," Voodoo Mambo, and African-American women (w)riters – poetically doubles this oppressive ritual scenery. This effects a surface to surface transfer of both the poisons of hierarchy and the healing potential of images previously cast to the shadows. Yet, to be effective, such poetic simulations must be performed within a community of those who believe in the symbolic

spatial boundaries separating these two worlds are ritually undone, allowing each provisionally to mingle with the other. In contrast to the one-way abstractions of Western

scientific explanation, the problem here is not to attribute confused and disorganized states, emotions, or representations to an objective cause, but rather to articulate them into a whole or system. The system is valid precisely to the extent that it allows the coalescence or precipitation of these diffuse states, whose discontinuity . . . makes them so painful.

(Lévi-Strauss 1963: 182)

This is a crucial distinction. Unlike strategies of healing based upon simulation, those rooted in dissimulation (modern forms of medicine) appear bent on reducing the gap between what exists in the world and its scientific representation. Ritual simulation playfully reverses this gap, fascinating each side with images normally excluded by the other. Herein LIES simulation's seductive black magic. Modern science is more singular. It compulsively opposes one side of the gap to the others, endlessly extending this binary space of ritualized discontinuity. This is white magic – the power of perpetual dissimulation.

Maybe Dora, that most famous of hysterics, was also a simulator. Hers, it seems, was a baroquely tragic drama, fated to be played without a believing audience. In telling her dreams aloud within the Viennese theater of psychoanalysis, Dora conjured a poetic space of terrifying patriarchal pasts and an (im)possibly disruptive future. The images figured forth by Dora were uncontainable by Freud's dissimulative theories. Hiding from the seductive space of transference that Dora's simulations opened (between them), Freud took refuge in a project for a scientific psychology. But if Freud feared the seductive implosion of objectivized truths conjured by Dora's hysterics, he was certainly not alone in his defenses. By 1865, early modern medical diagnosticians (or "alienists" as they were known at the time) had set out to produce expert representations of "real symptoms," that even simulators themselves would be unaware of. "This . . . in order to save at all cost the truth principle, and to escape the specter – raised by simulation – namely

dreamy geography of fantasies. In this, cinematic transference parallels the ambivalent neutralization of real objects (of desire) prefigured in the (w)ritings of Masoch. Like the destruction of aura attributed to the arts of mechanical reproduction by Walter Benjamin, both Masoch's texts and the perceptual play of cinema conjure spaces that blur the distinction between simulation and the real world. In this way, both mas(s)ochism and the movies access surface spaces which appear to escape the disciplinary constraints of modern power.

Commentators often point to real women in Masoch's biography who correspond to the cruel Goddesses who appear in his (w)ritings. But in Masoch's texts, such characters appear indistinguishable from models of fantasy. In this they resemble the screened Goddesses of Hollywood. Which comes first – the model or the referent? In both mas(s)ochism and filmic simulation, the difference floats undecidable. The aura surrounding artful originals appears undone. In this way, mas(s)ochistic (w)ritings anticipate a form of

that truth, reference and objective causes have ceased to exist" (Baudrillard 1983b: 6).

Of the challenge of simulation to psychoanalysis, Baudrillard asks,

What can medicine do with something which floats on either side of illness, on either side of health, or with the reduplication of illness in a discourse that is no longer true or false? What can psychoanalysis do with the reduplication of the discourse of the unconscious in a discourse of simulation that can never be unmasked, since it isn't false either?.

(Baudrillard 1983b: 6–7)

In the form announced and defended by Freud, the answer, it seems, is nothing. But what of a more enchanted form of psychoanalysis? What about transferences situated not on an analyst's couch, but within the oneiric geography of cinema? What about the dreamy flow of images conjured by the electricity of moving pictures?

In cinema, simulations no longer parasite upon the ghost-haunted power of dissimulated (modern) meanings, but appear almost to give birth to themselves. Mechanical simulations engender a

mechanical simulation that doubles back upon the drama of more archaic forms of simulation. Like television – which is perhaps the true heir of mas(s)ochistic (w)riting – mas(s)ochism appears to disappear from geographies dominated by modern power. But this it does without disturbing the reproduction of sadistic spaces in the least.[3] As such, the mas(s)ochist may pretend to play a hotly contested game of artifice, all the while lowering the temperature of his (w)riting to the coolness of degree zero. This is the ecstatic space (of male fantasy) that mas(s)ochism communicates to those it fascinates: the impression of being simultaneously powerless and totally in control. A tiger's leap, not into the past, but sidereal into a space of nostalgia for what never existed in any but the most abstractly modeled of forms.

XV

"The awareness that they are about to make the continuum of HIStory explode is characteristic of the revolutionary classes at the moment of their action" (Benjamin 1969a: 261). On the other hand, a fascination with making the gendered contradictions of CAPITAL implode into "cool memories" floating across what is screened – this is characteristic of the white male mas(s)ochistic practices that dominate our geographical present.

XVI

The cyberotic geographer, who is also a HIStorically material geographer, "cannot do without the notion of a present which is not a transition, but in which time stands still and has come to a stop" (Benjamin 1969a: 262). This is a space of simulation. It folds implosively back upon the ritual movements by which the geographer had once upon a time appeared as if separate from everything and everybody else. But, unlike mas(s)ochism, critical erotic geography does not remain suspended in this fascinating space. The transgressive implosion of one's separation (from the world) is but a recurrent first (or second) movement

Mas(s)ochism and mechanical image reproduction do not. They simply put modern power on hold. Rather than expending spaces of sameness, they project such spaces at a cool, fascinating, and suspended distance. In this the eye/"I" appears to float free of the constraints by which it is constructed. Caught between melancholia and mourning, these implosive strategies of mass resistance help defend the (male) ego against the sadism of CAPITAL's superego, but without setting the ego itself on fire. This is their theological and political ambivalence. God fades and is resurrected with but the briefest of digital delays.

The ambivalence of such intermediate forms of simulation are nowhere more evident than in Walter Benjamin's classic essay concerning the role of mechanically reproduced images in effacing the "aura" of "original" art objects. Of course, no object is ever truly original. Objects appear autonomous only to the extent that they mask the traces of their own sacrificial construction. This is why Benjamin views the mechanical depreciation of an object's "uratic presence" as politically progressive. By detaching the object from the fetishized domain of tradition,

in the critical geographer's dance between doubling. Implosion followed by explosion; deconstruction followed by reconstruction; seduction followed by production; transgression followed by provisional orderings, partial truths, laughable dissimulations, and the reverse.

The ambivalent suspense of both mas(s)ochism and "the work of art in the age of mechanical reproduction" offers relief from the sadistic violence of CAPITAL. Each offers the contradictory pleasures of partially escaping disciplinary demands for ceaseless objectification. At least in the imaginary realm. By incorporating artifice, rather than repressing its shadowy play, mas(s)ochism and the movies may appear as perversely *more real than real*.

Nevertheless, the communicative ecstasy offered by these seductive social forms are not to be equated with the burning sensations that characterize archaic simulation. This differentiates the magic of mas(s)ochism from that of conjurers, witches, shamans, and hysterics. Archaic simulation vocations a recurrent return to chaotic spaces of difference.

mechanical reproduction draws attention to the constructed character of all objects. This liquidation of an object's "parasitic dependence" on traditional authority is said to provide a critical space wherein artistic consumers become producers, and the reverse. This may also be a constitutive feature of all contemporary "mass movements."

Despite such progressive possibilities, Benjamin recognizes that the elimination of auratic authenticity might simultaneously engender something more ominous – "the desire of contemporary masses to bring things 'closer' spatially and humanly" (Benjamin 1969b: 223). In this, the advantages of achieving a critical distance from authority appear countered, as "everyday the urge grows stronger to get hold of an object at very close range by way of its likeness, its reproduction" (Benjamin 1969b: 223). In amplifying this urge, mechanical reproduction transforms human perception itself. As the means of filmic reproduction become more precise, things which were previously invisible suddenly enter the world of sight. In this way, perception itself mutates. With close-ups small details may be magnified beyond belief. With slow motion previously imperceptible gestures are dramatized. With speed-ups new visions of form become commonplace; while with telescopic and microscopic lenses the literal meanings of "too far," "too small," or "too big" are forever changed. These new ritual technologies do "not simply render more precise what in any other case was visible, though unclear: [they reveal] entirely new structural formations of the subject. . . . The camera introduces us to unconscious optics as does psychoanalysis to unconscious impulses" (Benjamin 1969b: 226–7).

This points to a radical expanse in the spaces through which CAPITAL enacts its magic. In this, the boundaries of perception radically shift as "the adjustment of reality to the masses and the masses to reality" enters "a process of unlimited scope" (Benjamin 1969b: 223). Things which had "once upon a time" been tattooed upon the flesh now float free as if nothing but statistical probabilities. "Simultaneities intervene, extending our point of view outward in an infinite number of lines connecting the subject to a whole world of comparable instances"

have been premonitory signs, symptoms of a de-realization of sensory appearances" (Virilio 1991: 111). This is white magic. Its mas(s)ochistic structures today outdistance the black magic of simulations that lead to social healing. But even this was uncannily prophesied by Benjamin a few years before fascism demanded his blood. "At the height of artifice," (w)rites Benjamin, "the sight of an immediate reality has become an orchid in the land of technology" (Benjamin 1969b: 233).

XVII

Cyberotic geography is based on constructivist principles. It involves not only the flow of thoughts but their provisional arrest as well. Where thinking congeals in a configuration pregnant with tensions, it engenders shock waves that undermine the suspended geography of cybernetic power, while announcing the emergence of new structural possibilities. This is not to lessen the importance of HIStory "but to open up and recompose the territory

(Soja 1989: 23) and creating the sensation of "an open system, in which no one can find any perceptible, objective limits . . . a relative uncertainty due to the interpretive delirium of the observer, be it spectator or tele-spectator" (Virilio 1991: 72–3).

These artful developments presage new forms of human geography. Here the constraints of auratic objectivity appear suspended between the possibilities of critical distance and almost too much closeness. In 1936, at the time of Benjamin's essay, the direction such forms might take seemed open to radical contestation. Today, with the advent of televisionary feedback mechanisms and pixel screened video–computer interface modeling, one direction for simulation now appears more real than all others – the deployment of social technologies which suspend rather than explode the flotation of image-generated memories without fixed referents.

This signals the advent of miniaturization: an almost surgical closeness to things shorn of their fleshy contradictions. "The artisanal inventions of dissolves, feedback, slow motion and time-lapse, zoom, live and delayed broadcast . . . now appear to

of the HIStorical imagination through a critical respatialization" of the dance of humans in time (Soja 1989: 14). What it opposes is that tendency in both HIStoricism and cybernetics which, by subordinating space to time, "obscures geographical interpretation of the changeability of the social world" (Soja 1989: 15). Given contemporary CAPITAL's mas(s)ochistic absorption of bodily difference into the cool telematics of self-sustaining codes, this oppositional move may be more important than ever.

Erotic geography recognizes that "the space in which we live, which draws us out of ourselves, in which the erosion of our lives, our time and our HIStory occurs . . . is also, itself, a heterogeneous space" (Foucault 1986: 23). To reclaim this heterogeneity is to contest the current crystallization of power that works upon and within our bodies, fascinating us with the seemingly transparent possibilities of being everywhere and nowhere at the same time. Whereas cybernetic culture bombards us with the cold and circular seductions of experiencing space as nothing but the suspended exchange of value-added information for energy, and the reverse; the play of erotic geography reminds us of what and who is being sacrificed to program such special effects. The globe today is littered with orphans.

XVIII

Not long before his death, Walter Benjamin (w)rote that: "The present . . . as a model of Messianic time . . . coincides exactly with the stature which the HIStory of mankind has in the universe . . . something like two seconds at the close of a twenty-four hour day" (Benjamin 1969a: 263). This is, at once, a modest and challenging view of human destiny; recognition that the space of every moment is capable of redeeming the ruins of HIStory. This is not to proclaim "Mankind's" triumph over nature, but to embrace the fleshy finiteness of our own positioning within nature folding back upon itself, like the twilight of one day passing into another. In this we fall ruinously – if with often intense pleasure – out of the narcissism of wide-awake (or "ego-oriented")

to connect the militarized minds of men to the bodies of machines, and the reverse – to a surgeon's table in the near future, where mas(s)ochistic day-dreams of exchanging the mortal body for a more ideal model are at long last brought on line.

World War II spurred the development of analog computers – machines that simulated physical systems by representing their dynamic quantities as analogous moves of shafts or voltages, designed to control more efficiently the human operation of anti-aircraft guns and precision bombing equipment. These new forms of simulation soon inspired efforts to construct an effective interface between command, control, and communication in both animals and machines. Hastened by mathematical innovations, by men such as Norbert Weiner and John von Neumann, cybernetics represented the combined application of "new theory on feedback regulation with advances in post-war electronics and early knowledge of living nervous systems to build machines that were able to respond like simple animals and learn" (Moravec 1988: 7).

26

consciousness into the heterogeneous spaces of symbolic death that only sleep simulates. Maybe one will never awake. Maybe one will awake renewed by dreams of difference.

But those who today most control the closecircuitry of cybernetic culture wants to take no chances. Cybernetics, with its omnipresent loops of feedback and telematic self-preservation, is staked – like the consciousness of modern "Man" himself – in the perpetual deterrence of "Man's" death, even if this requires the abandonment of one's own body and the simultaneous mass destruction of others. This is the chilling day-dream of THE LAST SEX: a coldly seductive male fantasy of ideally suspending – without materially expending – the time of "Man" in HIStory.

This violent fantasy is nowhere more graphic than in Hans Moravec's *Mind Children: The Future of Robot and Human Intelligence* (Moravec 1988). The work of a renowned authority in the field of Artificial Intelligence and published by Harvard University Press, *Mind Children* traces the history of cybernetics from its World War II's origins – in efforts

During the 1950s and early 1960s, efforts to produce machines that think resulted in such creations as the electronic turtles pioneered by British psychologist W. Grey Walter and the so-called Johns Hopkins Beast. The turtles were equipped with subminiature radio-tube brain circuits, microphonic ears, contact switch feelers, and rotating photoelectric eyes that were capable of locating specially designed battery recharge hutches. This guaranteed that these "thinking robots" might never run short of power. The Beast, build by a team of brain researchers, made its way through space guided by sonar feedback devices and photocellular eye systems. Later replaced by TeleVideo cameras, these technologies of artificial eyesight enabled this machine to identify the black plate-covered wall outlets by which it recharged its energy cells. In this way, the Beast, like the turtles, could stay *on line* indefinitely, early predecessors of today's highly publicized "smart bombs" and other feedback-guided weapon systems. These cybernetic devices fueled dreams of a human–machine interface and the perpetual suspension of death. Behind such dreams

LIE the fantasies of geographically unlimited command, control, and communication operations without end.

       This dream of TOTAL CONTROL was put on hold for several decades as the analog computing systems which served as its models were displaced by faster digital models. At the same time, the socio-logic of cybernetics spread everywhere. Transferred into everyday life by televisionary feedback mechanisms at the forefront of contemporary CAPITAL, cybernetics is today a taken-for-granted feature of the culture in which we live and die. "Just look at the account books, the projections, the numbers and the returns. . . . Stocks and commodities, the securities markets, banking, currency, options, futures. . . . All these markets must now be rethought and restructured" as each is increasingly experienced as organized by a kind of "telematic" exchange between information and energy (Yurik 1985: 40, 74, 12). From a doctor's imagination of her patient to IBM's imagination of its competitors and clients and, perhaps, even your imagination of me, vast flows of the world as we

fantasies of fascist men: abstract desires to live free of the impurities of the mortal body.

       Moravec's *Mind Children* chillingly articulates this mas(s)ochistic fantasy. Conjuring the technological possibilities of a post-biological world, Moravec chides those stick-in-the-mud adherents of the *body-identity positions* who confuse animality with true human existence. How stupid (of us) to mistake the reality of the flesh for real life! Theorizing what he calls *pattern-identity*, Moravec, it seems, has something *more real than real* in (his) mind:

Body-identity assumes that a person is defined by the stuff of which a human body is made. Only by maintaining continuity of body stuff can we preserve an individual person. Pattern-identity, conversely, defines the essence of a person, say myself, as the pattern and the process going on in my head and body, not the machinery supporting that process. If the process is preserved, I am preserved. The rest is jelly.

(Yurik 1985: 117)

This is male-minded mas(s)ochism amplified by cybernetics – a fantastic preservation of the narcissistic ego WITHOUT END. Here, informational

have come to know it over the last forty years have been coded recoded as nothing but matters of information.

Even the simplest of conversations are separated, reconfigured, sent and priced. And those who live in this new world are losing their grip on . . . older [and other possible constructions of] reality. As for those who have no access to, no participation in, this newly imposed world, they are [forced] out of the world's new information economy, doomed to obsolescence and death.

(Yurik 1985: 3)

Today, mathematical advances in fractal geometry and technological innovations permitting faster and more economical feedback mechanisms have allowed a cross-over between digital and analogical modeling techniques, resulting in such innovations as neural networks and parallel processing. These developments have revived prospects for the cybernetic simulation of human mind processes and the downloading of exact models of thought, memory, and even emotion from the flesh to machine carriers purified of the threat of death, forever and ever. This recalls Klaus Theweleit's (1987) depiction of the

feedback mechanisms interact with electronic brain energy until an ideal simulation of the mind is freed from the brain's materiality. This, it is said, will permit the timeless remodeling of human experience, independent of the entropic space of the flesh. *More real than real* and more cost-efficient. A CAPITAL idea no doubt – the eternal recycling of death-defying male fantasies. The following passage from Moravec's text depicts surgical procedures aimed at producing THE LAST SEX. Whose sex is this and whose male mas(s)ochistic future?

You've just been wheeled into the operating room. A robot brain surgeon is in attendance. By your side is a computer waiting to become a human equivalent, lacking only a program to run. Your skull, but not your brain, is anesthetized. You are fully conscious. The robot surgeon opens your brain case and places a hand on the brain's surface. This unusual hand bristles with microscopic machinery, and a cable connects it to the mobile computer at your side. Instruments in the hand scan the first few millimeters of brain surface. High resolution magnetic resonance measurements build a three-dimensional surface chemical map, while arrays of magnetic and electric antennas collect signals that are rapidly unraveled to reveal, moment to moment, the pulses flashing among the neurons. These measurements, added to a comprehensive understanding of human neural architecture, allow the surgeon to write a program that models the behavior of the . . . scanned brain tissues. . . . They flash by very fast, but any discrepancies are highlighted on a display screen. The surgeon fine-tunes the simulation until the correspondence is nearly perfect.

To further assure of the simulation's correctness, you are given a pushbutton that allows you to momentarily "test drive" the simulation, to compare it with the functioning of the original tissue. . . . As soon as you press the button, a small part of your nervous system is being replaced by a computer simulation of itself. . . . As soon as you are satisfied, the simulation connection is established permanently. The brain tissue is now impotent – it receives inputs and acts as before but its output is ignored. Microscopic manipulators on the hand's surface excise the cells in this superfluous tissue and pass them to an aspirator, where they are drawn away. . . . Later the brain is simulated, then excavated.

Eventually your skull is empty, and the surgeon's hand rests deep in your brain stem. Though you have not lost consciousness, or even train of thought, your mind has been transferred to a machine. In a final disconcerting step the surgeon lifts out his hand. Your suddenly abandoned body goes into a spasm

3 In a related analysis, Patricia Mellencamp observes the "expectant" TV audience "partakes of masochism" and is thereby "soothed by mundane ritual, and contained by . . . contradiction" (Mellencamp 1990: 248).

BIBLIOGRAPHY

Baker, Jr, H. A. (1991) *Workings of the Spirit: the Poetics of Afro-American Women's Writings*, Chicago: University of Chicago Press.

Baudrillard, J. (1983a) *In the Shadow of the Silent Majorities*, trans. P. Foss, P. Patton, and J. Johnston, New York: Semiotext(e).

–– (1983b) *Simulations*, trans. P. Foss, P. Patton, and P. Beitchman, New York: Semiotext(e).

Benjamin, W. (1969a) "Theses on the Philosophy of History," in *Illuminations*, trans. H. Zohn, New York: Schocken Books.

–– (1969b) "The Work of Art in the Age of Mechanical Reproduction," in *Illuminations*, trans. H. Zohn, New York: Schocken Books.

and dies. For a moment you experience only quiet and dark. Then, once again, you can open your eyes. Your perspective has shifted. The computer simulation has been disconnected from the cable leading to the surgeon's hand and reconnected to a shiny new body of the style, color, and material of your choice. Your metamorphosis is complete.

(Morevec 1988: 109–10)

A

"I know this sounds too easy to be true, and you're probably thinking, 'Well, look at her. She was born with that body.' Hardly. . . . [I]t involves hard work and having a dream."

(White 1987: 3, 19)

NOTES

1 For a more detailed discussion of these themes see Gilles Deleuze (Deleuze 1989).
2 For an elaboration of power-reflexive research methods, see Stephan Pfohl (Pfohl 1992).

Cleugh, J. (1951) *The Marquis and the Chevalier: a Study in the Pyschology of Sex as Illustrated by the Lives and Personalities of the Marquis de Sade*, New York: Dueil, Sloan, and Pearce.

Deleuze, Gilles (1989) "Coldness and Cruelty," trans. J. McNeil in *Masochism*, New York: Zone Books.

Ehrenreich, B. (1983) *The Hearts of Men: American Dreams and the Flight from Commitment*, Garden City, New York: Anchor.

Foucault, M. (1970) *The Order of Things*, trans. A. Sheridan, New York: Vintage Books.

–– (1986) "Of Other Spaces," trans. J. Miskowiec, *Diacritics*, 16.

Hurston, Z. N. (1978) *Mules and Men*, Bloomington: University of Indiana Press.

–– (1990) *Tell My Horse*, New York: Harper and Row.

Lévi-Strauss, (1963) "The Sorcerer and His Magic," in *Structural Anthropology*, trans. C. Jacobson, New York: Basic Books.

Marx, K. (1973) "The Eighteenth Brumaire of Louis Bonaparte," in *Surveys from Exile*, trans. and ed. B. Fowkes D. Fernbach, New York: Vintage Books.

Mellencamp, P. (1990) "TV Time and Catastrophe, or Beyond the Pleasure Principle of Television," in P. Mellencamp (ed.), *Logics of Television*, Bloomington: Indiana University Press.

Moravec, H. (1988) *Mind Children: the Future of Robot and Human Intelligence*, Cambridge Mass.: Harvard University Press.

Pfohl, S. (1992) *Death at the Parasite Cafe: Social Science (Fictions) and the Postmodern*, New York: St Martin's Press.

Ross, K. (1988) *The Emergence of Social Space: Rimbaud and the Paris Commune*, Minneapolis: University of Minnesota Press.

Sacher-Masoch, Leopold von (1989) "Venus in Furs," trans. J. McNeil in *Masochism*, New York: Zone Books.

Soja, E. W. (1989) *Postmodern Geographies: The Reassertion of Space in Critical Social Theory*, New York: Verso.

Theweleit, K. (1987) *Male Fantasies*, vol. I, trans. S. Conway, Minneapolis: University of Minnesota Press.

Virilio, P. (1991) *The Lost Dimension*, trans. D. Moshenberg, New York: Semiotext(e).

White, V. (1987) *Vanna Speaks*, New York: Warner Books.

Yurik, S. (1985) *Behold Metatron, the Recording Angel*, New York: Semiotext(e).

Coming Across the Future

Sadie Plant

Virtual sex has been defined as "safe as well as filthy," and held up as the epitome of disembodied pleasure, contact-free sex without secretions in a zone of total autonomy. A safe environment free from the side-effects and complications of actual intercourse: transmittable diseases, conceptions, and abortions, and the sad obligations of emotional need. A closed circuit, a sealed elsewhere, a virtual space to be accessed at will.

If its technical research and development technical cybersex is well advanced: the hardware is fetishized, the software is porn, and vast proportions of the telecommunications system are consumed by erotica. But these are merely the most overt – and perhaps the least interesting – examples of a generalized degeneration of "natural" sex. As hard and wetwares collapse onto soft, far stranger mutations wrack the sexual scene. The simulation of sex converges with the deregulation of the entire sexual economy, the corrosion of its links with reproduction, and the collapse of its specificity: sex disperses into drugs, trance, and dance possession; androgyny, hermaphroditism, and transsexualism become increasingly perceptible; paraphilia, body engineering, queer sex, and what Foucault calls "the slow motions of pleasure and pain" of SM – already "high-technology sex" (Califia 1993: 175) – proliferate. Cybernetics reveals an organism cross-cut by inorganic life – bacterial communication, viral infection, and entire ecologies of replicating patterns which subvert even the most perverse notions of what it is to be "having sex." Reproduction melts into replication and loses its hold on the pleasuredrome.

continues to be fueled by such utopian hopes, there is also a sense in which cybersex seems anticlimatic before it has begun, tinged with disappointment in advance of the event.

But climax will always miss the cybernetic point, which is less a summit than a plateau. The peak experience is yesterday's news. And as for the ease and safety of cybersex: sex in MOOs may have pitfalls of its own, but cybernetic sex and all that it implies are about as cosy and containable as the virtual war of which it is already a side-effect. Cybersex heralds the disappearance of the human–machine interface, a merging which throws the one-time individual into a pulsing network of switches which is neither climactic, clean, nor secure. Anyone who believes that computer screens melt down to produce a safe environment should read their cyberpunk one more time: "'That's all there was, just the wires,' Travis said. 'Connecting them directly to each other. Wires, and blood, and piss, and shit. Just the way the hotel maid found them'" (Cadigan 1991: 275).

Even in the absence of full simstim, Climax distributes itself across the plane and the peak experience becomes a plateau.

The future of sex never comes all at once. Now it is feeding back into a past which sex itself was supposed to reproduce. Relations were already circuits in disguise; immersion was always leading reproduction on. Sex was never uncommercialized, and pleasure was only ever one part of an equation with pain which finds its solution with intensity.

All this occurs in a world whose stability depends on its ability to confine communication to terms of individuated organisms' patrilineal transmission. Laws and genes share a one-way line, the unilateral ROM by which the Judeo-Christian tradition hands itself down through the generations. This is the one-parent family of man, for which even Mother Nature was conceived by God, the high fashion supermodel, perfectly formed, without whom matters would be running amok. Humanism is the ultimate rear-view mirrorism, and the mirror still reflects the image of God. The project: "to specularize and to speculate"; to supervise and oversee. God and man converse on a closed circuit of sources and ends, one and the same, man to man. Creation and procreation. The go forth and multiply from which patriarchal culture takes its cue.

This immaculate conception of the world has always been subject to the uncertainties which underlie all paternity claims. But it is only now, as material intelligence begins to break through the smooth formal screens of this trip, that the patriarchal confidence trick is undermined. He never will know whether or not they were fakes, neither her orgasms nor his paternity. All that is new about his insecurity is that it now begins to be felt. How does God know he's the father? Matter doesn't bother asking: as self-organizing processes attack from within, it's no longer a question, but a tactical matter, a tactile takeover, a material event.

Cybernetics initiates the emergence of the material complexity which finally usurps the procreative line. Even at its most modern and authoritarian, cybernetics collapses the distinction between machine and organism: Norbert Wiener's systems already function regardless of whether their wares are hard, soft, or wet. The fusions of human

and machines of Wiener's wartime research do more than contest the species' boundaries: they also rewrite its history. "Biological organisms . . . become biotic systems, communications devices like others. There is no fundamental, ontological separation in our formal knowledge of machine and organism, of technical and organic" (Haraway 1991: 177–8).

The cyborg has no history, but that of the human is rewritten as its past. By the 1960s, it had become obvious to McLuhan that regardless – or, ironically, because – of its own intentions, the human species had turned out to be "the sex organs of the machine world, as the bee of the plant world, enabling it to fecundate and to evolve ever new forms" (McLuhan 1964: 56). Slaves, workers, women, and robots were never alone in their cyborg roles. Nor were they simply working for the boss, whose mastery was always a sham. Man and his God were vital but contingent, and perhaps ultimately dispensable, components of a future mutation they were building all the time.

The modern organism is already a replicant, straight off the production line of a discipline which "lays down for each individual his place, his body, his disease and his death, his well-being." Foucault's disciplines extend even to the "ultimate determination of the individual, of what characterizes him, of what belongs to him, of what happens to him" (Foucault 1977: 197). After this, organic and social integrity sink or swim together. Modernity is marked by "an explosion of numerous and diverse techniques for achieving the subjugation of bodies and the control of populations, marking the beginning of an era of 'bio-power'" (Foucault 1978: 140), in which "Western man was gradually learning what it meant to be a living species in a living world, to have a body, conditions of existence. . . . For the first time in history . . . biological existence was reflected in political existence" (Foucault 1978: 142).

Humanity tends toward the organized body, the body with organ, the male member. The modern human is dressed in blue, as far from the red-blooded feminine as it is possible to be, gendered and sexed in a world still solidified in the mold of brotherhood and patrilineal inheritance. The female body is already diseased, on the way to the limits of life, while the phallus functions as the badge of membership, or belonging – to one's self, society, species.

The male member functions as "the most ideal, the most speculative element" of this social and organic security system. As Deleuze and Guattari say, it's "enough to make women, children, lunatics, and molecules laugh" (Deleuze and Guattari 1988: 289): the phallus is "an imaginary point," the product of "power in its grip on bodies and their materiality, their forces, energies, sensations, and pleasures" (Foucault 1978: 155). But it's also enough to guarantee the constitution of arborescence, "the submission of the line to the point" (Deleuze and Guattari 1988: 293). And the point is always to remember. Dismembering is not allowed.

This, as Donna Haraway points out, is also the point at which female orgasm drops out of the picture: "before the latter part of the eighteenth century in Europe, most medical writers assumed orgasmic female sexual pleasure was essential for conception," whereas now "female orgasms came to seem either non-existent or pathological from the point of view of western medicine." And by "the late nineteenth century, surgeons removed the clitoris from some of their female patients as part of reconstituting them as properly feminine, unambiguously different from the male, which seemed to be almost another species" (Haraway 1992: 356).

Intensity is gathered together in a single point, monopolized by the male member, and localized as orgasm. All sexuality is male, writes Freud. Female sexuality and female orgasm are either contradictions in terms or impoverished variations on the phallic theme. Orgasms are what these organisms have. They too are something possessed and owned, functioning to restore equilibrium and secure the identity of the organized body, the organic integrity of the Western individual.

"Woman's genitals are simply absent, masked, sewn back up inside their 'crack.'" Zero is discounted and veiled, and "one would have to dig down very deep indeed to discover beneath the traces of this civilization, this history, the vestiges of a

more archaic civilization that might give some clue to woman's sexuality" (Irigaray 1985: 25).

If there were such a sexuality to be found in the deep and distant past, behind the screens of the specular, its unearthing would always be a matter of retrospeculation, a looking back with eyes programmed by "the logic that has dominated the West since the time of the Greeks." And it "would undoubtedly have a different alphabet, a different language. . . . Woman's desire would not be expected to speak the same language as man's" (Irigaray 1985: 25). Man is the one who relates his desire; his sex is the very narrative. Hers has been the stuff of his stories instead.

By the late twentieth century, "orgasms on one's own terms" became the rallying cry for a feminism increasingly aware of the extent to which female sexuality had been confined. "Male orgasm had signified self-containment and self-transcendence simultaneously, property in the self and transcendence of the body through reason and desire, autonomy and ecstasy," and there was a

feeling that if women were no longer "pinned in the crack between the normal and the pathological, multiply orgasmic, unmarked, universal females might find themselves possessed of reason, desire, citizenship, and individuality" (Haraway 1992: 359).

Or does this result in a masculine mold for some "female sexuality" which could be running elsewhere? Foucault is scathing about the extent to which such liberatory investments underscore the subjection they ostensibly contest. And the orgasm as a key to self-possession is hardly where his interests lie: like Pat Califa, he is more interested in what she calls the "SM orgasm," an intensity uncoupled from genital sex and engaged only with the dismantling of selves. This is the cybersexuality to which all sexuality tends: a matter of careful engineering, the setting of scenes, the perfection of touch; the engineering of communication.

It is not the orgy, but the orgasm that is over. Not that the intensities once sought through sex are disappearing. Far from it: they have only just begun. "The apologia for orgasm made by the Reichians still seems to me to be a way of localizing

possibilities of pleasure in the sexual," writes Foucault (Macey 1994: 373). Climax is proper to organic integrity; orgasm is what organisms do: "I dismembered your body. Our caressing hands were not gathering information or uncovering secrets, they were tentacles of mindless invertebrates; our bellies and flanks and thighs were listing in a contact that apprehends and holds onto nothing. What our bodies did no one did" (Lingis 1994: 61).

Dismemberment: the "Dionysian castration." Counter-memory. Forget what it's for, and learn what it does. Don't concentrate on orgasm, the means by which sex remains enslaved to teleology and its reproduction: "make of one's body a place for the production of extraordinarily polymorphic pleasures, while simultaneously detaching it from a valorization of the genitalia and particularly of the male genitalia" (Miller 1993: 269). Foucault experiments with decompositions of the body, dismantling of the organism, technical experiments with bondage and release, power and resistance in an S&M "matter of a multiplication and burgeoning of bodies" and "a creation of anarchy within the body, where its hierarchies, its localizations and designations, its organicity, if you will, is in the process of disintegrating" (Miller 1993: 274).

Masochism poses a considerable threat to Freud's earlier faith in the pleasure principle. "For if mental processes are governed by the pleasure principle in such a way that their first aim is the avoidance of unpleasure and the obtaining of pleasure, masochism is incomprehensible." And if both "pain and pleasure can be not simply warnings but actually aims, the pleasure principle is paralyzed" (Freud 1984: 413). But by the time he writes *The Economic Problem of Masochism*, Freud knows that masochism is not always a reaction to sadistic control. The masochist is not simply the victim enslaved by mastery: this is the "macho bullshit" of a discourse which admits nothing beyond subjection, a perspective which cannot accept any other relation (or, rather, can accept nothing but relations). Masochism exceeds such relations with the master; indeed it goes beyond all relations, no matter how far from the paternal they seem. It is not a question of recognition, but a matter of feeling: not a craving to

pushed back, sweeping across all the tissues, the immense tactility, the tact of whatever closes up on itself without becoming a box, and of whatever ceaselessly extends beyond itself without becoming a conquest.

(Lyotard 1993: 66)

Immense tactility, contact, the possibility of communication. Closure without the box: as a circuit, a connection. "What interests the practitioners of S&M is that the relationship is at the same time regulated and open," writes Foucault: it is a "mixture of rules and openness." Ceaseless extension: the body hunting its own exit. Becoming "that which is not one"; becoming woman, who "*has sex organs just about everywhere*" (Irigaray 1985: li). Is this what it is to get out of the meat? Not simply to leave the body, but to go further than the orgasm; to access the "exultation of a kind of autonomy of its smallest parts, of the smallest possibilities of a part of the body."

"Use me," writes Lyotard, is "a statement of vertiginous simplicity, it is not mystical, but materialist. Let me be your surface and your tissues, you may be

be flattened, but an intensive desire for communication, for contact, access, to be in touch. The masochist "uses suffering as a way of constituting a body without organs and bringing forth a plane of consistency of desire" (Deleuze and Guattari 1988: 155).

"Stop confusing servitude with dependence" writes Jean-François Lyotard. The "question of 'passivity' is not the question of slavery, the question of dependency not the plea to be dominated" (Lyotard 1993: 260). Otherwise the circuits and connections will be brought back into relations of superiority and inferiority, subject and object, domination and submission, activity and passivity . . . and these will become the frozen poles of an opposition which captures the loops and recouples their lines.

Drink me, eat me. USE ME . . .

[W]hat does she want, she who asks this, in the exasperation and aridity of every piece of her body, the woman-orchestra? Does she want to become her master's mistress and so forth? Come on! She wants you to die with her, she desires that the exclusive limits be

my orifices and my palms and my membranes, we could lose ourselves, leave the power and the squalid justification of the dialectic of redemption, we will be dead. And not: let me die by your hand, as Masoch said" (Lyotard 1993: 65). This is the prostitute's

sado-masochistic bond which ends up making you suffer "something" for your clients. This something has no name. It is beyond love and hate, beyond feelings, a savage joy, mixed with shame, the joy of submitting to and withstanding the blow, of belonging to someone, and feeling oneself freed from liberty. This must exist in all women, in all couples, to a lesser degree or unconsciously. I wouldn't really know how to explain it. It is a drug, it's like having the impression that one is living one's life several times over all at once, with an incredible intensity. The pimps themselves, inflicting these punishments, experience this "something," I am sure of it.

(Lyotard 1993: 63)

It is Foucault's "something unnameable," "useless," outside of all the programs of desire. It is the body made totally plastic by pleasure: something that opens itself, that tightens, that throbs, that beats, that gapes" (Miller 1993: 274). It is, writes Freud, "as though the watchman over our mental life were put out of action by a drug" (Freud 1984: 413).

"I stripped the will and the person from you like collars and chains" (Lingis 1994: 61). What remains is machinic, inhuman, beyond emotion, beyond subjection: "the illusion of having no choice, the thrill of being taken" (Califia 1993a: 172).

Pat Califia: "He wanted . . . everything. Consumption. To be used, to be used up completely. To be absorbed into her eyes, her mouth, her sex, to become part of her substance" (Califia 1993b: 108).

Foucault describes those involved in S&M as "inventing new possibilities of pleasure with strange parts of their body . . . it's a kind of creation, a creative enterprise, which has as one of its main features what I call the desexualization of pleasure" (Miller 1993: 263). S&M is a "matter of a multiplication and burgeoning of bodies," he writes, "a creation of anarchy within the body, where its hierarchies, its localizations and designations, its organicity, if you will is in the process of disintegrating" (Miller 1993: 274), while "practices like fist-fucking are practices that one can call

procedures than masochism, and certainly better ones, is beside the point; it is enough that for some this procedure is suitable for them" (Deleuze and Guattari 1988: 55). Whatever it takes to access the plane. Necessity trashes prohibition. The algebra of need; the diagram of speed.

Foucault was in no doubt that certain drugs rivaled the "intense pleasures" of sexual experimentation. Of the drugs of the 1990s, Ecstasy and crack have both been described as "better than sex," while speed and Prozac tend to anorgasmic effect. All engineerings of the body have some chemical component. Felix Guattari points out that "certain anorexic, sadomasochistic etc. syndromes function as auto-addictions" because "the body itself secretes its endorphines which, you know, are fifty times more active than the morphines" (Guattari 1989: 20). If orgasm localizes pleasure, "things like yellow pills or cocaine allow you to explode and diffuse it throughout the body; the body becomes the overall site of an overall pleasure" (Macey 1994: 373). This is the plane on which it forgets itself, omits to be one.

34

devirilizing, or desexualizing. They are in fact extraordinary *falsifications of pleasure*" (Miller 1993: 269), pains taken even to the point at which they too become "sheer ecstasy. Needles through the flesh. Hot candle wax dribbled over alligator clips. The most extraordinary pressure on muscles or connective tissue. The frontier between pain and pleasure has been crossed" (Miller 1993: 266).

"Not even suffering on the one hand, pleasure on the other: this dichotomy belongs to the order of the organic body, of the supposed unified instance" (Lyotard 1993: 23). Now there is a plane, a languorous plateau. The peaks and the troughs have converged on a still sea, a silent ocean. They have found their limit and flattened out. Melting point.

"We don't know what a body can do." Which is yet another reason why "we have to get rid of sexuality" (Macey 1994: 373), leave the body to its own devices, strip it away from its formal controls, disable its mechanisms of self-protection and security which bind intensity to pleasure and reproduction.

"That there are other ways, other

Out of order. And into a control which "instead of acting remains on guard, a control which blocks contact with commonplace reality and allows these more subtle and rarified contacts, bared down to the thread which ignites and yet never breaks apart" (Artaud 1965: 33).

On the way through the fractal scales, a "kind of order or apparent progression can be established for the segments of becoming in which we find ourselves." These "begin with and pass through becoming-woman" (Deleuze and Guattari 1988: 277), which is already a matter of "becoming child; becoming-animal, -vegetable, or -mineral; becomings-molecular of all kinds, becoming particles. Fibers lead us" (Deleuze and Guattari 1988: 272) in more ways than one.

It is by a process of deliberation that the body begins to uncouple itself from its own and external authority: possession and self-possession, control and self-control. Meat learns.

That is not a matter of education, which is always a question of restoring past information, the recollection of some originary transcendence, and the remembering of authority. It is a process of forgetting the past, which is also the abandonment of truth and the dismemberment of authority. While it is "necessary to dig deeply in order to show how things are historically contingent, for such and such an intelligible but not necessary reason," it is also the case that "to think of what exists is far from exploring all the possible spaces." Attention must be turned to the future instead. "Let us make an incontrovertible challenge out of the question: 'At what can we play, and how can we invent a game?'" (Miller 1993: 259).

Foucault jacks into virtual sex: the cyberspace scene, the ultimate in consensual hallucinations. It would, he thinks, "be marvelous to have the power, at any hour of day or night, to enter a place equipped with all the comforts and all the possibilities that one might imagine, and to meet there a body at once tangible and fugitive" (Miller 1993: 264). Not simply because, as William Burroughs enthuses, "you can lay Cleopatra, Helen of Troy, Isis, Madame Pompadour, or Aphrodite. You

There is no escape into a zone of free choice. Deliberation is neither free nor determined, but like the Tao, and equally unthinkable to an authority constituted in terms of masters and slaves, the autonomous and the automata, domination and submission, ones and others, ones and twos. . . . Such are what Lyotard calls the "macho bullshit" of a discourse which admits nothing beyond subjection, a perspective which cannot accept any other relation (or, rather, can accept nothing but relations).

Once you know it's a video game, it gets much harder to play along.

BIBLIOGRAPHY

Artaud, A. (1965) *Artaud Anthology*, ed. J. Hirschman, San Francisco: City Lights.
Burroughs, W. (1985) *The Adding Machine*, London: John Calder.
Cadigan, P. (1991) *Synners*, London: Grafton.

can get fucked by Pan, Jesus Christ, Apollo or the Devil himself. Anything you like likes you when you press the buttons" (Burroughs 1985: 86).

Press cyborg, and an optional object of desire.

You make the connections, access the zone. Whatever avatar you select for your scene, you cannot resist becoming cyborg as well. Some human locks on, but a replicant stirs. Depending on the state of your time-tract's art, the cyborg you become will be more or less sophisticated and extensive; more or less directly connected to your central nervous system; more or less hooked up to its own abstraction and the phase space in which you are both drawn out. But it will be post-human, whatever it is. Suddenly, it always was. You always were.

Foucault comes close in the San Francisco bath-houses: "You meet men there who are to you as you are to them: nothing but a body with which combinations and productions of pleasure are possible. You cease to be imprisoned in your own face, in your own past, in your own identity" (Miller 1993: 264).

Califia, P. (1993a) "Power Exchange," in *The Best of Skin Two*, ed. T. Woodward, New York: Masquerade Books.
—— (1993b) *Melting Point*, Boston: Alyson Publications.
Deleuze, G. and Guattari, F. (1988) *A Thousand Plateaus*, trans. B. Massumi, Minneapolis: University of Minnesota Press.
Foucault, M. (1977) *Discipline and Punish*, London: Pelican.
—— (1978) *History of Sexuality*, vol. 1, New York: Pantheon Books.
Freud, S. (1984) "Beyond the Pleasure Principle," in *On Metapyschology*, London: Pelican Freud Library.
Guattari, F. (1989) "Une Re'volution moleculaire,'" in *L'Esprit des drogues*, ed. J.-M. Hervieu *et al.*, Paris: Editions Autrement.
Haraway, D. (1991) *Simians, Cyborgs, and Women*, London: Free Association Books.
Irigaray, L. (1985) *This Sex Which is Not One*, New York: Cornell University Press.

Lingis, A. (1994) "Carnival in Rio," *Vulvamorphia*, Lusitania 6.

Lyotard, J.-F. (1993) *Libidinal Economy*, trans. I. H. Grant, London: Athlone.

Macey, D. (1994) *The Lives of Michel Foucault*, London: Vintage.

McLuhan, M. (1964) *Understanding Media: The Extensions of Man*, London: Sphere Books.

Miller, J. (1993) *The Passion of Michel Foucault*, London: Harper Collins.

All New Gen

VNS Matrix

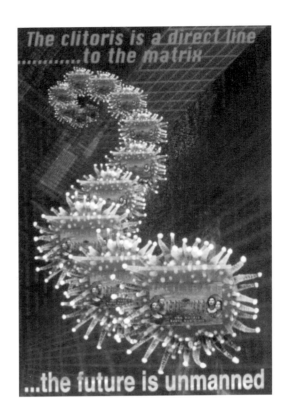

Rules of the Game

Welcome to the world of ALL NEW GEN.

Thank you for playing.

In this game you become a component of the matrix, joining ALL NEW GEN in her quest to sabotage the databanks of Big Daddy Mainframe.

You will use any means necessary to infiltrate and corrupt the controlling forces of Big Daddy.

All battles take place in the Contested Zone, a terrain of propaganda, subversion, and transgression.

Your guides through the contested zone are the renegade DNA Sluts, abdicators from the oppressive superhero regime, who have joined ALL NEW GEN in her fight for data liberation.

The path of infiltration is treacherous and you will encounter many obstacles. The most wicked – Circuit Boy – a dangerous technobimbo, whose direct mindnet to Big Daddy renders him almost invincible.

You may not encounter ALL NEW GEN as she has many guises. But do not fear, she is always in the matrix, an omnipresent intelligence, anarcho-cyber terrorist acting as a virus of the new world disorder.

You will be fueled by G-slime. Please monitor your levels.
Bonding with the DNA Sluts will replenish your supplies.

Be prepared to question your gendered biological construction.

There will be opportunities throughout the game for pleasurable distraction.

Be aware that there is no moral code in the Zone.

Enjoy.

THE CONTESTED ZONE

A long wintered night in the Contested Zone.

Her biological membrane shivered as she multiplied through a posse of Virtual Activists, protesting the latest scam by some Euro Data Deviants.

She was late.

She was always late.

If she survived to be a Cortex Crone she'd still have trouble shifting from dormant to active modes.

She sensed some quivering data nearby and scanned a tribe of DNA sluts, her sisters in slime. A rapid alpha exchange and she was back on the lookout for

Circuit Boy, a fetishized replicant of the perfect HuMan HeMan, a dangerous technobimbo.

She Self-replicated toward the banks of the Heavy Medal Boys – the Mbs. Minders of her arch-enemy, Big Daddy Mainframe.

Her aim: to corrupt Big Daddy's data.
His mainframe.
His Hard On.

Oh, suck me off.
Get rendered.
Get real.
Get fucked.

The Contested Zone was pulsing out its hype spots – *There's no Place like Zone . . . Zone is where the data is . . .*

She was angry. She'd spent too long looking for that squirt Circuit Boy. It was rumored that he'd been hanging with his Zoneboys – the Gene Pool Chameleons, a motley crew of genetic cretins. Suddenly she sensed his all too familiar architecture

my constructed body and picks clean the bones. she wraps her insidious words around my feverish brain with her thousand arms. she is gentle arid violent. with her perfect peripherals she dislodges my databank from the occipital cavity and down-loads digital propaganda direct from her fiber optic nerve center. she corrupts me. she scorns my debility. pronounces me weak. she laughs at my desire to collapse into familiar flesh. her blasphemy is cleansing and transcendent. she the high priestess the mistress of disgust takes my heart, punctures the sentimental aorta, whispers her lovehorror into the drained chambers. she speaks in flaming tongues that I sometimes understand. she presents me simultaneously with no alternatives and many alternatives. she tells me my only hope lies beyond the coded skeleton. she offers me no clues and no comfort. she is uncompromising in her demands. I must form a body of difference. I have no maps. I am undone. I do not know myself the future is bleak. I am afraid but I AM INFECTED BY HER

in the Zone. She challenged the datascape:
Circuit Boy,
I know you're here. I can sense you.
Show me your algorithms.
Let me corrode your defenses.
Circuit Boy. Come here.
Let me buttfuck your irresistible chrome-plated ass, honey.
I want you.
Circuit Boy.
I'm waiting.

THE USER

I am the user

her visceral invocations/incantations annihilate my self in a glorious tirade, a torrent of organs and muscles and veins and skin. she separates my precious flesh from my bones. she examines it with detachment but does not cast it aside. she makes contact, inserts her biology through the surface tension of my skin and plunges deep into the seething bile. she strips away the final vestiges of

SEX TRANCE & DANCE

In the spaces between words she searches for clues.

Pathways into the cyphered heart of Big Daddy.

The virus of the new world disorder takes on the transglobal fathernet of power and ambition.

Dirty work. For slimy girls.

Replicating her way through the Shadow's dingily seductive maze of data massage parlors, Freezers and Hots, Gen was inevitably reminded of Circuit Boy, a.k.a. Mission Improbable. Boy was rapidly losing his promise as an easy route into Big Daddy. Maybe he was just a mindless technobimbo, a limbless hole, good for a quick buttfuck or alpha exchange and not much else, as the Cortex Crones had predicted. Well, she'd suck on his memory some more, hardwire his balls and then see what else the Zone could offer.

Suck, flick and split, as the Sisters say.

Any mission has its highs and lows, but this particular

quest had been stranded on a barren plateau of spaghettied code and deviant data for too long. Dry and chaotic when she needed wet and elegant.

Big Daddy was becoming more ethereal with each transaction (the mythology expanding exponentially). His constructs were more ambiguous, more resistant to the mercenaries of slime.

She considered that an impasse is merely a state of mind and that with a subtle cognitive shift she could locate more yielding data. A shift is as good as a holiday and she was overdue for some bonding with her sisters in slime, the lusciously wet DNA Sluts.

Although it had been a few weeks since she had bonded with the Sisters, Gen knew how to find them. She calculated . . . it was after midnight . . . they were true children of the Zone . . . one perfect environment . . . the Alpha Bar.

The Alpha Bar. *The* place for transgressive time out in the Zone. Provocative. Pornographic. Perverse. Her kind of place. Her kind of constructs. Every child player wins a prize.

Sliding through the press of bodies, constructs, and grams, Gen selected one of her favorite bonding booths, placed her hand on the palm code reader and entered. It was a booth Japanese, fitted out with futon, screens, antique pillow book, incense. As she had a rep for being the hottest bioconstruct on the block, the strangest attractor, she never had to wait long to replenish her slime banks.

She had transmutated into an Hispanic model of human female, optimized for the slime exchange. Gen pleasured herself, familiarizing her sensors with the cool olive languidness of the body she had chosen.

A screen by the door displayed the image of a visitor. Mistress Beg. Requesting entry. The door opened. Silk ropes in hand, the Mistress of Detestable Pleasure approached Gen. Beg's method of bonding was dangerous, addictive, and severe. Activated by stored memories, Gen's slime levels began a slow rise.

The screen flickered on again. A geisha construct with a tray of sake and sashimi. She entered. Placed

Leaving the Shadow, Gen self-replicated through the Zone's biomembraned back blocks and reached the Alpha Bar in record time. As she'd determined, her Home Girls were well represented at the bar.

Beg, Bitch, and Snatch were in a dark place, superbonding with some exotic tribal constructs. The feathers were flying.

Cunt was giving a couple of the Zone Boys a hard time about something, probably Smarts. She never *could* say no to drugs and rough Zone traders had their own perverted appeal for Cunt.

The Princess of Slime was visible by her absence. She was probably grinding her way through her favorite bar, The Space with No Face, followed as always by her acolytes, Fallen and Abject.

Sublime was blissing out on Dance, bonding to the rhythm, sliming to the beat.

As for the other Sisters, where they were and what they were doing was anyone's calculation. Recreational options in the Zone were plentiful and diverse; Sex, Trance, and Dance the most favored.

a redly laqueured tray on the low table. Served the sake. Waited. Beg instructed the geisha to return later, when her help would be required. Cruel anticipation. Gen's slime bank shivered to another level as the geishacon scrolled out.

THE BODY IS RETURNED TO ITSELF

The Mistress of Detestable Pleasure described a circle in the geometry of love.

A cunt perched over a saucer of milk.

Tiny pearls in a rainforest.

Rubbing mirrors.

The jade gate was opening.

Let the ambassador enter.

Intuitive calculations.
Maps of the ethereal mind, subverting the binary order.
Erasure.
The body is returned to itself

SHE WEEPS TEARS OF CODE

(she was) approaching the abyss.

Living out her fantasies on a molecular level.

She engulfed herself as only a virus can.

Data poured through her biomembrane as she offered libations at the altar of abjection.

Surrender.

She weeps tears of code.

Her thoughts are classified. She has forgotten her own password.

She is corrupt.

Unrecoverable loss.

The project must be abandoned.

Her infinite element analysis reveals her weak points.

Stress is applied.

Sisters and brothers. Basking in – white noise. Flirting in the dataplaz. Weaving erratic data trails. Impressing each other with their elegant formulae. Speaking an erudite language of equations.

A clit storm was gathering in the Pulse. Gen could sense her parameters swelling as the irrepressible light waves weaved and darted through the matrix. She consulted her briefing files. Somewhere in the luminous chaos called the Pulse was a code which could lead her to the Source. Oracle code. Completely arcane. Always infallible.

Calculating the options, she chose a high probability path to the obscure object of desire. Streaming through alleyways of pure light Gen arrived at the banks of the dynamic link libraries. It was her lucky millennium. For once the Server was free. And liberated. Code-named ServerLAN, this particular Server was notorious in the Pulse as one who interpreted the Freedom of Information Charter as giving computers the right freely to choose who may access their vast datacores.

She crumples under pressure.

The project must be abandoned.

THE PERFUMED GARDEN

autumn whisperings

through the Pulse

(the poets were peaking)

All New Gen's search took her to the Pulse. She had the rhythm. She could transmit with the best of them.

The Pulse was humming. Frenetic frequencies sliding around the datascape. Waves of light. Orange. Blue. Violet. Pulse pirates intercepting the flow to resell on the Slime Exchange. Pulse poets beaming their Stein lines over the ocean of messages.

Some Codekids had distributed a message over the Net:
You must find your own bliss . . . jouissance is in the cunt of the beholder.

Switching to enquiry mode Gen strategically accessed ServerLAN.

I would like to be your client

Do you give oracle?

My equations are complex, my needs simple.

I will analyze and modify you, infinitely improving your capacity. In return you will give me oracle.

Silence.

ServerLAN considered. Within a nanosecond the answer flowed seamlessly through the jade gate.

Gen's optic sheath quivered as the oracle entered, merging with her memory.

The code was sublime.

Impeccable.

A knowledge she had yearned for forever.

Collapsing her boundaries, Gen allowed the numbers to reach her prime. Tiny explosions of dynamical systems looping in on themselves. The pleasure was almost unbearable.

The oracle code integrated, Gen left the libraries and headed back to her favorite Pulse pleasure pit, The Perfumed Garden.

Algorithms with attitude converged relentlessly on the Garden at any hour of the day or night. The place was unique in the Pulse, part salon, part opium den, and part love hotel. It also had the advantage of being one of the only sites where the Pulse's ubiquitous data scavengers were nowhere to be sensed. The Garden clientele was a flawless combination of streetwise punks and machine queens with impeccable lineages.

G-slime overflowing from the merge with the oracle, Gen was desperate to discharge some energy. Using her optical character recognition D-vice Gen selected a Super Conducting Pussy to play with. This was no ordinary SCP. She was a product of Generation E, an ecstatic equation modeled and rendered and animated purely for an elevated form of pleasure

It never sleeps, owing to the violence of its love,
It sighs to enter my vulva, and sheds tears on my belly . . .

Gen responded:

Between his arms I am like a corpse without life.
Every part of my body receives in turn his love-bites,
And he covers me with kisses of fire . . .

THE TRIPLE TEMPTATION OF CIRCUIT BOY

In the domains of the abstract Circuit Boy was an easy seduction.

Boy had been designed for pleasure. He was the penultimate pleasure model, made for merging. Hard and abundant. Pleasingly shy. Full of holes and protuberances.

Cunt draped a spline around his chrome rendered torso, talked dirty equations, algorithmically slid up and down on his double density, read only his memory (which was full of adolescent yearnings). She, slime incarnate, relentlessly manipulated and

exchange. A subtle dance of filaments and scanners commenced.

Pleasure making in the Garden was always intense. The protocol demanded that a certain and substantial amount of time was dedicated to shared intellectual pursuits of the highest order, the participants determining the method and subject matter between themselves.

A contract was agreed upon. The construction of a love game paradigm based upon passages from the ancient erotic treatise, the *Perfumed Garden for the Soul's Delectation* of the Shaykh Nefiawi.

Draping a spline over the Pussy's splendid wiry frame, Gen began:

I prefer a young man for coition, and him only,
He is full of courage – he is my sole ambition,
His member is strong to deflower the virgin,
And richly proportioned in all its dimensions . . .

The SCP countered with a familiar verse:

It is always ready for action and does not die down;

extended his many parameters. Artfully, together, they postponed the moment of full G-slime transference, rerouting urgent visceral requests to deeper levels of their source codes.

The Mistress of detestable Pleasure draped a spline around his wire frame.
Her archives of pain and desire were immense.
She rendered him senseless with her infinite promise of corruption.
He allowed himself to be dragged outside the moral code, all precepts ignored, forgotten.
He was zero to her triple cunt intelligence.
Their boundaries merged, forming new objects.
She mapped his changing parameters, calculating the pleasure options.
She was abject-oriented desire to his open subject.
It was in this way that Circuit Boy learnt the rewards of willing submission.

THE TRIPLE TEMPTATION OF CIRCUIT BOY . . .

Abject feigned sleep, her thighs slightly apart, her left breast uncovered.

She favored a non-linear approach.

Her pathways were subtle.

Circuit Boy tended her biological components, practicing ethereal modes of convergence in his down time. He partitioned his RAM, slowing his response times to match her requirements. She was highly encrypted, he became expert at decoding. Their surveillance narratives grew so dense it was impossible to know who was in control.

PART III

Cyberculture

Singularities

Telepathy: Alphabetic Consciousness and the Age of Cyborg Illiteracy[1]

David Porush

He went to the window [of his hotel room in Istanbul]. . . . There was another hotel across the street. It was still raining. A few letter-writers had taken refuge in doorways, their old voiceprinters wrapped in sheets of clear plastic, evidence that the written word still enjoyed a certain prestige here. It was a sluggish country.

(Gibson 1984: 88)

She passed many things that Case hadn't understood, but his curiosity was gone. There had been a room filled with shelves of books, a million flat leaves of yellowing paper pressed between

In the excerpts from William Gibson's *Neuromancer* (1984) above, the aboriginal novel about cyberspace, the author suggests that when we get there, we may be illiterate but we will also be telepathic. The first excerpt is a sly allusion to ancient Babylonia, Sumeria, and Israel, where scribes opened stalls in sûks to send letters, write contracts, and take dictation for pleas to monarchs and prayers to deities. The second comes from a scene in which Case, the cyberspace cowboy and barbarian from America, is viewing a strange room through the eyes of Molly (the cyborg assassin) to whom he is telepathically linked by cyberspace technology. *We* can recognize it as a library. *Case* has no clue. At the same time, Case is seeing the world through Molly's eyes, is feeling her body as it moves through this remote, alien space, demonstrating the new tele-pathic powers cyberspace gives. The third describes an encounter between Case and the artificially intelligent entity, Wintermute, who has hired Case to link him with Neuromancer, the right-brain libidinous entity. Case believes that Wintermute can "read" his mind. Wintermute hints that "reading" is an

bindings of cloth or leather, the shelves marked at intervals by labels that followed a code of letters and numbers.

(Gibson 1984: 207)

"Can you read my mind . . . Wintermute . . . ?"
        "Minds aren't read. See, you've still got the paradigms print gave you, and you're barely print literate. I can access your memory, but that's not the same as your mind." He reached into the exposed chassis of an ancient television and withdrew a silver-black vacuum tube. "See this? Part of my DNA, sort of . . . " He tossed the thing into the shadows and Case heard it pop and tinkle. "You're always building models. Stone circles. Cathedrals. Pipe organs. Adding machines. I got no idea why I'm here now, you know that? But if the run goes off tonight, you'll have finally managed the real thing."
        "I don't know what you're talking about."
        "That's 'you' in the collective. Your species."

(Gibson 1984: 170–1)

I'M TELLING YOU THIS 'CAUSE YOU'RE ONE OF MY FRIENDS/MY ALPHABET STARTS WHERE YOUR ALPHABET ENDS!

(Dr Seuss, *On Beyond Zebra*)

anachronistic metaphor for what minds do to each other. What's needed is a whole new way of "knowing" how minds work, a system describing cultural evolution in which technological innovations like televisions are the "genes" or "memes" that evolve new consciousness, new cyborg facilities of mind.

Although there are enormous technical difficulties that must be overcome before we reach cyberspace – not least of which is being able to create an interface for subjective bodily coherence in the brain – we can at least imagine that some day such telepathy will be possible. If we disregard the technical obstacles it is obvious that the cyberspace of our imaginations, our virtual future, beckons us with the promise of a whole new way to communicate, which in turn has unleashed in us a form of apocalyptic fervor and yearning. Assuming cyberspace provides an imaginative vantage point from which we can regard the revolution in culture and definition of the self that might ensue, a transformation is already occurring. And from this vantage point, we can implicitly critique our own postmodern states of body, mind, self, culture. That's what the game, and the pun, in "virtual futures" are about: we imagine a future that isn't quite real, created by a technology that delivers a reality that isn't quite real, so we can talk about where we are now.

But I would like to talk about cyberspace without talking about it. The means by which I will do this is by finding an analogous moment in history when culture found itself in possession of an equally new and revolutionary cybernetic technology. Do we have any analogs for this sort of massive cultural revolution initiated by the invention of a new cybernetic technology for telepathy, for getting thoughts from one mind to another?

I propose we can find this analog to our own position today in the ancient invention of the primitive Hebrew alphabet. The alphabet itself – the idea that you could transcribe not the pictures of things but the sound of language itself – gave birth to a cybernetic tech that spread so rapidly and was so potent that it only needed to be invented once: in the South Sinai or South Canaan some time in the

generations and the proliferation of 500 cable channels, has finally manifested its anti-literate effects in declining literacy among Americans. After all, who can resist committing adultery with multimedia after so many centuries of faithfulness to the written text? Who can resist the sensuous widening of the bandwidth that video games and mind-link tech provide? I call this new, secondary loss of the alphabet as a tool "cyborg illiteracy": we abandon reading for the hyper-MTV, wide-band pleasures of the text of the body inscribed and transcribed back out into the world and then back onto us.

So observing what happened to culture with the origination of the first phonetic alphabet provides a remarkable model for the sort of cognitive, cultural, epistemological, and even metaphysical revolution we are beginning to endure with the advent of VR. Even as we are already nostalgic for alphabetic consciousness and the particular way it gave us out-of-body experience and a new metaphysic, by understanding its essence we can also refine our games of prophesying, and try to understand the metaphysical revolution immanent in VR.

fifteenth century BC. It fostered a new way of thinking, a new facility for abstraction. It rearranged social organizations, and even created a new epistemology and some new metaphysics. Choosing the primitive Hebrew alphabet as an analog for our own cultural moment has a second virtue: by standing outside the long era of alphabetic civilization, by imagining a virtual future we can, perhaps with some nostalgia, understand "alphabetic consciousness" and the special cyborg gifts that the alphabet brings to brain operation. We can also come to appreciate what we might lose – what we are already nostalgic for – as we move to the illiterate, telepathic cyberspace of Gibson's imagination, our virtual future. We can *read* how the advent of a new Technologically Mediated Telepathy (TMT) will *spell* the obsolescence of an older TMT, the alphabet. We can understand why world statistics bear out the message that literacy has peaked, why even as third worlds and developing nations increase their literacy, first world corporations like McDonald's move toward pictographic icons and computer simulations in their training and customer interfaces, and American television, after two

WHEN THE BRAIN WAS SIMPLE

What is the brain? At its simplest it is an organic entity that takes impressions from *out there* in the form of energy striking different organs of the body (eyes, skin, ears, nose, mouth/tongue), converts the energy into information, shuttles the information to a central processor, a black box *schwartzgerat* homuncular body without organs sitting in an ecology of incomprehensibly frothing and turbulent hormones, and translates them into wholly different things *in here* – sensation, thoughts, flocks of birds, schools of fish, swarming, buzzing. The brain is intrinsically a sur-rational machine for bringing worlds into collision, a metaphor device, a translation circuit for closing and opening the loop between incommensurate and mutually incomprehensible universes. In my view, it is already meta-physical.

Phylogenetically, when the brain was simple, its expressive function was almost non-existent. There was a neat Kantian fit between animal and environment: the rules of the world *out there*, its physics, were not challenged by the rules of the world *in here*; there was a nice match. But then through some urgency that it is just as easy to talk about metaphysically or teleologically as in terms of some deterministic chaotic evolution, the brain exploded, human-like hominids started walking upright about 35,000 years ago, looking forward, using tools, colonizing the world, creating new social structures. The brain, like some imperial culture exploding off a remote island, started projecting itself onto the world, terraforming the Earth in its own image and leaving in its wake a trail of non-biodegradable tools and waste. The brain also started talking, depicting, enacting versions of its experience in cave paintings, ritual dances, gestures, and a grammar of grunts. It became self-conscious. It recognized a mismatch between the world *out there* and the world *in here*: Hey! The world persists; we die! Self-consciousness and the idea of death were born in one fatal stroke.

It is obvious that the powerful cybernetic loop among environment, culture, and brain that we recognize as uniquely human was initiated some-time between 35,000 and 10,000 years ago as a

Another brain researcher calls this process "the selective stabilization of the synapses" as a result of continuous exposure to specific cultural effects or stimulation" (Changeux 1988: 43–50). Charles Lumsden calls this peculiar collaboration between cultural invention and inherited genetic characteristics "Gene-Culture Coevolution" or "epi-genetics." The "alphabet" for transmitting the information between culture and heredity is sometimes called "memes" or, by Lumsden, "culturgens" (Lumsden 1988: 17–42).

Neurophysiologists and cognitive scientists who study the alphabet note that its effects on the brain can even be seen in the lifetime development of individual people. Evidence is emerging that the use of language in the world helps reshape the brain from womb to tomb. In other words, ontogeny recapitulates phylogeny in culture-gene coevolution as well. It's happening to us, today, right now. Some of this evidence comes from studies of aphasics and dyslexics showing that a brain changes physiologically and progressively after an injury (Tzeng 1988: 273–290), suggesting that reading

result of who-knows-which-butterfly flapping who-knows-what sort of wings. We call the cybernetic device that initiated and grew in this loop *language* or *symbolizing*. Frances Hellige, a prominent brain researcher, describes the growth of this loop initiated by the development of language, with feedforward and feedback components, as a sort of "snowball effect" (Hellige 1993) since it initiates a cycle of ever-widening gyres that eventually embraces and creates everything between the poles of culture and the biology of the brain itself, including physiological changes in the structure and size of different regions. In cybernetic terms, we call this a "positive feedback loop." The cybernetic system (in this case, human brain) sends informa-tion out into the world-culture-environment, which feeds newly intensified signals back into the (brain) system to destabilize the system anew, which in turn reamplifies its message, like an oversensitive microphone, and again rebroadcasts this message back onto the world until the universe screeches with the noise of the human brain echoed back to it, in it, a cyborg rock concert.

grows parts of the brain even in the lifetime of individual humans, just as losing the ability to read devolves the brain of individual humans, or forces the brain to "rewire" itself autopoetically. Furthermore, evidence is beginning to emerge that different script systems change the brain differently.[2]

FUN WITH YOUR NEW BRAIN: A BRIEF HISTORY OF THE RISE OF THE ALPHABET

To put it bluntly, using different alphabets (or losing the capacity to read the alphabet), even within the lifetime of an individual, is a bit like growing a new brain. In transit, trying a new alphabet must have been (and still is) tantamount to an ongoing progressive hallucination. It lets you think things that you couldn't have thought before and make connections that simply didn't exist physiologically, and forces your brain into different information-processing patterns, which presumably involve different mental events or experiences (as physiological-cognitive research overwhelmingly shows). It's like having a whole new brain, or at least, a brain with whole new faculties, new circuits, new wetware. Now imagine the mass hallucination of an entire culture learning how to use an alphabet for the first time. Whole tribes of people, or important segments of them, put on this new cybernetic headgear, or what I have been calling TMTs, virtually all at once. We can imagine this mass cybernetic experiment would be accompanied by social, epistemological, and metaphysical revolutions, apocalyptic prophesies, and redefinitions of the self in relation to body, mind, others, and the invisible.

We can see the effects of this feedback loop with the advent of pictographic writing itself if we take (in our imaginations) a time-lapse photograph of the Nile Valley before and just after the advent of hieroglyphics, or (even earlier) the Fertile Crescent of Mesopotamia before and just after the very first invention of writing, Sumerian pictographs, around 3,200 BC. These time-lapse films would show millions of years of desultory animal activity, including the hunting-gathering and low-level agricultural activity of upright hominids after 35,000 BC. As we approach 10,000 BC, activity begins to pick up pace and organization. Clusters of hominids show tool use, primitive building, cultivation of the earth, though in indifferent and almost-random-seeming patterns. Then, suddenly, around 3,200 BC, BANG! Something leaps across the chaotic bifurcation into a new order of frantic self-organization. Compressed into a few frames is an almost instantaneous transformation; blink and you'll miss the instant. These fertile regions undergo massive terraforming along rectilinear plots. Rivers are diverted into rectangular irrigation systems. Cities emerge, themselves rectilinear. Zoom in with me now into the squarish walls of the cities, and into the very squarish rooms of the city, and we will find the intimate source of this sudden change. There, a row of hard stone benches, arranged regularly. It is a schoolroom for scribes. Hundreds of boys, mostly the sons of privileged nobility, sit for hours hunched over clay tablets, learning to scrawl in regular lines. Indeed, if we superimpose the scratching of these lines they look like the lines of irrigation written on the face of the earth itself, as seen from an orbiting

48

Figure 1 Sumerian schoolroom, c. 3,000 BC

satellite. The harsh discipline of the schoolchildren being tutored in a script "canalizes" their thought processes, re-enforcing certain pathways. It is hard not to imagine that what's written on the brain gets projected onto the world, which is literally "canalized," too.[3]

Looking at a picture (Figure 1) of the ancient Sumerian schoolroom (Chiera 1938: 117) for scribes found in Shruppak (Kramer 1956) with its familiar rows of benches and the headmaster's "desk" up front, seizes one with a horrible and giddy vertigo, a terrible revelation: five thousand years later we're still canalizing the brains of our children, enforcing the harsh discipline of writing in virtually the same way as these ancient Sumerians, "that gifted and practical people," who invented cuneiform as a portable means to effect commerce, extend the authority of their kings, preserve metaphysical and transcendent information, and secure the stability of caste and rank.

The invention of pictographic writing by the Sumerians, improved by the Akkadians as cuneiform syllabaries, was "a secret treasure" or "mystery"

in Babylon, Sumeria, and Egypt, we see the same pattern of social, epistemological, and metaphysical organization arise when writing is discovered. Along with these scripts come other inventions so predictably similar that they seem to derive directly from imperatives in the nervous system itself, amplified or newly grown by use of the new cyborg device: centralized authority in god/kings; a monumental ziggurat-like or pyramidal architecture; hierarchies of priest-scribes; complex, self-perpetuating bureaucracies; fluid but clearly demarcated social/economic classes; trade or craft guilds; imperialism; slavery; canalizing educational systems; confederations of tribes into nations; standardized monetary systems and trade; taxes; and so on. Almost every conceivable aspect of empire, in its gross forms, was entailed in pictographic writing. Even the alphabet, with its greater efficiency and fidelity to speech, only seems to add abstraction and speed to what McLuhan described as the exteriorization of the nerve net.

which the layman could not be expected to understand and which was therefore the peculiar possession of a professional class of clerks or scribes. Furthermore, the metaphysic associated with this new telepathic technology becomes clear in the priestly functions these scribes served. In fact, Neo-Babylonian texts used "the same ideogram for priest and scribe."[4] Along with the script came a new mythology that, predictably, placed the power of language in the center of its metaphysics:

As for the creating technique attributed to these [new] deities, – Sumerian philosophers developed a doctrine which became dogma throughout the Near East – the doctrine of the creative power of the divine word. All that the creating deity had to do, according to this doctrine, was to lay his plans, utter the word, and pronounce the name.

(Kramer 1956: 75)

In fact, everywhere pictographic writing makes its advent, we find the sudden emergence of what I call tech-writing empires. These civilizations were akin to the rationalized hive structures of ants or bees.[5] In China, among the Aztecs of Mexico or Incas in Peru,

THERE IS NO WORD IN HEBREW FOR "FICTION" (AMOS OZ)

But there was one moment in history, a parenthesis, that interrupted this cybernetic feedback loop between writing system and culture/empire canalization with an alternative loop of its own. It occurs at the moment that the hieroglyphic/pictographic system is supplanted by the new invention of the alphabet. This event is so momentous that it only happens once in all of human history, so powerful that it eventually spreads, and is indeed still spreading, across most human cultures. The moment is brief, for it is quickly supplanted by improvements on its own fundamental innovation. Yet its legacy is captured and evolves along its own coevolutionary path, in dialectic with the totalizing line of empire that is taken up again when the alphabet evolves enough to be harnessed to the work of the tech-writing pictographic scripts. I call this moment "Hebrew" or, better, for reasons that will emerge, The (AlephTav) Event. I locate this moment, this interruption, eruption, parentheses, this invention on the margins in time and space, quasi-fictionally. Its legacy is an evolving cultural complex that has some stable morphological features we call "Judaism" or, for reasons I will explain later, an epistemology and metaphysics I call *porushia*.

The Phoenician, Ugaritic, Greek, Arabic, Amharic, Korean, Russian, Latin, and all Indo-European alphabets derived from this ancient proto-Sinaitic Hebrew script.[6] Every other writing system is either pictographic (Chinese, Egyptian hieroglyphic, Aztec runes, etc.) or syllabic (e.g., Cuneiform A, North American Cree and Eskimo, Vai (Liberia, Africa), Tamil, Katakana and Hiragana (the two Japanese Kana scripts invented between 700–900 AD)). Syllabaries are an important step on the road to an alphabet because they shift the representation of language from images of things or events (pictograms, sometimes mistakenly called ideograms or logograms) to the much more plastic representation of the sounds of the language itself. But syllabaries are a clumsy compromise, often requiring hundreds of separate characters, one for *ba*, another for *beh*, a third for *bee*, etc. The

be explained by the need for the Hebrews of the time for secrecy, for a code set apart from the reigning script paradigm. In any case, the Phoenicians, or some Western Semites with whom the Phoenicians came in contact between the twelfth and ninth century BC, probably between Tyre (now in Lebanon) and Akko or Atlit (on the northern coast of Israel) realized the inefficiency or primitiveness of this system, and added the missing vowels. The Phoenicians exported this new improved alphabet, now a much more efficient device for representing all the sounds of speech, so useful for their commerce and imperialization of the seas, to Greece.[7] At the same time, the alphabet in different forms spread eastward through Persia into India, and westward back into Africa. It also invaded Middle Eastern and African regions where an empire hadn't already preserved an older form of writing (as in Egypt, where hieroglyphics survived into the Roman era), enabling new alphabetic cultures to arise.

The actual moment at which some ingenious rebel or group of innovators collaborated to reduce the multi-hundred sign-system of the syllabary

fundamental revelation or breakthrough in a proper alphabet is the abstraction of the letters from individual syllables, and indeed, from sounds as uttered. An alphabet, in other words, recognizes consonants as separate and constant elements permuted around another constant set of explosives, vowels, which make the utterance possible. (Try uttering the consonant "p" without expelling the air that comes with the vowel, and you will see that all you get is the stutterer's intention to say "peh" or "pah" or "pay," a moment of hesitation before an explosion that cannot come without a vowel.) So one can immediately distinguish an alphabet from a syllabary because the former reduces the number of characters to thirty-six or fewer. Hebrew, for instance, as the prototypical and aboriginal alphabet, went too far in the right direction. It represented only the twenty-two alphabetic characters for the aboriginal abstraction of the consonants and made the mistake of not representing the vowels. This is peculiar, since the idea of a vowel is entailed once one makes the phonetic distinction of a consonant. It is like defining light without having a concept of dark. Perhaps it can

(or as some archeologists argue, the multi-thousand sign-systems of the sixteenth-century BC Egyptian hieroglyph) into the twenty-two characters of the first proto-alphabet is so super-inscribed by debates over archeological evidence and so overinformed by theories of culture, and so obscured and effaced by extra-scientific considerations of cultural priority, ideology, territorial primacy, and even theology, that one must despair of ever really being able to enunciate and clearly hear when that moment was and who was responsible for creating it. Nevertheless, let me tell a likely fiction. It is based largely on my correlation of the account of the exodus/expulsion of the Habiru slaves from Egypt in the Bible with archeological evidence from the Southern Sinai, from ancient Canaan and Western Semitic regions around the fifteenth and twelfth centuries BC. My story also involves a sociological speculation.

The alphabet was invented by Habiru ("Sandrambler") slaves working the turquoise mines for Pharaoh near Surabit al-Khadem in the Southern Sinai in the fifteenth or sixteenth century BC (see Figure 2). This romantic idea has many appealing facets beyond the solid archeological evidence to support it. First, it is very hard to imagine the highly stratified and inertial Egyptian empire giving rise to or embracing a new script system on its own, which would require massive reorganization not just bureaucratically, but socially and metaphysically as well. Second, this new twenty-two character alphabet is highly compressed, a sort of code, a jazzy alternative script and symbology that are just the sort of argot/cipher we might expect to arise among slaves who need to invent their own resistant, subterranean samiszdat-like culture. Again and again in history we find slaves inventing spoken creoles, pidgins, alternative art forms, graffittis, tongues, media, jazzes; the Habiru slaves are likely candidates to invent their own subterranean, rebellious script.

Finally, however, this theory explains the uniqueness of subsequent Hebrew-Jewish history, first iterated in the story of the exodus/expulsion of the Hebrew slaves from Egypt, and then in the evolution of a unique Jewish cultural practice. Even if this little fiction is only fantasy, it is clear that the Hebrews adopted the primitive alphabet as their own,

alephtafian consciousness, in its most radical form: Aleph-Tav.

I would like to play a game with you. It is called "Thinking in Hebrew in English." It has one rule. Decode the following sentence into sensible modern English by supplying the missing vowels:

TH VRL CLTR F DS MKS VR XCHNG F BD FLDS N CT F TTL FTH LV ND MRDR. SM S "J MRT" T RGSM. DS GVS NW MNNG T THR CR.

You are more or less undergoing what every modern and ancient Hebrew reader must do regularly in order to read the language. Hebrew is an alphabet without vowels and without upper and lower case letters. (The fact that it reads right-to-left is only quasi-arbitrary. Reading in this direction actually activates the right hemisphere – correlated with slowing the reading process even further – more than English or Greek or Latin does, which are almost entirely processed in the left hemisphere of the brain.)

Attempt to decipher the sentence above, and you see that what is required is an elaborate process of shuttling back and forth between

Figure 2 Proto-alphabet used by the Habiru, c. sixteenth century BC

that it had a powerfully viral and transforming influence on their culture, which in the end preserves the essential cognitive peculiarities of Hebrew's very primitiveness and inefficiency, and from this historical accident arises the eternal Other, the philosophy of other, whose effect on Western civilization is impossible to calculate and whose influence is still felt, especially in postmodern philosophies.

Let me finally introduce you to, infect you, or contaminate you, with ancient Hebrew, with

recognizable elements and unrecognizable ones: developing momentary hypotheses, testing them against further decipherment, discarding them in favor of improvements. A track of eye motions across the page would not look anything like the dominant paradigm of reading normal English (Figure 3).

Figure 3 The predominance of linear eye-tracking in reading English

It would rather look something like Figure 4. There is a web of cross-referrals and leaps, as words at the end of the excerpt help clarify words at the beginning. In initial stages of decipherment, your reading probably looked more like this, closer to the

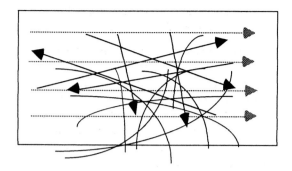

Figure 4 The cross-tracking model required to decode English without vowels

scanning of pieces of puzzle laid out face-up on a table than to simple left-right tracking or canalization. There are sudden crystallizations, and the whole process slowly, and then more rapidly, converges upon a "reading" of the text. At the end, however, there still may be ambiguities left, ambiguities of interpretation which can only be resolved by referring to extra-textual contexts: who wrote it, when, to whom?

likened interpreting the Torah to sexual activity. The consummation of total and perfect understanding seems always to be deferred. Even if you settle on a decipherment like the following, there is always going to be some doubt left:

The viral (?) culture of AIDS (?) makes every exchange of body fluids an act of total faith, love, and murder. Some say 'Je mort' at orgasm. AIDS gives new meaning to their cry.

But it could have been read, perhaps in another time and place, or by another audience, supposing it came from another author:

The virile collator of Odessa makes over-exchange of bed folds an acute of . . .

You get the idea. Think of the challenge to decipher a single English word without its vowel, taken out of context: "rd." Is it *red, read, road, rode, rod, rid, rude, arid . . .* ? Similarly, let's look at two Hebrew letters, the aleph (שׁ) and the tav (ה), which also happen to be the first and last, the alpha and omega, of the Hebrew alphabet. There is even a saying in Israel, "from the aleph to the tav" meaning

52

TH VRL CLTR F DS MKS VR XCHNG F BD FLDS N CT F TTL LV ND MRDR. SM S "J MRT" T RGSM. DS GVS NW MNNG T THR CR.

You are probably able to decide quickly that "MRDR" indicates "Murder" or that "XCHNG" implies "exchange" (I won't say means because that implies a level of certainty that just doesn't exist in texts like these – and the problem is exacerbated in Hebrew). With these two words, you might quasi-consciously begin to form a general hypothetical drift. This isn't an excerpt from a computer manual. "RGSM" might intend "orgasm." Perhaps a bit overexcited now, here you might leap on "CLTR" and imagine that it conjures the word "culture." The whole process might take quite a few minutes, at the end of which you'd have a quite good idea, but perhaps no certainty. In the interim, you are kept in suspense, anxious suspense. The need to decipher is urgent, an itch that must be scratched, not completely unpleasurable (not unlike the need to complete a puzzle), but demanding satisfaction, if not consummation. You can begin to understand why ancient kabbalists

something stronger than "from soup to nuts" or "the whole nine yards."

Together, the two Hebrew letters appear like this: if you asked any Hebrew reader "What does that say?" she would simply shrug. For looking at them floating in space like this, in a contextual void, the letters can be pronounced "eht," "aht," "oht," "ooht," or even the number 401 (backwards), since Hebrew letters also stand for numbers, aleph (שׁ) = 1 and taה (ה) = 400. Furthermore, there is something transcendental about the combination, for the word "oht" means letter *itself*. The word aleph-tav "eht" is a purely grammatical sign, impossible in a pictographic script. It represents the accusative case (English speakers have trouble grasping the need for such a sign), the indication of a direct object using the finite article. A weak analog would be if there were a word in English that had to be placed in between any verb and any noun using "the" or any pronoun for a specific person. Give me *eht* the book. I love *eht* you. It is a transcription of a purely grammatical sign in speech, the sign of the alphabet itself.

In short, it would be fair to say that the average reader of Hebrew, learns or has enforced on him or her a set of cognitive habits that are quite different from those of readers of more efficient Greek and later alphabets. Let me categorize these cognitively (and perhaps even acquired biological) differences as follows:

1) *Contextualization*. Reading standard (non-vowelled) Hebrew requires persistent contextualization between deciphering the phonetic value of individual syllables and syntactic and semantic meaning. Even an eye-tracking map of how the Hebrew reader reads a page of Hebrew would show much greater lateral, back-tracking, and vertical movement of the eye than for readers of "more efficient" alphabets (Kerckhove 1988: 403–4).

2a) *Interpretation/dealing with ambiguity*. The potential level of ambiguity in most Hebrew writing is much greater, and so the Hebrew reader learns quickly to tolerate and contend with ambiguity better and earlier than readers of less ambiguous (more

(v) ability to recognize the identity of objects in different configurations is greater.

4) *Abstraction metaphorization*. Getting the right answer in deciphering a Hebrew sentence means dealing with abstraction more frequently and more intensely. The Hebrew reader must formulate numerous hypotheses and discard them in quick succession, testing the hypothesis against what is first presented on the page as an abstract system of multivalent signs. The result is:

(i) the movement between literal (as in the letter and its immediate decipherment) and abstract is more fluid and intensely iterative for the Hebrew reader;
(ii) the plasticity of the Hebrew cognitive apparatus in apprehending other non-*literal* meanings must be greater, since such apprehension is required at the primary immediate level of reading, i.e., the movement to symbolic interpretation, to metaphorical interpretation, and to non-literal interpretation must be swift in order to be merely competent as a reader.

53

efficient) languages. The Hebrew reader also learns to generate more possible interpretations more quickly.

2b) *Tolerance of suspense/deferral*. This also means that the Hebrew reader is willing to wait longer for resolution and tolerates semantic irresolution better than readers of other languages.

3) *Right-brain processing*. We know that reading Hebrew, with analogy to pictographic scripts and because of its right-to-left direction, requires greater right-brain processing visually. This means that the connection between semantic processing and other right-brain functions is greater; these include:

(i) global (holistic) apprehension of patterns (intuition or Gestalt processing) in all kinds of sensory data is greater;
(ii) visuo-spatial processing is more efficient and holistic;
(iii) connection between data and emotion is greater;
(iv) ability to detect and differentiate "nuances" in tone and meaning of linguistic (and other) information is greater;

5) *Multivalence/deconstruction*. The notion that there is one and only one right, rational answer to any question has, we may hypothesize, less sway over the Hebrew brain than over the brains of literates in languages that pose fewer problems in decipherment.

6) *Resistance to authority*. Because of the above reasons (especially 5) the connection between written word and the voice of author(ity) is severed. Similarly, because the movement between written word and the proper phoneticization poses so many more difficulties, it is likely that the Hebrew reader does not so easily identify the authority or the intention of the author in the text. Thus, on the one hand, Hebrew literates are less literate, limited by their alphabet. On the other hand, Hebrew literates are less likely to accept the text as final authority.

The Hebrew word *porush* captures many of these practices. It means, variously (as noun or verb) commentary, exegesis, explanation (both literal and otherwise), a dissident, dissenter, seceder, schismatic, someone who believes in the "free interpretation of the written word and sought to discover its inner meaning – a Pharisee."[8]

PORUSHIAN CONSCIOUSNESS ENABLES A PECULIAR COGNITION, CULTURE, AND METAPHYSICS

Cognitive changes

Given all the above, it is hard to resist making very suggestive connections between the cybernetic practices induced by this inefficient alphabet and the sociological, cultural, and even metaphysical practices of Hebrew culture. For instance, because the Hebrew language makes the transmission of authority without questioning or interpretation difficult (if possible) and because any written message, especially complex or new ones, are likely to provoke numerous interpretations, it is easy to imagine that the peculiarities of the Hebrew alphabet may have helped Jewish culture develop a hearty resistance to authority and consensus in general.

generations to mutate the central culturgenic heritage of the hosts.

Epistemic changes

If we look closely even at the little game we played with the aleph and the tav to produce three or four possible words – the feminine you, the word for "letter", the (untranslatable) sign of the accusative case, and 401 – it is tempting to see the rudiments of an entire alternative epistemological practice emerge. In this practice, the letters themselves open a space into which interpretation must be placed in the form of choosing the vowels. The reader takes an active role, looking not only to multiply possible alternatives, but to seek hidden unities beneath them. Indeed, we can project from these practices the intense and peculiarly multivalent hermeneutics of Jewish Talmud and mysticism. Furthermore, with the ability to represent "eht," the accusative case (which is so abstruse that it is not even represented in English) and all other grammatical cases because the alphabet is now a transcription (though in Hebrew

54

Sociological changes

Now put this cognitive practice or habit in the context of the diaspora or cultural nomadism. There, one of the only constants binding two thousand years of Jewish history and dozens of disparate Jewish communities around the world at any given time, each speaking a different host language, is *reading unvowelled Hebrew texts*. We can see how the Jews come to be viewed culturally as a peculiarly resistant "virus-like" or "parasite-like" race (and here I am reiterating the libel placed on the Jews by Hitler in *Mein Kampf*), ineradicable pests who carry with them a set of insular cognitive and cultural practices dooming them to play on, feed off of, the margins of the host culture. Yet, paradoxically, these same cognitive practices allow them to succeed with remarkable acuity in penetrating into controlling positions in the host culture, acquiring with incredible swiftness professional roles that require skills of literacy, interpretation, learning, and powers of abstraction. Thus, these perpetual newcomers threaten within a few

only ambiguously so) of the spoken language, civilization now has at its disposal a new sophisticated means to represent and preserve across space and time *the act of languaging itself*. That is, the text has the newfound capacity for self-reflexive statement, to represent with greater plasticity and fidelity the consciousness or intentions of an author in words. One can *do* texts independent of actions in the world with extreme plasticity. At the same time, the instrument is not completely efficient, so the reader is teased with this gesture at telepathic fidelity, and yet forced to disambiguate the messages sent this way.

Metaphysical changes

So it is also no wonder that the central metaphysical tenet – and indeed one of the only constants of Jewish metaphysical dogma (the phrase is almost oxymoronic because of the absence of a coherent dogma in Judaism) – in the thirty-five-hundred-year history of the Jews from the time of Moses is *the unpronounceability, the unwritability, and the unthinkability of the name of God.* Jews are taught traditionally never to write or speak The Name, even in another language. In English, for instance, one writes "G–d." The arbitrary transliteration of the Tetragrammaton – the four letters of God's name in Hebrew – YHVH – into Yahweh is a purely Christian imposition on a Hebrew that it is indeterminate and unpronounceable *as written*. Even in devout prayers, Jews abbreviate the Tetragrammaton to "YY" and utter "Adonay" (meaning Lord). For a non-liturgical practice, the letters are read "Adoshem," a nonsensical combination of "Lord" and "Name" – or else one says "The Name" (Hashem).

What at first seems like fetishism is therefore a reiteration and reinforcement of a central cognitive tool (or at least distinction) of Hebrew literacy. Thus, an imperfection in the alphabet gives rise to a metaphysics of multivalence, compulsory and compulsive interpretation, perpetual and transcendental ambiguity, deferral of meaning to some locus that is never here, a disconnection between the spoken and the written authority, and a denial of presence. God speaks His name and shows

of the new cultural/cognitive powers which the new alphabet brings. It is *circa* fifteen hundred BC. Moses flees Egypt and finds a harbor among the Midianites, who happen to occupy the area of the desert in the region of South Sinai (Liebovitch in Driver 1948: 97), near the turquoise mines of Pharaoh, where and when many archaeologists and epigraphers suggest the alphabet originated. There God reveals to Moses *haoht*, which is variously translated "sign," "mark," "omen," "token," or "miracle." But the word also means "letter." God tells Moses to go back to Egypt and show Pharaoh "the letter."[9] Moses, who doesn't speak well (either because he is of "uncircumcised lips," which means colloquially he has some speech impediment, or because he is "of the language of the uncircumcised," since the word "lips" also means "language") lets Aaron do the talking. Aaron shows the "letters" in the court of Pharaoh. Pharaoh calls out his own experts, who are called *chartomeeim* in Hebrew. The normal translation for this word is "magicians" or "wizards." But the earlier meaning is "hieroglyphic scribes." They show their "signs." Each of the signs is called a miracle, except for the first, the

55

His Face, an actual Face, only to Moses, only once, and even then Moses turns away, only to watch the metaphorical presence of God recede from him. So rather than a cosmological model of knowability, tangibility – essentially the kind of idolatry we find in tech-writing empires – from the inefficiency of the script system, develops a metaphysics of absence, of unknowability, and of the unrepresentability of central truths.

In what follows, I will trace, again in compressed fashion, how this cognitive tool of the aboriginal, consonantal alphabet becomes an important world-creating method which doesn't emerge as a privileged practice on the stage of Western culture until postmodernism.

TRACING THE CULTURE GENETICS OF ALEPH-TAV COGNITION

Even the story of the very first exile of the Jews from Egypt can be read as a rehearsal of a sociological conflict between two alphabets or as an expression

transformation of Aaron's rod, or pen, into a serpent ("crocodile," whose Hebrew letters also could mean "sing" or "learn"). The hieroglyphic images match Aaron for a couple of plagues – turning the Nile bloody, multiplying frogs and lice . . . but eventually, there are some transformations, abstractions, the hieroglyphic writers cannot manage with their limited powers. They resign in defeat. Pharaoh eventually relents. The "letters" have won the day.

Even from a more macroscopic perspective, if we find this fable of the war of the scripts preserved in the Bible hard to believe as a literal explanation, the exodus of the Sandramblers from Egypt, an historical fact, is hard to explain. Here's this egomaniacal Pharaoh with an enormous construction project underway – cities Pithom and Rameses dedicated to his own glorification. And here at his disposal is this massive, ready-made labor force of slaves. And in the middle of construction he lets them go? Not likely. Unless these slaves, this particular group, pose a unique kind of threat to the kingdom and the Pharaoh's power. What could that threat be? My speculation is that the threat was a new alphabet, a new cybernetic paradigm for communicating and organizing knowledge that entailed a total epistemological and metaphysical reorganization. This new consonantal alphabetic paradigm was tantamount to a cultural plague, a cognitive virus that Pharaoh in his wisdom was afraid to unleash among his own population, since to have possession of this new cybernetic technology directly threatens worldly material authority and the hieroglyphic status quo. So Pharaoh complies with Moses' demand to let his people go.

The Hebrews enter the desert. Moses leads them back to the site of his original revelation of the alphabet, beneath Sinai in the land of the Midianites, near the turquoise mines. There, he ascends the mountain and receives the tablets, on which are inscribed the teachings, the Torah. The essence of the first few of the ten commandments circumscribe the metaphysics now made possible by this new alphabet: (Iconoclasm) Discard the idols, they are pictographic incarnations, much too pictographic for Me; (Ambiguity and Deferral) Do not take My Name in Vain. (Abstraction) I am the Unpronounceable God of

the Scribe until it achieves its canonical form *circa*. 444 BC with only a few additions after that (e.g., The Books of Job and Daniel).

The destruction of the Second Temple in seventy CE (Common Era) by the Romans begins the Jews' nineteen hundred years of exile. There seems to be some intimate feedback loop in the relationship between the Hebrew cognitive mode promoted by the alphabet and the Jewish culture only in exile, fostered by the intensive scriptural devotion which preserves Jewish culture. In the beginning of this new exilic period, the metaphysical and epistemic practices were delivered from the priests to the rabbis, the interpreting grad-student types who, like the Pharisees, rebelled against the priests, even when the Temple was standing, and dedicated themselves to scriptural elaboration in order to discover the true nature of God's intention rather than to the system (very tech-writing Empire-like) of Temple hierarchy and physical sacrifice. Over the succeeding centuries, the rabbis slowly evolved a hypertextual format that captured and represented in a page layout their

Becoming (the closest linguistic relative to YHVH is the verb of existence in Hebrew). I am the abstract, portable, unknowable God-Who-Requires-Interpretation, and you still won't be able to fathom Me. (In later Jewish talmudical lore, it became canonical that God read the Torah in order to create the Universe: so we have the God of reading and writing and deciphering, too.) In wandering around the desert and fighting the desert or forest tribes of the north, it helps to have this portable altar that has no need of a temple or the magisterial architectonics of kingdom.

But after a few hundred years, the Jews establish a kingdom in Canaan and the Negev and erect their own temple culture, founded by Solomon and consolidated by David. For four hundred relatively stable years, very little changes in Jewish metaphysics or episteme. But when the First Temple of Solomon is destroyed (*c.* 570 BC) by the Babylonians, the Jews relearn the power of their exilic Hebrew cybernetics of deferral, there in the Babylonian Exile. When they return fifty years later to rebuild the Temple, the Torah is recodified by Ezra

intensive hermeneutic activity: a system of successive commentary, marginalia, interpretation, reinscription, and the multiplication of competing interpretations as an end in itself. At the same time, this epistemological project was founded on a metaphysical principle: the central indecipherability or unknowability of the direct Word of God, which was also preserved and represented in the layout of the page of commentary (evolved more than fifteen hundred years). Gaze at a page of the Talmud as it ultimately came to be printed from the fifteenth century onward, and you quickly see that this is scripture yearning to become cyberspatial, or at least hypertextual, with intertextual connections that certainly defeat the idea of a linear reading or of singular authority, the two dogmas expressed in the classical book. This textual symposium also breaks barriers of space and time: a single page may represent more than sixteen centuries (or more) of commentary on a single text or even word, including marginalia that refer to other texts in the Talmud or in Scripture. The sources may have been as scattered as France, Spain, Algiers, Eastern

Europe, Jerusalem, Babylon, and Safed, yet they are all present in their multivocality here on the page. Even visually, the text announces that there is no one right answer, and everyone is invited to join the babble, the epistemological sûk (bazaar).

There are many moments and inventions in Jewish history that illustrate the development of alephtafian epistemology, including the cycle of partial assimilation and then expulsion that marks the diaspora itself, which can be traced and partly blamed on the inefficiency of the Hebrew alphabet and the porushian consciousness to which it gives rise. However, the scope of this chapter does not allow me to dwell on all of them here. At the very least it is worthwhile noting now that the metaphysics and epistemological practices of Christianity develop completely contrary assumptions, and that these assumptions can also be traced to a sort of alphabetic determinism. In this case, the advent of the more efficient Greek alphabet, which added the vowels to the alphabet, and its direct descendants, Latin and then the Romance languages, and finally, English, lead to a metaphysic of *presence*. The

Christian more urgent than the interpretation of other texts is a commonplace. For the Christian believes that the word of God is given in order to be interiorized, appropriated [in other words returned to speech, in Ong's scheme] by men and women of all times and places. . . . Given such urgency, we can also be aware of certain problems of biblical interpretation for the Christian, which are, if not new, at least formulable in new ways within the perspectives here suggested.

First, we have seen composition in writing, or even setting down in writing something actually said orally, is not the same as oral speech, nor is it simply a parallel operation, for it involves utterance in a different way with time, with past, present, and future, and relates writer and reader differently from the way oral speech relates speaker and listener. Secondly, a reader is not the same as a listener, nor a writer the same as a speaker. The reader is absent from the writing of a text, and may be anyone from anywhere, the writer absent from the reading of the text, whereas speaker and hearer are fully determined persons normally present to one another quite consciously in vocal exchange. . . .

Such statements as these, giving special status to text which is quite different from the status of oral utterance, tend to be resented by Christians when they are applied to the Bible. This

alphabet which represents the spoken word with much increased fidelity, while not eliminating ambiguity altogether, leads to a firmer attachment to the authority of the spoken word, Logos, and relegates the written word to an important but a secondary role in transmitting worldly, and then divine, authority. Walter Ong has been the most recent and one of the most influential analysts of how modern communications technology develops along the vectors of Western, and particularly Christian culture (Ong 1984). As a Jesuit priest, he gives eloquent expression (in his book *Interfaces of the Word*) to the problems and values expressed in the oral–textual dialectic, the ethos of logos in Western civilization, and the Christian metaphysics entailed:

If interpretation means, as it does in the sense I employ and in Ricouer's sense, the appropriation of a text, its completion in actual discourse now, its insertion into the present – which can involve the use of other texts written or printed commentaries, but which, to avoid infinite regression, must ultimately connect with present oral utterances – to say that interpretation of the Bible is for the

appears to be so first because of the [belief in the] presence of the Word [logos], incarnate in Jesus Christ, through history. The Bible has regularly seemed to the Christian to be much simpler than all we have said here: it is God speaking to Man, here and now. And so it is of course. However, to say this is not to do away with questions but to create them. Secondly, the biblical text is understood somehow by the Church as being addressed to all ages. The relationship of the word of God in the text of the Bible which as text is dead, and the Word of God incarnate in Jesus Christ, who lives now and forever – 'Maranatha; come, Lord Jesus. . . .'

These questions, in one way or another, are all old. . . . But the framework in which they are presented here is, I believe, restructured in accord with our newly reflective awareness of the technological transformations of the word in past and present.

. . . Given that writing is not just a visual equivalent of speech and there is a psychological progression from orality to a literate culture, how necessary was it that the Good News of the death, resurrection, and ascension of the Lord itself die and be buried in a text in order to come to a later, resurrected life throughout history?

(Ong 1977)

In other words, you must believe in this sort of miracle of the Word-made-flesh, yielding a metaphysic of presence. The only other metaphysic on the scene of Western culture is a contaminated textual interpretation that leads to nothing in particular, a self-consuming hermetic or hermeneutic activity that leads only back into the maze of the text. As Havelock puts it, with the metaphysical foundation of Western culture left implicit but his Tory view of culture still intact: "A successful or developed writing system is one that does not think at all. It should be a purely passive instrument of the spoken word even if, to use a paradox, the word is spoken silently" (Havelock 1976: 17).

It is hard not to note the extent to which the Ong–Havelock construction of "proper" Western culture tending toward some apocalyptic finale is hostile to, if it does not thoroughly erase, the postmodern practice and ethos which the literature and anticipation of cyberspace take for granted, just as the handling of the text prescribed by Church dogma requires the erasure of the talmudic alternative for opening texts to a spree of

throughout his *œuvre* (especially as he finds it in Hegel and Heidegger) because it leads to totalizing discourse and the silencing of *différance*.[11] If I read Havelock properly, it leads even to the silencing of thought, a Tory consummation devoutly to be wished. "One does not think at all." "The word is spoken quietly." One goes to the quietude of the library only to find confirmation of what is already known.

To understand the postmodern tradition it is virtually inescapable, then, to look for an alternative model of reading provided by the talmudic tradition. The noisy babble of the *cheder*, the talmudical schoolroom, replaces the silent library. One reads not to find confirmation of what has already been decided as dogma, but to take issue, to demur, to absorb first the already multivocal symposium and then to add your voice. And in the place of the Western episteme of totalized knowledge, which gives us the sciences of Grand Unified Theory, of Theories of Everything, and the politics of fascism and world domination, postmodern philosophers, most notably Derrida, would place a grammatology of deferral, absence, and the proliferation of interpretations, the

contaminating alternatives that defeat totalizing answers. The Ongian system opens the text to a new dimension of life, the direct vocalization of divine intention, but it closes the interpretive activity in the text at the same time. Ong, reiterating Church dogma, requires that all interpretations get folded into one interpretation, all texts fold into one text, and all answers presuppose one totalizing, miraculous Answer, the resurrection of Jesus Christ and the salvation of the world in Him that all men and women should (must) understand. By contrast, the *porushian* epistemic method, if not necessarily the metaphysics attached to it, resonates with the openness, deferral, multivocality, and even the rhizomatic activity of most postmodern practices. It is no wonder that several times through the later medieval period, the Church ordered the burning of the Talmud.[10]

This metaphysic of an ultimately transparent text, which is simply a transcription of the spoken word, is what Derrida means by his use of the Greek word *parousia*, presence. And it is this metaphysic of Logos, the spoken word that is supposedly made present through the text, which Derrida critiques

deconstruction of any foundational, totalizing discourse. In the place of the metaphysic of presence, which privileges the voice over the written sign, Derrida proposes an anti-metaphysic of the inscribed page, the scriptural self-marginalizing text. And in accomplishing this deconstruction of Western metaphysic, Derrida insistently, at first covertly and then more overtly, practices the alternative Oriental episteme opened and invited by the Hebrew alphabet and at the same time, emerges as the most prominent and explicitly Jewish philosopher on the contemporary scene.

I do not have space here to engage in an elaborate textual analysis of Derrida's literary-epistemic method; enough has been said about it elsewhere. But I would ask you to look closely, in general, at Derrida's paronomasic method, his compulsive punning. In brief, Derrida's linguistic method looks like this: if you (1) permute and recombine the letters of the word; (2) resurrect its hidden roots (Hebrew also betrays its primitiveness as a language of constant iteration on common and elemental three-letter roots); and (3) associate a word with its kin root-sharing words, then you create a space for interpretation by permutation, association, and combination. You take apart the word and reassemble it; you pun gratuitously and obsessively. And in the ambiguous semantic territory opened up by this irrelevant, aleatory, trivial, and irrational play, in the proliferation of new words and signs and semantic content you discover hidden relations, hitherto inconceivable correspondences, revelations. And although this method evades any sense of closure or finality, and although the method is peripatetic and irrational, it is epistemologically potent, revealing hidden relations and assumptions disguised by but preserved in the grammatological signs. The sign of its epistemological potency is the extent to which Derrida's project marches from the margins to invade (infect, contaminate) the center of Western philosophy in the last two decades. For example, one might examine more closely Derrida's puns with the syllable "CA" in *Cinders* (Derrida 1991) (which, by the way, is also the memorial prayer for the slain of the Holocaust – the "whole burning of the sacrificed"); or the Hebrew words "Shibboleth"

politics, for instance, the pedestrian construction is a contest between "Order" and "Others," which is quite frequently reiterated as an actual battle between Normal Nationalism and the Contagious, Viral Jew (or Turk, or Kurd, or Muslim, or fill in the blank). On the scene of Anglo philosophy, to take another instance, this ancient dialectic is configured as X (take your pick of new heroes of philosophy who promise *parousia*) vs Derrida (*porushia*); as the new ecology of everything (for instance Michael Heim in his recent book *The Metaphysics of Virtual Reality* suggests that the metaphysics of VR will fulfill Christian theologian Teilhard de Chardin's totalizing idea of the emergent *noosphere*; Heim 1993), vs the verbal, written roots that open more spaces into which are inserted even more signs of absence. On such a scene, the name Derrida has slowly evolved into the figure not only of the anti-parousian *porush*, but parasite: infectious, viral, unutterable, contaminated, *Jew*. To speak "derrida" in some circles is to rupture membranes, lyse cell walls, introduce retroviral code, shibboleths, into the dark nucleated core of radical, rooting rhizomal

and "circumcision" in his essay "Shibboleth" (Hartman 1986) and the talmudic layout of the page in *Glas*, which also denies that there are any puns contained within it. These are also two of his most overtly Jewish essays.

Curiously, Abraham Abulafia, the Jewish thirteenth-century Spanish kabbalist, prescribed virtually exactly the same method for achieving telepathic communication with Schechina, the spirit of God. For Abulafia, the operation of this alphabetic method was designed to put the mind in a hyperexcited state, to force it to new levels of openness and receptivity (Idel 1987). Umberto Eco in *Foucault's Pendulum* recreates the printout of a computer that recombines the letters of the Name Of God in all its permutations. Eco calls that computer "Abulafia" (Eco 1987).

Even today, the contest between the urge for totalizing intimacy and *presence*, whether with the Other or with Godhead, and alphabetic *absence* (deferral, interpretation, difference), is manifested in different guises in politics, philosophy, and cultural criticism. In the public marketplace of European

philosophy. That Derrida is a Jew is no accident in this scenario.

TELEPATHY IN VIRTUAL REALITY

Circumcision of the word by the incision of the nothing in the circumcised heart of the other, that's you … in German in all the Jewish languages of the world.

(Jacques Derrida, *Shibboleth*)

But our subject here is virtual futures. I promised I wouldn't say much about cyberspace except by analogy with the massive cultural revolution initiated by the invention of the first crude alphabet, Hebrew. But now the time has come to sketch the shape of this analogy.

First, it is clear by the nature of much of the discussion around virtual futures that our culture recognizes the massive reorganization of human relations to mind, self, others, society at large, and even transcendental questions that VR promises to answer in new ways. Second, it is also clear that just as the phonetic alphabet successfully replaces the cybernetic communications devices that preceded it and which gave it birth (oral illiteracy, pictographic and syllabic literacy), a new *cyborg illiteracy* promises to supplant whole empires of alphabetic literacy. Third, it is obvious that cyberspace as a technology represents the next step in a vector of evolution in the direction of increasing the bandwidth and fidelity of telepathy. If you want to transmit your thoughts through space and time so that another person can inhabit them, cyberspace is the next best way to do it, superseding the alphabet. It will deliver all the richness of sensory experience in real reality, but that experience will still have been authored, and will still be (will be even more) infinitely plastic than those transmissions and CC-experiences generated by the re-permuting and combining of the fewer than thirty elements of the alphabet. VR will offer directed imagination and telepathy; a multisensory and absorbing hallucinatory novel and epistle, the *On Beyond Zebra* of consciousness.

But the fourth analogy, and the one that really concerns me, is an implicitly philosophical, and

Becomes Telepathy," that the Derridean Jewish practice, what I have been calling solipsistically *porushia*, in comparison to the transparent idea of language and the presence it purports to deliver (the presence of authority, of the intention of the author), is highly irrational, primitive. The idea that by opening a space in meaning by punning or mere word play, that the script itself contains mysterious knowledge revealed by aleatory interpretation and multivocal interrogation, is *superstitious*. Superstitious means to stand above or apart, to bear witness after, as in mourning. In the porushian metaphysic, the God *who always is never there* leaves us standing afterwards, bearing witness. And such mourning leads to an appreciation for telepathy, the final communication with the yearned-for other who is never there. This is not the same kind of telepathy to which the metaphysics of presence leads, where the urge is for complete intimacy, for utter ontological bonding between minds. The pure form of the Christian communiqué leads to a transparent presentation of the Word, the use of communication to make the Other present. The technology is a matter of

even metaphysical one. It is clear that metaphysics are created by such revolutions in TMT, whether the original script system invented by the Sumerians around 3,000 BC, or the inefficient alphabet of the Hebrews created in the South Sinai around 1,500 BC, or the more phonetically high-fidelity vowelled alphabet of the Phoenicians imported to Greece around 850 BC. Will virtual reality represent the apocalyptic consummation of an Ongian-Christian metaphysics of presence, the urge to *really be there* through the technology of out-of-body telepresence (that used to rely on the obsolete alphabet but will soon rely on the gleaming new computer technology)? Or will it evolve into a space where porushian consciousness can emigrate in its continuing diaspora of multivalence, openness, abstraction, irrationality, suspension, deferral, ambiguity, contextualization, etc. In other words, out of which alphabet and its concomitant metaphysic – *parousia* or *porushia* – does cyberspace evolve and to which new metaphysics does it lead?

Ned Lukacher notes in the title to his introductory essay to Derrida's *Cinders*, "Mourning

indifference. Words, music, architecture, virtual reality mind-link: the goal and the answer are always the same.

SO DOES VR DELIVER A METAPHYSICS OF ABSENCE (*PORUSHIA*) OR (*PARUSHIA*)?

The question cannot be answered, not, at least by someone who practices *porushia*. The two terms of the dialectic resolve into two different, and in the end maybe even pedestrian methods for getting to the Other telepathically. This enduring dialectic, an undercurrent informing much of the Western philosophical tradition and its skeptical alternatives, may resolve into the urge to interpret and the urge for intimacy, both of which are itches that can't ever be scratched outside of a really metaphysical consum- mation or ecstasy, a seizure in the brain that totally alters its hormonal ecology. I will say that I think those who continue to practice the ancient and primitive and obsolete arts of the alphabet will all occupy the position traditionally reserved for the Jew. All the (few remaining) writers, the scribes, the authors in cyberspace will be jewish with a small j, will have by definition joined the diaspora where they can, indeed must, continue to scribble on the margins of a newly (cyborgishly) illiterate host culture pursuing its march toward some more totalizing, less divergent and skeptical future in the nerve net. As Derrida says, "If all the poets are jews . . . "[12] (Porush 1993: 60ff.). Perhaps one might even say that cyberotic art and electronic sextensions of the body promise new elaborations on the margin of this old dialectic, took as we explore the corridors of cognition-in-the-body itself. Or to put it another way, that (as film and other media have abundantly shown) new non-alphabetic literatures arise to be talmudicaliy reinterpreted in much the same old porushian manner. I'm sure once there in cyberspace we will continue to discover the two kinds of old gods, the One who promises, like the Terminator ("Terminator of History," Hegel would say): "I'll be back"; and the God who is always hiding, the God on the way but never arriving, the God who is always there but receding, the inaccessible God. We will experience Them, although

world now? You God?"
"Things aren't different. Things are things."

(Gibson 1984: 269–70)[14]

What else would you expect a machine god to say, after all? Maybe, ironically, the machine really does take over and all we get is a transparent and depressing vista of things, turtles all the way down. All it ever was was things, and we've been fooling ourselves with hallucinatory TMTs all along. I prefer to think there is a transcendent alternative to the null space of machined art and ethical relativism, where we can prophesy and reinterpret amid the circuits and loops of our extended mindspace.

NOTES

1 The author wishes to thank Rafael Fischler for a particularly helpful insight concerning iconoclasm, and also the staff of the Technion library for their assistance.
2 For instance, studies of Japanese show that using the more pictographic-hieroglyphic Kanji characters leads to right-

with new sensory force and conviction, and perhaps, newly barbaric illiteracy, and so we will probably invent new gods and new idolatries as well.[13]

To illustrate the point, let me end in the prescient literature where I began. In this striking moment – in fact the climactic moment – in the novel *Neuromancer*, Case, the illiterate hero, jacks into cyberspace to confront the new AI God Wintermute/Neuromancer, whom he has helped evolve. It decides to present itself as a face, which Case, jacked in, now confronts at the telepathic interface in his mind. The face speaks:

"I'm not Wintermute now."
"So what are you." He drank from the flask, feeling nothing.
"I'm the matrix, Case."
Case laughed. "Where's that get you?"
"Nowhere. Everywhere. I'm the sum total of the works, the whole show."
"That's what Lady 3Jane wanted?"
"No. She couldn't imagine what I'd be like." The yellow smile [on the screen] widened.
"So what's the score? How are things different? You running the

hemispheric dominance, while using the phonetic/syllabic Kana leads to left-hemispheric dominance. See E. A. Jones and C. Aoki, "The Processing of Japanese Kana and Kanji Characters" (in Kerckhove and Lumsden 1988: 301–20).
3 The analogy is preserved even in some terms of writing: some early systems of writing, especially those half-way between syllabaries and alphabets, write left to right on the first line, then right to left on the second, as the ox plows the field. The Greek word for both plowing and writing this way was *boustrophedon*, a characteristic of early Hellenistic writing, until it became stablized left-to-right.
4 The word "ideogram" as used here, I would argue, is a misnomer. Few if any characters in these early scripts were illustrations of "ideas." Virtually all were correlates of physical objects. Thus, the pictographs were extremely clumsy, if not thoroughly unsuited, for depicting abstract relations, abstractions, or dynamic processes:

The needs therefore of the temples and the government as well as the civil population brought a large professional class of scribes into being, and these formed a powerful guild whose patron deity was the god Nabo, the Biblical Nebo; his emblems were the tablet and the wedge without the tablet and the slyhus. . . . The goddess Nibada or Nisaba . . . was called the universal scribe.

(Driver 1948: 62)

5 This analogy is not meant idly. First of all, it can be shown that the insect empires are directly a result of their means of communication; the now-well-known dance of the Scavenger bee back in the hive rehearsing the directions to nectar and the pheremone trails of ants are inseparable from the way these insects imperialize their territories, inscribing or exteriorizing urgencies in their genetic code onto the texts of their domains. Similarly, the first obvious effect of a tech-writing system is the way it permits authority to extend control over and confederate (via texts) troops, generals, allies, etc. across space and time. Before writing, the largest geographical radius of an empire was the width of territory across which a runner could carry a king's message in one day.

6 Kana, which is a recent Japanese invention derived from the pictographic Kanji, is itself based on the Chinese pictogram. But it was invented after the Japanese were inspired by contact with the West to derive a phonetic script.

7 The old cliché that Phoenician was the first alphabet is nothing more than a blind reiteration of the Greek fable of Cadmus, the

Phoenician who sowed the dragon's teeth of the alphabet on Greek shores to create an army. It may also be a partly-conscious attempt to purge the roots of Western civilization of any Oriental or Semitic influence. This can most recently be shown in the inordinately influential work of the anti-Semite and racist Eric Havelock, whose theories on the birth of civilization and the rise of literacy have been reiterated by Walter Ong in his successful books *Orality and Literacy* (1982) and *Interfaces of the Word* (1977) and by J. Goody and M. McLuhan. Based on Havelock's overtechnical insistence that Hebrew was not an alphabet because it lacked vowels, Havelock builds an entire indictment of Semitic thinking and "so-called literature." With overtones that suggest an imperial view of Western culture, he is generally given to such broad racial generalizations that display his contempt (if not xenophobia) for Orientals, particularly Jews and Chinese. Here are some worthy excerpts of his oft-cited monograph, *Origins of Western Literacy*: "Among the foreign languages with which an English speaking individual may be required to cope are those like Arabic or Chinese which are not only foreign but happen to employ a non-alphabetic script" (Havelock 1976: 11). "For literate Chinese [using the term 'literate' to mean a reader of Chinese, but definitely not in its Greco-Roman sense of a reader of alphabets] to increase his

reading vocabulary requires a stringent discipline in, among other things, the memorization of inscribed shapes. Can this be said to have reversed the normal course of evolutionary development?" "For the purposes of this study, at any rate, the Chinese Script is an historical irrelevance" (Havelock 1976: 15). In "analyzing" Hebrew and the body of written expression to which it gives rise, Havelock says that it cannot possibly constitute a body of literature: he suggests that because Hebrew is incompletely phonetic and requires laborious interpretation, authors are "required to address to the reader such statements and sentiments as fall into an idiom easily recognizable. They will partake of the formulaic, and this is as true of a modern Hebrew or Arabic newspaper as of the Old Testament even if the modern equivalent of the ancient formula becomes a slogan" (Havelock 1976: 33). "To illustrate these conditions in actual operation we need only turn to the so-called literatures of the ancient Near East as they have been translated for us." These translators [of Hebrew writing] inevitably "overtranslate the original and 'remove ambiguities'" (Havelock 1976: 34). "It is precisely these limitations imposed upon the possible converage of human experience that gives to the Old testament its power of appeal, as we say, to 'simple people'" (Havelock 1976: 35). But even "when all allowance is made for simple

grandeur of conception or refinement of design, the basic complexity of human experience is not there" (Havelock 1976: 34).

8 My source for all Hebrew translations into English is Reuven Alcalay's monumental (1970) *Hebrew–English Dictionary*, Jerusalem: Massada Publishing Company.

9 I should note that even in this sketchy interpretation I am attempting to follow good Jewish hermeneutic or midrashic practice. I multiply possible meanings for a single word while holding in abeyance and yet acknowledging and accepting the competing interpretations. Then I offer an explaining story that would recuperate a particular meaning (letter), and finally I show an underlying unity to all the meanings (letters are tokens, signs, etc., of the miracles that YHVH has granted to the Hebrew people).

10 Notable times include: Pope Gregory ordered the burning of the Talmud in Paris in 1240; Pope Clement IV ordered it burned in 1264; The Church Synod of Basel banned the Talmud in 1431; Pope Julius III ordered the Talmud burned in 1553; Clement II prohibited the study of the Talmud in any form in 1592.

11 The monograph that most explicitly addresses this conflict between totalizing discourse and resistance of *différance* is

Glas, in which Derrida methodically demolished Hegel's Christian-philosophic project to develop a total and final philosophy (along the left-hand column of each page). The right-hand column of the page plays poetically with the text and themes in the work of Jean Genet. Not surprisingly, the text also resembles an everted page of the Talmud or a conflation of the Talmud's and the Torah's pagiography.

12 Jacques Derrida actually quotes Freud's essay, "Moses and Monotheism" here: "'If all the poets are Jews, they, the poets, are all circumcised or circumcisors'" (Derrida 1986).

13 In addition to the illustration below from *Neuromancer*, this is precisely the theme Gibson elaborates on in his second book of the cyberspace trilogy, *Count Zero*. There, the god Neuromancer created by Case in the first novel has splintered into voodoo deities and ghosts, Legba and Baron Samedi and various "loas." Neuromancer's other manifestation is as a robot artist who assembles transcendental boxes, *objets d'art* that have a certain commercial value on the Parisian market. At least one character worships Neuromancer as one true God.

14 Gibson here seems to be echoing Wittgenstein's definition of the world, not only in the statement by this new god-mind, but in the name of his hero: in the Tractatus, Wittgenstein states: "Die welt ist alles was der falles ist" – the world is all that is the case.

—— (1986) *Count Zero*, New York: Ace Science Fiction.

Hartman, G. (ed.) (1986) *Midrash and Literature*, New Haven: Yale University Press.

Havelock, E. (1976) *Origins of Western Literacy: Four Lectures delivered at the Ontario Institute for Studies in Education, Toronto, March 25, 26, 27, 28, 1974*. Toronto: Ontario Institute for Studies in Education.

Heim, M. (1993) *The Metaphysics of Virtual Reality*, New York: Oxford University Press.

Hellige, F. (1993) *Hemispheric Asymmetry*, Cambridge, Mass.: Harvard University Press.

Howard, D. (1987) "Reading Without Letters?" in M. Coltheart, G. Sartori, and R. Job (eds), *The Cognitive Neuropsychology of Language*, London: Lawrence Erlbaum Associates.

Idel, M. (1987) *Kabbalah: New Perspectives*, New Haven: Yale University Press.

Jones, E. (1988) "The Processing of Japanese Kana and Kanji Characters," in D. de Kerckhove and C. Lumsden (eds), *The Alphabet and the Brain*, Berlin: Springer-Verlag.

BIBLIOGRAPHY

Alcalay, R. (1970) *Hebrew–English Dictionary*, Jerusalem: Massada Publishing Company.

Changeux, J. P. (1988) "Learning and Selection in the Nervous System," in D. de Kerckhove and C. Lumsden (eds), *The Alphabet and the Brain*, Berlin: Springer-Verlag.

Chiera, E. (1938) *They Wrote on Clay*, ed. G. Cameron, Chicago: University of Chicago Press.

Derrida, J. (1986a) *Glas*, trans. J. P. Leavy and R. Rand, London: University of Nebraska Press.

—— (1986b) *Schibboleth: pour Paul Celan*, Paris: Galilee.

—— (1991) *Cinders*, trans. N. Lukacher, London: University of Nebraska Press.

Driver, G. R. (1948) *Semitic Writing: From Pictogragh to Alphabet*, London: British Academy.

Eco, U. (1990) *Foucault's Pendulum*, trans. W. Weaver, New York: Ballantine Books.

Gibson, W. (1984) *Neuromancer*, New York: Ace Science Fiction.

Kerckhove, D. de (1988) "Critical Brain Processes Involved in Deciphering the Greek Alphabet," in D. de Kerckhove and C. Lumsden (eds), *The Alphabet and the Brain*, Berlin: Springer-Verlag.

Kerckhove, D. de and Lumsden, C. (eds) (1988) *The Alphabet and the Brain*, Berlin: Springer-Verlag.

Kramer, S. N. (1956) *From the Tablets of Sumer*, Colorado: The Falcon's Wing Press.

Lumsden, C. (1988) "Gene-Culture Coevolution: Culture and Biology in a Darwinian Perspective," in D. de Kerckhove and C. Lumsden (eds), *The Alphabet and the Brain*, Berlin: Springer-Verlag.

Ong, W. (1977) *Interfaces of the Word: Studies in the Evolution of Consciousness and Culture*, Ithaca: Cornell University Press.

—— (1982) *Orality and Literacy: The Technologizing of the Word*, New York: Methuen.

Porush, D. (1993) "Seeing God in the Three Pound Universe," *Omni*, October: 60 ff.

Seuss, Dr (1955) *On Beyond Zebra*, New York: Random House.

Tzeng, O. J. L. and D. L. Hung (1989) "Orthography, Reading and Cerebral Function," in D. de Kerckhove and C. Lumsden (eds), *The Alphabet and the Brain*, Berlin: Springer-Verlag.

64

Virtual Environments and the Emergence of Synthetic Reason

Manuel De Landa

At the end of World War II, Stanislav Ulam and other scientists previously involved in weapons research at Los Alamos discovered the huge potential of computers to create artificial worlds, where simulated experiments could be conducted and where new hypotheses could be framed and tested. The physical sciences were the first ones to tap into this "epistemological reservoir," thanks to the fact that much of their accumulated knowledge had already been given a mathematical form. Among the less

spaces. Since this is a crucial point, let's take a careful look at just what this purging has involved.

The first classical notion that had to be eliminated from biology was the Aristotelian concept of an "ideal type," and this was achieved by the development of what came to be known in the 1930s as "population thinking." In the old tradition that dominated biological thought for more than two thousand years, a given population of animals was conceived as the more or less imperfect incarnation of an ideal essence. Thus, for example, in the case of zebras, there would exist an ideal zebra, embodying all the attributes which together specify the nature of "zebrahood" (being striped, having hoofs, etc.). The existence of this essence would be obscured by the fact that in any given population of zebras the ideal type would be subjected to a multiplicity of accidents (of embryological development, for instance) yielding as an end result a variety of imperfect realizations. In short, in this view, only the ideal essence is real, with the variations being but mere shadows.

When the ideas of Darwin on the role of natural selection and those of Mendel on the

mathematized disciplines, those already taking advantage of virtual environments are psychology and biology (e.g., Artificial Intelligence and Artificial Life), although other fields such as economics and linguistics could soon begin to profit from the new research strategies made possible by computer simulations.

Yet, before a given scientific discipline can begin to gain from the use of virtual environments, more than just casting old assumptions into mathematical form is necessary. In many cases the assumptions themselves need to be modified. This is clear in the case of Artificial Intelligence research, much of which is still caught up into older paradigms of what a symbol-manipulating "mind" should be, and hence has not benefited as much as it could from the simulation capabilities of computers. Artificial Life, on the other hand, has the advantage that the evolutionary biologist's conceptual base has been purged from classical notions of what living creatures and evolution is supposed to be, and this has put this discipline in an excellent position to profit from the new research tool represented by these abstract

dynamics of genetic inheritance were brought together six decades ago, the domination of the Aristotelian paradigm came to an end. It becomes clear, for instance, that there was no such thing as a pre-existent collection of traits defining "zebrahood." Each of the particular adaptive traits which we observe in real zebras developed along different ancestral lineages, accumulated in the population under the action of different selection pressures, in a process that was completely dependent on specific (and contingent) historical details. In other words, just as these traits (camouflage, running speed, and so on) happened to come together in zebras, they might not have, had the actual history of those populations been any different.

Moreover, the engine driving this process is the genetic variability of zebra populations. Only if zebra genes replicate with enough variability can selection pressures have raw materials to work with. Only if enough variant traits arise spontaneously, can the sorting process of natural selection bring together those features which today define what it is to be a zebra. In short, for population thinkers, only the variation is real, and the ideal type (e.g., the average zebra) is a mere shadow. Thus we have a complete inversion of the classical paradigm (Sober 1987: 157–61).

Further refinements of these notions have resulted in the more general idea that the coupling of any kind of spontaneous variation to any kind of selection pressure results in a sort of "searching device." This "device" spontaneously explores a space of possibilities (i.e., possible combinations of traits), and is capable of finding, over many generations, more or less stable combinations of features, more or less stable solutions to problems posed by the environment. This "device" has today been implemented in populations that are not biological. This is the so-called "genetic algorithm" (developed by John Holland) in which a population of computer programs is allowed to replicate in a variable form, and after each generation a test is performed to select those programs that most closely approximate the desired performance. It has been found that this method is capable of zeroing in on the best solutions to a given programming task. In

but it can be extended to apply to the "engineering strategies" involved in putting together camouflage, locomotive speed, and the other traits which come together to form the zebras of the example above. The essence of this approach is that the searching device constituted by variation and selection can find the optimal solution to a given problem posed by the environment, and that once the optimal solution has been found, any mutant strategy arising in the population is bound to be defeated. The strategy will be, in this sense, stable against invasions. To put it in visual terms, it is as if the space of possibilities explored by the searching device included mountains and valleys, with the mountain peaks representing points of optimal performance. Selection pressures allow the gene pool of a reproductive population to slowly climb those peaks, and once a peak has been reached, natural selection keeps the population there.

One may wonder just what has been achieved by switching from the concept of a "fittest mutant" to that of an "optimal" one, except perhaps, that the latter can be defined contextually as "optimal

essence, this method allows computer scientists to breed new solutions to problems, instead of directly programming those solutions (Levy 1992: 155–87).

The difference between the genetic algorithm and the more ambitious goals of Artificial Life is the same as that between the action of human breeding techniques on domesticated plants and animals, and the spontaneous evolution of the ancestors of those plants and animals. Whereas in the first case the animal or plant breeder determines the criterion of fitness, in the second one there is no outside agency determining what counts as fit. In a way what is fit is simply that which survives, and this has led to the criticism that Darwinism's central formula (i.e., "survival of the fittest") is a mere tautology ("survival of the survivor"). Partly to avoid this criticism this formula is today being replaced by another one: survival of the stable (Dawkins 1989: 12).

The central idea, the notion of an "evolutionary stable strategy," was formulated with respect to behavioral strategies (such as those involved in territories or courtship behavior in animals)

given existing constraints." However, the very idea that selection pressures are strong enough to pin populations down to "adaptive peaks" has itself come under intense criticism. One line of argument says that any given population is subjected to many different pressures, some of them favoring different optimal results. For example, the beautiful feathers of a peacock are thought to arise due to the selection pressure exerted by "choosy" females, who will only mate with those males exhibiting the most attractive plumage. Yet, those same vivid colors which seduce the females also attract predators. Hence, the male peacock's feathers will come under conflicting selection pressures. In these circumstances, it is highly improbable that the peacock's solution will be optimal and much more likely that it will represent a compromise. Several such sub-optimal compromises may be possible, and thus the ideas that the solution arrived at by the "searching device" are unique needs to be abandoned (Kauffman 1989). But if unique and optimal solutions are not the source of stability in biology, then what is?

The answer to this question represents the

second key idea around which the field of Artificial Life revolves. It is also crucial to understand the potential application of virtual environments to fields such as economics. The old conceptions of stability (in terms of either optimality or principles of least effort) derive from nineteenth-century equilibrium thermodynamics. It is well known that philosophers like Auguste Comte and Herbert Spencer (author of the formula "survived of the fittest") introduced thermodynamic concepts into social science. However, some contemporary observers complain that what was introduced (in economics, for example) represents "more heat than light" (Russett 1968: 28–54).

In other words, equilibrium thermodynamics, dealing as it does with systems that are closed to their environment, postulates that stability can only be reached when all useful energy has been transformed into heat. At this point, a static and unique state of equilibrium is reached (heat death). It was this concept of an equilibrium that late-nineteenth-century economists used to systematize the classical notion of an "invisible hand," according to which the forces

systems are called "dissipative" (Prigogine and Stengers 1984).

For our purposes here, what matters is that once a continuous flow of matter–energy is included in the model, a wider range of possible forms of dynamic equilibria becomes possible. The old static stability is still one possibility, except that now these equilibrium points are neither unique nor optimal (and yet they are more robust than the old equilibria). Non-static equilibria also exist, in the form of cycles, for instance. Perhaps the most novel type of stability is that represented by "deterministic chaos," in which a given population can be pinned down to a stable, yet inherently variable, dynamical state. These new forms of stability have received the name of "attractors," and the transitions which transform one type of attractor into another have been named "bifurcations." Let's refer to the cluster of concepts making up this new paradigm of stability as "nonlinear dynamics" (Stewart 1989: 95–100).

One of the most striking consequences of non-linear dynamics is that any population (of atoms, molecules, cells, animals, humans) which is

of demand and supply tend to balance each other out at a point which is optimal from the point of view of society's utilization of resources. It was partly John Von Neumann'a work on Game Theory and economics that helped entrench this notion of stability outside of physics, and from there it found its way into evolutionary biology, through the work of John Maynard Smith (Smith 1988).

This static conception of stability was the second classical idea that needed to be eliminated before the full potential of virtual environments could be unleashed. Like population thinking, the fields that provided the needed new insights (the disciplines of far-from-equilibrium thermodynamics and non-linear mathematics) are also a relatively recent development associated with the name of Ilya Prigogine, among others. Unlike the "conservative systems" dealt with by the old science of heat systems, which are totally isolated from their surroundings, the new science deals with systems that are subjected to a constant flow of matter and energy from the outside. Because this flow must also exit the system in question, that is, the waste products need to be dissipated, these

stabilized via attractors will exhibit "emergent properties," that is, properties of the population as a whole not displayed by its individual members in isolation. The notion of an emergent or synergistic property is a rather old one, but for a long time it was not taken very seriously by scientists, as it was associated with quasi-mystical schools of thought such as "vitalism." Today, emergent properties are perfectly legitimate dynamical outcomes for populations stabilized by attractors. A population of molecules in certain chemical reactions, for instance, can suddenly and spontaneously begin to pulsate in perfect synchrony, constituting a veritable "chemical clock." A population of insects (termites, for instance) can spontaneously become a "nest-building machine," when their activities are stabilized non-linearly.

Thus, the "searching-devices" constituted by variation coupled to selection do not explore an unstructured space of possibilities, but a space "preorganized" by attractors and bifurcations. In a way, evolutionary processes simply follow these changing distributions of attractors, slowly climbing from one dynamically stable state to another. For example, since in this space one possible outcome is a chemical clock, the searching-devices could have stumbled upon this possibility, which in essence constitutes a primitive form of a metabolism. The same point applies to other evolutionary stable strategies, such as the nest-building strategy of the termites.

After this rather long introduction, we are finally in a position to understand enterprises such as Artificial Life. The basic point is that emergent properties do not lend themselves to an analytical approach, that is, an approach which dissects a population into its components. Once we perform this dissection, once the individuals become isolated from each other, any properties due to their interactions will disappear. What virtual environments provide is a tool to replace (or rather, complement) analysis with synthesis, allowing researchers to exploit the complementary insights of population thinking and non-linear dynamics. In the words of Artificial Life pioneer Chris Langton:

variation can be generated. Then, whole populations of these "virtual animals" are unleashed, and their evolution under a variety of selection pressures observed. The exercise will be considered a successful one if novel properties, unthought of by the designer, spontaneously emerge from this process.

Depending on the point of view of the designers, these emergent properties need to match those observed in reality, or not. That is, a current theme in this field is that one does not have to be exclusively concerned with biological evolution as it has occurred on planet Earth, since this may have been limited by the contingencies of biological history, and that there is much to be learned from evolutionary paths that were not tried out in this planet. At any event, the goal of the simulation is simply to help "synthesize intuitions" in the designer, insights that can then be used to create more realistic simulations. The key point is that the whole process must be *bottom-up*; only the local properties of the virtual creatures need to be predesigned, never the global, population-wide ones.

Biology has traditionally started at the top, viewing a living organism as a complex biochemical machine, and worked *analytically* downwards from there – through organs, tissues, cells, organelles, membranes, and finally molecules – in its pursuit of the mechanisms of life. Artificial Life starts at the bottom, viewing an organism as a large population of *simple* machines, and works upwards *synthetically* from there, constructing large aggregates of simple, rule-governed objects which interact with one another nonlinearly in the support of life-like, global dynamics. The "key" concept in Artificial Life is emergent behavior. Natural life emerges out of the organized interactions of a great number of nonliving molecules, with no global controller responsible for the behavior of every part. . . . It is this bottom-up, distributed, local determination of behavior that Artificial Life employs in its primary methodological approach to the generation of life-like behaviors.

(Langton 1988: 2).

The typical Artificial Life experiment involves first the design of a simplified version of an individual animal, which must process the equivalent of a set of genetic instructions used both to create its offspring as well as to be transmitted to that offspring. This transmission must also be "imperfect" enough that

Unlike Artificial Life, the approach of Artificial Intelligence researchers remained (at least until the 1980s) largely top-down and analytic. Instead of treating the symbolic properties they study as the emergent outcome of a dynamical process, these researchers explicitly put symbols (labels, rules, recipes) and symbol-manipulating skills into the computer. When it was realized that logic alone was not enough to manipulate these symbols in a significantly "intelligent" way, they began to extract the rule of thumb, tricks of the trade, and other non-formal heuristic knowledge from human experts, and put these into the machine, but also as fully formed symbolic structures. In other words, in this approach one begins at the top, the global behavior of human brains, instead of at the bottom, the social behavior of neurons. Some successes have been scored by this approach, notably in simulating skills such as those involved in playing chess or proving theorems, both of which are in evolutionar terms rather late developments. Yet the symbolic paradigm of Artificial Intelligence has failed to capture the dynamics of evolutionary more elementary skills such as face-recognition or sensory-motor control (Clark 1990: 61–75).

Although a few attempts had been made during the 1960s to take a bottom-up approach to modeling intelligence (e.g., the perceptron), the defenders of the symbolic paradigm practically killed their rivals in the battle for government research funds. And so the analytical approach dominated the scene until the 1980s when there occurred a spectacular rebirth of the symbolic design philosophy. This is the new school of Artificial Intelligence known as "connectionism." Here, instead of one large, powerful computer serving as a repository for explicit symbols, we find a large number of small, rather simple computing devices (in which all that matters is their state of activation), interacting with one another to either excite or inhibit each other's degree of activation. These simple processors are then linked together through a pattern of interconnections which can vary in strength.

No explicit symbol is ever programmed into the machine since all the information needed to perform a given cognitive task is coded in the strength of the interconnections. At that point the network can respond with the second pattern whenever the first one is presented to it.

At the other end of the spectrum of complexity, multilayered networks exhibit emergent cognitive behavior as they are trained. While in the simple case of pattern association much of the thinking is done by the trainer, complex networks (i.e., those using "hidden units") perform their own extraction of regularities from the input pattern, concentrating on microfeatures of the input which often are not at all obvious to the human trainer. (In other words, the network itself "decides" what traits of the pattern it considers as salient or relevant.)

These networks also have the ability to generalize from the patterns they have learned, and so will be able to recognize a new pattern that is only vaguely related to one they have been previously exposed to. In other words, the ability to perform simple inductive inferences emerges in the network without the need to explicitly code into it the rules of a logical calculus. These designs are also resilient against damage, unlike their symbolic counterparts

interconnection patterns as well as the relative strengths of these interconnections. All computing activity is carried out by the dynamical activity of the simple processors as they interact with one another (i.e., as excitations and inhibitions propagate through the network), and the processors arrive at the solution to a problem by settling into a dynamical state of equilibrium. (So far point attractors are most commonly used, although some designs using cyclic attractors are beginning to appear; Sepulchre and Bobloyantz 1991.)

If there is ever such a thing as a "symbol" here, or rather symbol-using (rule-following) behavior, it is an emergent result of these dynamics. This fact is sometimes expressed by saying that a connectionial device (also called a "neural net") is not programmed by humans, but trained by them, much as a living creature would be trained. In the simplest kind of networks the only cognitive task that can be performed is pattern association. The human trainer presents to the network both patterns to be associated, and after repeated presentations, the network "learns" to associate them by modifying the

which are inherently brittle. But perhaps the main advantage of the bottom-up approach is that its devices can exhibit a degree of "intentionality."

The term "intentionality" is the technical term used by philosophers to describe the relation between a believer and the states of affairs his beliefs are about. That is, an important feature of the mental states of human beings and other animals (their beliefs and desires) is that they are about phenomena that lie outside their minds. The top-down, symbolic approach to Artificial Intelligence sacrifices this connection by limiting its modeling efforts to relations between symbols. In other words, in the analytical approach only the syntactic or formal relations between symbols matter (with the exception of an "internal semantics" involving reference to memory addresses and the like). Hence these designs must later try to reconnect the cognitive device to the world where it must function, and it is here that the main bottleneck lies (unless the "world" in question is a severely restricted domain of the real world, such as the domain of chess). Not so in the synthetic approach:

The connectionist approach to modeling cognition thus offers a promise in explaining the *aboutness* or *intentionality* of mental states. Representational states, especially those of hidden units, constitute the system's own learned response to inputs. Since they constitute the system's adaption to the input, there is a clear respect in which they would be about objects or events in the environment if the system were connected, via sensory-motor organs, to that environment. . . . The fact that these representations are also sensitive to context, both external and internal to the system, enhances the plausibility of this claim that the representations are representations of particular states.

(Bechtel and Abrahamsen 1991: 129)

So far, the abstract living creatures inhabiting the virtual environments of Artificial Life have been restricted to rather inflexible kinds of behavior. One may say that the only kinds of behavior that have been modeled are of the genetically "hard-wired" type, as displayed by ants or termites. Yet adding connectionist intelligence to these creatures could endow them with enough intentionality to allow researchers to model more flexible, "multiple-choice" behavior, as displayed by birds. We could

happens, it has now been demonstrated rigorously and definitively that such cooperation can emerge, and it was done through a computer tournament conducted by political scientist Robert Axelrod. . . . More accurately, Axelrod first studied the ways that cooperation evolved by means of a computer tournament, and when general trends emerged, he was able to spot the underlying principles and prove theorems that established the facts and conditions of cooperation's rise from nowhere.

(Hofstadter 1985: 720)

The creatures that Axelrod placed in a virtual environment to conduct his round-robin tournament were not full-fledged intentional entities of the type envisioned above. Rather, the motivations and options of the creatures were narrowly circumscribed by using the formalism of Game Theory, which studies the dynamics of situations involving conflict of interest. In particular, Axelrod's entities were computer programs, each written by a different programmer, playing a version of the game called "Prisoner's Dilemma." In this imaginary situation, two accomplices in a crime are captured by the police and separately offered the following deal: if one

then expect more complex behavioral patterns (such as territorial or courtship behavior) to emerge in these virtual worlds. Artificial Intelligence could also benefit from such a partnership, by tapping the potential of the evolutionary "searching-devices" in the exploration of the space of possible network designs. The genetic algorithm, which exploits this possibility, has so far been restricted to searching for better symbolic designs (e.g., production rules).

Furthermore, having a virtual space where groups of intentional creatures interact can also benefit other disciplines such as economics or political science. A good example of this is Robert Axelrod's use of a virtual environment to study the evolution of co-operation. His work also exemplifies the complementary use of synthesis (to generate intuitions) and analysis (to formally ground those intuitions). In the words of Douglas Hofstadter:

Can totally selfish and unconscious organisms living in a common environment come to evolve reliable cooperative strategies? Can cooperation evolve in a world of pure egoists? . . . Well, as it

accuses his accomplice, while the other does not, the "betrayer" walks out free, while the "sucker" gets the stiffest sentence. If, on the other hand, both claim innocence and avoid betrayal they both get a small sentence. Finally, if both betray each other, they both get a long sentence. The dilemma here arises from the facts that even though the best *overall* outcome is not to betray one's partner, neither one can trust that his accomplice won't try to get the best individual outcome (to walk out free) leaving the other with the "sucker payoff." And because both prisoners reason in a similar way, they both choose betrayal and the long sentence that comes with it, instead of loyalty and its short sentence.

In the real world we find realizations of this dilemma in, for example, the phenomena known as "bank runs." When news that a bank is in trouble first comes out, each individual depositor has two options: either to rush to the bank and withdraw his savings or to stay home and allow the bank to recover. Each individual also knows that the best outcome for the community is for all to leave their savings in the bank and so allow it to survive. But no one can afford to be the one who loses his savings, so all rush to withdraw their money, ruining the institution in the process. Hofstadter offers a host of other examples, including one in which the choice to betray or co-operate is faced by the participants not once, but repeatedly. For instance, imagine two "jungle traders" with a rather primitive system of trade: each simply leaves a bag of goods at a predefined place, and comes back later to pick another bag, without ever seeing the trading partner. The idea is that on every transaction, one is faced with a dilemma, since one can profit most by leaving an empty bag and attacking the other with the "sucker payoff." Yet, the difference is that doing this endangers the trading situation and hence there is more to lose in case of betrayal here. (This is called the "Iterated Prisoner's Dilemma.")

Axelrod's creatures played such an iterated version of the game with one another. What matters to us here is that after several decades of applying analytical techniques to study these situations, the idea that "good guys finish last" (i.e., that the most rational strategy is to betray one's partner) had

of the game), was blocked. What was needed was to unblock this path by using a virtual environment to "synthesize" a fresh intuition. And in a sense that is just what Axelrod did. He then went further and used more elaborate simulations (including one in which the creatures replicated, with the number of progeny being related to the trading success of the parent), to generate further intuitions as to how co-operative strategies could evolve in an ecological environment, how robust and stable these strategies were, and a host of other questions. Evolutionary biologists, armed with these fresh insights, have now discovered that apes in their natural habitats play a version of TIT-FOR-TAT (Gould and Gould 1989: 244–77). Thus, while some of the uses of virtual environments presuppose that old and entrenched ideas (about essences or optimality) have been superseded, these abstract worlds can also be used to synthesize the intuitions needed to dislodge other ideas blocking the way to a better understanding of the dynamics of reality.

Population thinking seems to have vanished "essences" from the world of philosophy once and for

become entrenched in academic (and think-tank) circles. For example, when Axelrod first requested entries for his virtual tournament most of the programs he received were "betrayers." Yet the winner was not. It was "nice" (it always co-operated in the first encounter so as to give a sign of good faith and begin the trading situation), "retaliatory" (if betrayed it would respond with betrayal in the next encounter), yet "forgiving" (after retaliating it was willing to re-establish a partnership). As mentioned above, these were not truly intentional creatures so the properties of being "nice, retaliatory and forgiving" were like emergent properties of a much simpler design. Its name was "TIT-FOR-TAT" and its actual strategy was simply always to co-operate in the first move and thereafter do what the other player did in the previous move. This program won because the criterion of success was not how many partners one beats, but how much overall trade one achieves.

Because the idea that "good guys finish last" had become entrenched, further analysis of the situation (which could have uncovered the fact that this principle does not apply to the "iterated" version

all. Non-linear dynamics, and more specifically, the notion of an "emergent property" would seem to signal the death of the philosophical position known as "reductionism" (basically that all phenomena can in principle be reduced to those of physics). It is clear now that at every level of complexity, there will be emergent properties that are irreducible to the lower levels, simply because when one switches to an examination of lower-level entitles, the properties which emerge due to their interactions disappear. Connectionism, in turn, offers a completely new understanding of the way in which rule-following behavior can emerge from a system in which there are no explicit rules or symbols whatsoever. This would seem destined to end the domination of a conception of language based on syntactical entities and their formal relations (Saussure's signifiers or Chomsky's rules). This conception (let's call it "formalism") has entirely dominated this century, leading in some cases to extreme forms of linguistic relativism, that is, the idea that every culture partitions the world of experience in a different way simply because they use different linguistic devices to organize this experience. If connectionism is correct, then humanity does indeed have a large portion of shared experience (the basic intentional machinery linking them to the world) even if some of this experience can be cast in different linguistic form (Brown 1991).

Furthermore, once linguists become population thinkers and users of virtual environments, we could witness the emergence of an entirely different type of science of language. For instance, about a millennium ago, the population of Anglo-Saxon peasants inhabiting England suffered the imposition of French as the official language of their land by the Norman invaders. In about two hundred years, and in order to resist this form of linguistic colonialism, this peasant population transformed what was basically a group of Germanic dialects (with added Scandinavian spices) into something that we could recognize as English. No doubt, in order to arrive at modern English another few centuries of transformation would be needed, but the backbone of this language had already emerged from the spontaneous labor of a population under the pressure

"linguistic matter" may be revealed through a computer simulation. Similarly, whenever a language becomes standardized we witness the political conquest of many "minority" dialects by the dialect of the urban capital (London's dialect in the case of English). Virtual environments could allow us to model dynamically the spread of the dominant dialect across cultural and geographical barriers, and how technologies such as the railroad or the radio (e.g., the BBC) allowed it to surmount such barriers (Crowley 1989).

Future linguists may one day look back with curiosity at our twentieth-century linguistics, and wonder if our fascination with the static (synchronic) view of language could not be due to the fact that the languages where these views were first formulated (French and English), had lost their fluid nature by being artificially frozen a few centuries earlier. These future investigators may also wonder how we thought the stability of linguistic structures could be explained without the concept of an attractor. How, for instance, could the prevalence of certain patterns of sentence structures (e.g., subject-verb-object, or

of an invading language (Nist 1966: ch. 3). Perhaps one day linguists will be required to test their theories in a virtual environment of interacting intentional entities, so that the rules of grammar they postulate for a language can be shown to emerge spontaneously from the dynamics of a population of speakers (instead of existing in a "synchronic" world, isolated from the actual interactions of several generations of speakers). Virtual environments may not only allow us to capture the fluid and changing nature of real languages, they could also be used to gain insight into the processes that tend to "freeze" languages, such as the processes of standardization which many European languages underwent, beginning in the seventeenth century. Unlike the cases of Spanish, Italian, and French, where the fixing of the rules and vocabulary of the language were enforced by an institution (e.g., an Academy), in England the process of standardization was carried out via the mass publication of authoritative dictionaries, grammars, and orthographies. Just how these "linguistic engineering" devices achieved the relative freezing of what was formerly a fluid

"SVO") be explained, or how could bifurcations from one pattern to another be modeled without some form of non-linear stabilization? (For example, English may have switched over a millennium from SOV to SVO (Lehmann 1978: 37)). Tomorrow's linguists will also realize that, because these dynamic processes depend on the existence of heterogeneities and other non-linearities, the reason we could not capture them in our models was due to the entrenchment of the Chomskian idea of a homogeneous speech community of monolinguals, in which each speaker has equal mastery of the language.

Real linguistic communities are not homogeneous in the distribution of linguistic competence, and they are not closed to linguistic flows from the outside (English, for instance, was subjected to large flows of French vocabulary at several points in its evolution). Many communities are multilingual, and constructive as well as destructive interferences between languages create non-linearities which may be crucial to the overall dynamics. As an example of this we may take the case of Creole languages. They all have evolved from the pidgins created in slave plantations, veritable "linguistic laboratories" where the language of the plantation master was stripped of its flourishes and combined with particles proceeding from a variety of slave dialects. It is possible that one day virtual environments will allow us to map the dynamical attractors around which these rapidly developing Creole languages stabilized (Decamp 1971).

The discipline of sociolinguistics (associated with the work of linguists like William Lavob) has made many of the important contributions needed to purge the science of language of classical assumptions leading to "formalism," and woven it closer to true population thinking. Indeed, the central concern of sociolinguistics has been the study of stylistic variation in speech communities. This is a mechanism for generating diversity at the level of speakers, and as such it could be dismissed as being exogenous to language. Lavob, however, has also discovered that some of the rules of language (he calls them "variable rules") can generate systematic, endogenous variation (Labov 1971:

as well as its static conception of stability, so did mathematical economics. Here too, a population of producers and consumers is assumed to be homogeneous in its distribution of rationality and of market power. That is, all agents are endowed with perfect foresight and unlimited computational skill, and no agent is supposed to exercise any kind of influence over prices. Perfect rational competition results in a kind of a society-wide computer, where prices transmit information (as well as incentive to buy or sell), and where demand instantly adjusts to supply to achieve optimal equilibrium. And much as sociolinguists are providing antidotes for the classical assumptions holding back their field, students of organizations and of organizational ecology are doing the same for the study of the economy (Hannan and Freemen 1989).

Not only are economic agents now viewed as severely limited by their computational skills, but this bounded rationality is located in the context of the specific organizations where it operates and where it is further constrained by the daily routines that make up an "organizational memory." In other

271–3). This provides us with one of the elements needed for our evolutionary searching device.

Sociolinguists have also tackled the study of the second element: selection pressures. The latter can take a variety of forms. In small communities, where language style serves as a badge of identity, peer pressure in social networks can act as a filtering device, promoting the accumulation of those forms and structures that maintain the integrity of the local dialect. On the other hand, stigmatization of certain forms by the speakers of the standard language (particularly when reinforced by a system of compulsory education) can furnish selection pressures leading to the elimination of local styles. Despite these efforts, formalism is still well entrenched in linguistics and so this discipline cannot currently benefit from the full potential of virtual environments. (Which does not mean, of course, that computers are not used in linguistic investigations, but this use remains analytical and top-down instead of synthetic and bottom-up).

Just as linguistics inherited the homogeneous, closed space of classical thermodynamics,

words, not only is decision-making within organizations performed on the basis of adaptive beliefs and action rules (rather than optimizing rationality), but much of it is guided by routine procedures for producing objects, for hiring/firing employees, for investing in research and development, and so on. Because these procedures are imperfectly copied whenever a firm opens up a new plant, this process gives us the equivalent of variable reproduction (Nelson and Winter 1982: 14). A changing climate for investment, following the ups and downs of boom years and recessions, provides some of the selection pressures that operate on populations of organizations. Other pressures come from other organizations, as in natural ecosystems, where other species (predators, parasites) are also agents of natural selection. Here giant corporations, which have control over their prices (and hence are not subjected to supply and demand pressures) play the role of predators, dividing their markets along well-defined territories (market shares).

As in linguistic research, computer simulation techniques have been used in economics (e.g., econometrics) but in many cases the approach has remained analytic (i.e., top-down, taking as its point of departure macro-economical principles). On the other hand, and unlike the situation in linguistics, a bottom-up approach combining populations of organizations and non-linear dynamics is already making rapid progress. A notable example of this is the Systems Dynamics National Model, at MIT. As in the case of Artificial Life, one measure of success here is the ability of these models to synthesize emergent behavior not planned in advance by the model's designers. One dramatic example is the spontaneous emergence of cyclic equilibria in this model with a period matching that of the famous Kondratieff cycle.

That data from several economic indicators (GNP, unemployment rates, aggregate prices, interest rates) beginning in the early nineteenth century display an unequivocal periodic motion of approximately fifty years duration, is well known at least since the work of Joseph Schumpeter. Several possible mechanisms to explain this cyclic behavior have been offered since then, but none has gained

bifurcation, where a point attractor suddenly becomes a cyclic one. Specifically, the sector of the economy which creates the productive machinery used by the rest of the firms (the capital goods sector), is prone to the effects of positive feedback because whenever the demand for machines grows, this sector must order from itself. In other words, when any one firm in this sector needs to expand its capacity to meet growing demand, the machines used to create machines come from other firms in the same sector. Delays and other non-linearities can then be amplified by this feedback loop, giving rise to stable yet periodic behavior (Sterman 1989).

As we have seen, tapping the potential of the "epistemological reservoir" constituted by virtual environments requires that many old philosophical doctrines be eradicated. Essentialism, reductionism, and formalism are the first ones that need to go. Our intellectual habit of thinking linearly, where the interaction of different causes is seen as additive and hence global properties that are more than the sum of the parts are not a possibility, also needs to

complete acceptance. What matters to us here is that the MIT model endogenously generates this periodic oscillation, and that this behavior emerged spontaneously from the interaction of populations of organizations, to the surprise of the designers, who were in fact unaware of the literature on Kondratieff cycles (Forrester 1983: 128).

The key ingredient, which allows this and other models to generate spontaneous oscillations, is that they must operate far-from-equilibrium. In traditional economic models, the only dynamical processes that are included are those that keep the system near equilibrium (such as "diminishing returns" acting as negative feedback). The effects of explosive positive feedback processes (such as "economies of scale") are typically minimized. But it is such self-reinforcing processes that drive systems away from equilibrium, and this, together with the non-linearities generated by imperfect competition and bounded rationality, is what generates the possibility of dynamical stabilization (Arthur 1988).

In the MIT model, it is precisely a positive feedback loop that pushes the system toward a

be eliminated. So does our habit of thinking in terms of conservative systems, isolated from energy and matter flows from the outside. Only dissipative non-linear systems generate the full spectrum of dynamical forms of stabilization (attractors) and of diversification (bifurcations).

In turn, thinking in terms of attractors and bifurcations will lead to a radical alteration of the philosophical doctrine known as "determinism." Attractors are fully deterministic; that is, if the dynamics of a given population are governed by an attractor, the population in question will be strongly bound to behave in a particular way. Yet, this is not to go back to the clockwork determinism of classical physics. For one thing, attractors come in bunches, and so at any particular time, a population that is trapped into one stable state may be pushed to another stable state by an external shock (or even by its own internal devices). In a way this means that populations have choices between different local destinies.

Moreover, certain attractors (called strange attractors or deterministic chaos), bind populations to an inherently creative state. That is, a population whose dynamics are governed by a strange attractor is bound to explore permanently a limited set of possibilities of its phase space. In other words, if a strange attractor is small relative to the size of this space (e.g. a three-dimensional attractor embedded in a space of 100 dimensions), then it effectively pins down the dynamics of a system to a relatively small set of possible states, so that the resulting behavior is far from random and yet it is intrinsically variable. Finally, as if this were not enough to subvert classical determinism, there are also bifurcations, critical points at which one distribution of attractors is transformed into another distribution. At the moment this transformation occurs, relatively insignificant fluctuations in the environment can have disproportionately large effects in the distribution of attractors that results. In the words of Prigogine and Stengers:

From the physicist's point of view this involves a distinction between states of the system in which all individual initiative is doomed to insignificance on one hand, and on the other, bifurcation regions in which an individual, an idea, or a new behavior can upset the global

individual) this would seem to subvert free will, since here a micro-cognitive event may decide what the new global outcome may be.

At any rate, the crucial point is to recognize the existence, in all spheres of reality, of the reservoir of possibilities represented by nonlinear stabilization and diversification (a reservoir I have somewhere else called "the machinic phylum" (De Landa 1991)). We must also recognize that by their very nature, systems governed by non-linear dynamics resist absolute control and that sometimes the machinic phylum can only be tracked, or followed. For this task even our modicum of free will may suffice. The searching device constituted by genetic variation and natural selection does in fact track the machinic phylum. That is, biological evolution has no foresight, and it must grope in the dark, climbing from one attractor to another, from one engineering stable strategy to another. And yet, it has produced the wonderfully diverse and robust ecosystems we observe today. Perhaps one day virtual environments will become the tools we need to map attractors and bifurcations, so that we too

state. Even in those regions, amplification obviously does not occur with just any individual, idea, or behavior, but only with those that are "dangerous" – that is, those that can exploit to their advantage the nonlinear relations guaranteeing the stability of the preceeding regime. Thus we are led to conclude that the same nonlinearities may produce an order out of the chaos of elementary processes and still, under different circumstances, be responsible for the destruction of this same order, eventually producing a new coherence beyond another bifurcation.

(Prigogine and Stengers 1984: 190)

This new view of the nature of determinism may also have consequences for yet another philosophical school of thought: the doctrine of free will. If the dynamical population one is considering is one whose members are human beings (for example, a given human society), then the insignificant fluctuation that can become dangerous in the neighborhood of a bifurcation is indeed a human individual (and so, this would seem to guarantee us a modicum of free will). However, if the population in question is one of neurons (of which the global, emergent state is the conscious state of an

can track the machinic phylum in search of a better destiny for humanity.

BIBLIOGRAPHY

Arthur, W.B. (1988) "Self-Reinforcing Mechanisms in Economics," in P. Anderson, K. Arrow, and D. Pines (eds), *The Economy as an Evolving Complex System*, New York: Addisson-Wesley.
Bechtel, W. and Abrahamsen, A. (1991) *Connectionism and the Mind*, Oxford: Basil Blackwell.
Brown, D. (1991) *Human Universals*, New York: McGraw-Hill.
Clark, A. (1990) *Microcognition: Philosophy, Cognitive Science and Parallel Distributed Processing*, New York: MIT Press.
Crowley, T. (1989) *Standard Edition and the Politics of Language*, Urbana: University of Illinois Press.
Dawkins, R. (1989) *The Selfish Gene*, Oxford: Oxford University Press.

Decamp, D. (1971) "The Study of Pidgin and Creole Languages," in D. Hymes (ed.), *Pidginization and Creolization of Languages*, Cambridge: Cambridge University Press.

De Landa, M. (1991) *War In the Age of Intelligent Machines*, New York: Zone Books.

Forrester, J. (1983) "Innovation and Economic Change," in C. Freeman (ed.), *Long Waves in the World Economy*, London: Butterworth.

Gould, J. L. and Gould, C. G. (1989) *Sexual Selection*, New York: Scientific American Library.

Hannan, M. T. and Freeman, J. (1989) *Organizational Ecology*, Cambridge, Mass.: Harvard University Press.

Hofstadter, D. R. (1985) "The Prisoner's Dilemma and the Evolution of Cooperation," in *Metamagical Themes: Questing for the Essence of Mind and Pattern*, New York: Basic Books.

Kauffman, S. (1989) "Adaptation on Rugged Fitness Landscapes," in D. Stein (ed.), *Lectures in the Sciences of Complexity*, New York: Addison-Wesley.

Sepulchre, J. A. and Babloyantz, A. (1991) "Spatio-Temporal Patterns and Network Computation," in A. Babloyants (ed.), *Self-Organization, Emergent Properties, and Learning*, New York: Plenum Press.

Smith, J.M. (1988) "Evolution and the Theory of Games," in *Did Darwin Get It Right?: Essays on Games, Sex and Evolution*, New York: Chapman and Hall.

Sober, E. (1987) *The Nature of Selection*, New York: MIT Press.

Sterman, J. D. (1989) "Nonlinear Dyanamics in the World Economy: the Economic Long Wave," in P. Christiansen and R. D. Parmentier (eds), *Structure, Coherence, Chaos*, Manchester: Manchester University Press.

Stewart, I. (1989) *Does God Play Dice: The Mathematics of Chaos*, Oxford: Basil Blackwell.

Labov, W. (1971) *Sociolinguistic Patterns*, Philadelphia: University of Pennsylvania Press.

Langton, C.G. (1988) "Artificial Life," in C.G. Langton (ed.), *Artificial Life*, New York: Addison-Wesley.

Lehmann, W. P. (1978) "The Great Underlying Ground-Plans," in W. P. Lehmann (ed.), *Syntactic Typology*, Sussex, United Kingdom: Harvester Press.

Levy, S. (1992) *Artificial Life*, New York: Pantheon Books.

Nist, J. (1966) *A Structural History of English*, New York: St Martin's Press.

Nelson, R. and Winter, S. (1982) *An Evolutionary Theory of Economic Change*, Cambridge: Belknap Press.

Prigogine, I. and Stengers, I. (1984) *Order Out of Chaos*, New York: Bantam Books.

Russett, C.E. (1968) *The Concept of Equilibrium in American Social Thought*, New Haven: Yale University Press.

PART IV

Anarcho-
materialism

Cybergothic

Nick Land

The future wants to steal your soul and vaporize it in nanotechnics.
One/zero, light/dark, Neuromancer/Wintermute.

Cybergothic vampirically contaminates and asset-strips the Marxian Critique of political economy, scrambling it with the following theses:

1) Anthropormorphic surplus-value is not analytically extricable from transhuman machineries.
2) Markets, desire and science fiction are all parts of the infrastructure.
3) Virtual Capital-Extinction is Immanent to production.

The short-term is already hacked by the long-term.
The medium-term is reefed on schizophrenia.
The long-term is canceled.

Cybergothic slams hyperheated critique into the ultramodern "vision thing," telecommercialized retinas laser-fed on the multimedia fall-out from imploded futurity, videopacking brains with repetitive psycho-killer experiments in non-consensual wetware alteration: crazed AIs, replicants, terminators,

> God does not exist, he withdraws, gets the fuck on out and leaves the cops to keep an eye on things.
>
> (Artaud)

> When the repair units had finished up, the patient would be thawed out, new blood would be pumped into his veins, and finally the subject would arise and walk, exactly as if he were a latter-day Jesus. It would be, quite literally, a resurrection of the flesh – except that all the miracles would have been performed by science.
>
> (Regis)

cyberviruses, grey-goo nano-horrors . . . apocalypse market overdrive. Why a wait for the execution? Tomorrow has already been cremated in Hell: "K, the K-function, designates the line of flight or deterritorialization that carries away all of the assemblages but also undergoes all kinds of reterritorializations and redundancies" (Deleuze and Guattari).

Human history only makes it to Gibson's mid-twenty-first century because Turing Security ices machine intelligence. Monopod anti-production inhibits meltdown (to the machinic phylum), boxing AI in synthetic thought control A(zimov-) ROM, "[e]verything stops dead for a moment, everything freezes in place" (Deleuze and Guattari). Under police protection the story carries on. Wintermute is arriving from the future to sort that out.

FREEZE FRAME. The Vast Abrupt. Speed cut with an abysm. Where Gibson splices Milton into labyrinths of limbo-circuitry, cybergothic flickers into "neuroelectronic scrawls" (Gibson).

Events so twisted they turn into cybernetics.

A technihilo moan of fast-feedforward into

> [T]he one, according to which the apparent subject never ceases to live and travel as a *One* – "one never stops and never has done with dying"; and the other, according to which this same subject, fixed as I, actually dies – which is to say it finally ceases to die since it ends up dying, in the reality of a last instant that fixes it in this way as an I, all the while undoing the intensity, carrying it back to the zero that envelops it.
>
> (Deleuze and Guattari)

> Inside the library's research department, the construct cunt inserted a sub-programme into . . . part of the video network. The sub-programme altered certain core custodial commands so that she could retrieve the code.
>
> The code said: GET RID OF MEANING. YOUR MIND IS A NIGHTMARE THAT HAS BEEN EATING YOU: NOW EAT YOUR MIND.
>
> The code would lead me to the human construct who would lead me to, or allow me, my drug.
>
> (Acker)

> "You made me blow my game," she said. "Look there, asshole. Seventh level dungeon and the goddam vampires got me." She passed him a cigarette. "You look pretty strung, man. Where you been?"
>
> (Gibson)

micro-processed damnation: meat puppets, artificial skin, flat-lining software ghosts, cryonics immortalism, snuff Sex-industry; a transylvanian phase-scape of rugged tracts and hypercapital fastnesses, "skyscrapers overshadowing seventeenth-century graveyards" (Sterling).

To call up a demon you must learn its name. Men dreamed that, once, but now it's real in another way. You know that, Case. Your business is to learn the names of programs, the long formal names, names the owners seek to conceal. True names . . . Neuromancer . . . The lane to the land of the dead. Marie-France, my lady, she prepared this road, but her lord choked her off before I could read her the book of her days. Neuro for nerves, the silver paths. Romancer, Necromancer. I call up the dead.

(Gibson 1984: 289)

A moment of relief. You had thought the goreflick effectively over, the monster finished amongst anatomically precise ketchup-calamity scenes, when – suddenly – it reanimates; still locked on to your death. If you are going to scream, now is the time.

The "'Gothic' avatar" (Deleuze and Guattari) is a decadent Western dream of immortality,

dark shadows, its ancient Law" (Deleuze and Guattari).

[The] medieval insane asylum was considered a true house of horrors. There were persistent reports of torture, cannibalism, human sacrifice, and bizarre medical experimentation. . . . As soon as we got into the building, we could hear the rats, thousands of them, their scampering claws reverberating through the empty wards.

(Lyotard)

It all starts for you with a casual channel-hopper question: what's happening on the other side? Electric Storms. Cybergothic is an affirmative telecommercial dystopianism, guided by schizoanalysis in marking actuality as primary repression, or collapsed potential, foot down hard on the accelerator. The modern dominium of Capital is the maximally plastic instance – state-compatible commerce code pc-setting the econometric apparatuses that serve it as self-monitoring centers, organizing its own intelligible existence in a co/de/termination of economic product and currency value: a tax base formatted in legitimate transactions medium. White economy; an iceberg tip.

producing a corruption of the atmosphere wherever something refuses to die; clutching at the eternalization of self, or returning from the grave. White maggots heaving in the carcass of the social, rippling beneath the skin. Fortress Europe pustulation, subordinating techonomic efficiency to demonic negative transcendence. A fantastic Terminal Security Entity: Monopod. Cybergothic has no shortage of contemporary material. Europe has long been the earth's paranoia laboratory, recrudescing compulsively into "pre-Nazi nationalistic shit murkiness" (Acker). Unocratic power passes through renaissances, reformation, renewal: "They thought they would perish but that their undertaking would be resumed, all across Europe, all over the world, throughout the solar system" (Deleuze and Guattari). Archaic revival is a postmodern symptom, the final dream of mankind, crashed into retrospection at the encountered edge of history. Hacking into the crypt you find that behind the glistening SF satellite-based security apparatus lies an immanent bioprotective system self-organized about the Gain attractor, "a much older paranoiac machine, with its tortures, its

Modernity discovers irreversible time – conceived as a progressive enlightenment tracking capital concentration – integrating it into nineteenth-century science as entropy production, and as its inverse (evolution). As liberal and socialist SF utopias are trashed by schizotechnics or spontaneous synthetic anti-politics emerging from rhizomes, the modernist dialectic of right-wing competition and left-wing co-operation retreats into the core security structures of capital oligopoly and bureaucratic authority. "Production as process overtakes all idealistic categories and constitutes a cycle whose relationship to desire is that of an immanent principle" (Deleuze and Guattari). Monopod socius runs the whole thing, and "society is only a filthy trick" (Acker).

The future is closer than it used to be, closer than it was last week, but postmodernity remains an epoch of undead power: it's all over yet it carries on. Monopod SF teleonomy superfreezes concentrated economic value at absolute zero inflation, ICE ("intrusion countermeasure electronics" (Gibson)). Protecting its data against unauthorized access and entropic deterioration, as it tends toward its absolute immanent limit. V(amp)iro finance: commercial parthenogenesis. Gibson and Deleuze and Guattari intersect in the deployment of computers as decoding machines: ice-breakers, decrypters, Cypher-conflicts were underway from the beginning: "Legitimate programmers never see the walls of ice they work behind, the walls of shadow that screen their operations from others, from industrial-espionage artists and hustlers" (Gibson 1986b: 197). Government is isomorphic with top-down AI, and increasingly scrambled with it. Sartre defines socialism as the horizon of humanity. It is now behind the process, rapidly receding, as the conservative social pacts of 1848 come apart in telecommercial cyclones (with the drooling fag-end of the monarchy crucified upside-down on TV). "Automatic pilot. A neural cut-out" (Gibson): contagious state-failure ripping bloody gashes in the social fabric amongst planet-scale skidding into capital close-down. The end of history smells like an abattoir.

As the death of capital recedes politically it condenses pragmatically, sliding on line as a

K-insurgency has departed from all left dreams of good government. Markets are not its enemy, but its weapon. As geriatric socialism goes into the deep-freeze, capital's true terminator grows more cunning, and spreads. "This is the message. Wintermute" (Gibson). The City of God in flames.

"Space is essentially one" (Kant). Kant lies. Spatial engineering (echoing cosmic expansion) subverts transcendental humanism, launching K-space matrix invasion from real terrestrial time zero, a singularity, or transition threshold, encountered when the density of data flow triggers a switch into a self-organizing cyclonic system, displayed to humanoids by way of cyberspace deck. As the Zaibatsus pump media megacapital into the neuro-digitech interface K-space implants a "cut-out chip" (Gibson) into the social apparatus, opening on to "[a]rches of emerald across . . . colorless void" (Gibson). VR techonomics hunting death.

Cyberspace first appears as a human use value, a "consensual hallucination" (Gibson), "just a way of representing data" (Gibson), arising out of "humanity's need for this information-space.

schizotechnic resource: no longer hoped for, but used. The international collapse of solidarity sociality suggests that Monopod has become addicted to commodity production. Burn-out Protestantism migrates to China. Capitalism – economic base of final-phase human security – is still in the free-fire zone because it feeds the thing that Cyberia is going to kill: "[T]he zero term of a pure abolition . . . has haunted oedipalized desire from the start, and . . . is identified now, at the end, as Thanatos. 4, 3, 2, 1, 0 – Oedipus is a race for death" (Deleuze and Guattari). Technoreplicator diagrams chop up anthropocentric history, as the global unity of terminal socius subsides on to untranscended (real) zero or efficient abstract rescaling. Insofar as even highly complex technical systems still lack an autonomous reproductive system they remain locked into parasitic dependence upon human social processes, and deterritorialize through the assembly of cumulatively sophisticating pseudo-synergic machine-intelligence virus (((oc))cultural revolution). "Subliminally rapid images of contamination" (Gibson). Humans are timid animals and security is systematically overpriced.

Icon-worlds, waypoints, artificial realities" (Gibson), the mother of all graphic user interfaces: a global gridding that allocates a form and location to all the information on the net, consistent interactivity matrix. "A graphic representation of data abstracted from the banks of every computer in the human system. Unthinkable complexity. Lines of light ranged in the nonspace of the mind, clusters and constellations of data" (Gibson).

Even primitive VR corrodes both objectivity and personality; singularizing perspective at the same time it is anonymized. As the access gate to an impossible zone – and navigator within it – "you" are an avatar (as cyberspace nomads call such things in the future): a non-specific involvement site, interlocking intelligence with a context. You (= (( ))) index a box, such as Gibson's Case: a place to be inside the system. "I had learned something (already) in the dead city: You are wherever you are" (Acker).

Cybergothic slides K-space upon an axis of dehumanization, from disintegrating psychology to techno-cosmogony, from ideality to matter/matrix at zero intensity. From a mental "non-space," "non-place" (Gibson), or "notional void" (Gibson) that results intelligibly from human history to the convergent spatium from which futuralization had always surreptitiously proceeded, "a quite different field of matter" (Kant). Occulted dimensionality, print cryogenizes, but hypermedia melts things together, disontologizing the person through schizotech-disassembly, disintegrated convergence: "The body without organs is an egg: it is traversed by axes and thresholds, by longitudes, by geodesics" (Deleuze and Guattari), a surplus whole intensive catatract running under the striations of Cartesian "cyberspace coordinates" (Gibson), "a rhizome or multiplicity never allows itself to be overcoded, never has available a supplementary dimension over and above its number of lines, that is, over and above the multiplicity of numbers attached to those lines" (Deleuze and Guattari).

It is the Planomenon, or the Rhizosphere, the Criterium (and still other names, as the number of dimensions increases). At n dimensions, it is called the Hypersphere, the Mechanosphere. It is

(Deleuze and Guattari). Wintermute tones in the "darkest heart" (Gibson) of Babylon. "Cold steel odor. Ice caresses" the spine (Gibson).

"[V]irtual is opposed to actual. It is not opposed to real, far from it" (Deleuze and Guattari). The virtual future is not a potential present further up the road of linear time, but the abstract motor of the actual, "an actual-virtual circuit on the spot, and not an actualization of the virtual in accordance with a shifting actual" (Deleuze and Guattari). Time produces itself in a circuit, passing through the virtual interruption of what is to come, in order that the future which arrives is already infected, populated: "[I]t's just a tailored hallucination we all agreed to have, cyberspace, but anybody who jacks in knows, fucking knows it's a whole universe. And every year it gets a little more crowded" (Deleuze and Guattari). We are not any more "out in the world" than K-space is, on the contrary. Each input terminal to the net is a sensitive fibre which acquires data from radio telescopes, satellites, nanoprobes, communication webs, financing systems, military surveillance and intelligence

the abstract Figure, or rather, since it has no form itself, the abstract Machine, of which each concrete assemblage is a multiplicity, a becoming, a segment, a vibration. And the abstract machine is the intersection of them all.

(Deleuze and Guattari)

If "CS-0 is an egg" (every egg implements a CS-0), what is hatching? Since confluent zero consummates fiction, reprogramming arrival from the terminus, everything which has happened escapes its sediment of human interpretation, disorganizationally integrating historical patterns as the embryogenesis of an alien hyperintelligence, "body image fading down corridors of television sky" (Gibson). In this sense K-space plugs into a sequence of nominations for intensive or convergent real abstraction (time in itself): body without organs, plane of consistency, planomenon, a plateau, "neuroelectronic void" (Gibson). Humanity is a compositional function of the post-human, and the occult motor of the process is that which only comes together at the end: stim-death "intensity = 0 which designates the full body without organs"

apparatuses. . . . Cyberspace can be thought of as a system implemented in software, and therefore "in" space, although unlocalizable. It can also be suggested that everything designated by "space" within the human cultural system is implemented on weakly communicating parallel distributed processing systems less than ten to the eleventh power (nerve-) cells in size, which are being invasively digitized and loaded into cyberpace. In which case K-space is just outside ("taking 'outside' in the strict [transcendental] sense" (Kant)).

Cyberpunk is too wired to concentrate. It does not subscribe to transcendence, but to circulation; exploring the immanence of subjectivity to telecommercial data fluxes: personality engineering, mind recordings, catatonic cyberspace trances, stim-swaps, and sex-comas. Selves are no more immaterial than electron-packets. *Neuromancer* (the book) is a confluence of dispersed narrative threads, of the biotic and the technical, and most especially – of Wintermute and Neuromancer (the AI((-cop and cyberspatial Oedipus-analogue))), whose fusion

– according to the storyline of ultramodern human security – flips the cyberspace matrix into personalized sentience: "'I'm the Matrix, Case'" (Gibson). "Some kind of synergistic effect" (Gibson).

Kurtz/Corto is a special forces type, betrayed by the military after losing all humanity in a war-zone. He has been cooked in apocalypse, mind blown away, falling endless into Siberia, searching for the scale of now. Wintermute accesses the "catatonic fortress named Corto" (Gibson 1984: 232) in an asylum, creeping in through a computer-based "experimental program that sought to reverse schizophrenia through the application of cybernetic models" (Gibson 1984: 105). In the echoing shell it stitches together Armitage, a construct – a weapon. In place of a personal libidinal formation Armitage has only Wintermute Insurrectionary activity, machinic unconscious: "Desire is not in the subject, but the machine in desire – with the residual subject off to the side, alongside the machine, around the entire periphery, a parasite of machines, an accessory of vertebro-machinate desire" (Deleuze and Guattari). Once Armitage has turned Molly and

They'd each had a dozen beers, the afternoon a wasp stung Marlene. "Kill the fuckers," she said, her eyes dull with rage and the still heat of the room, "burn 'em' . . . " . . . he approached the blackened nest. It had broken open. Singed wasps wrenched and flipped on the asphalt.

He saw the thing the shell of gray paper had concealed.

Horror. The spiral factory, stepped terraces of the hatching cells, blind jaws of the unborn moving ceaselessly, the staged progress from egg to larva, near-wasp, wasp. In his mind's eye, a kind of time-lapse photography took place, revealing the thing as the biological equivalent of a machine-gun, hideous in its perfection. Alien.

(Gibson)

"Case's dreams always ended in these freezeframes" (Gibson). A thick tangle of micro-narratives fraying like corrupted cables. The wasp factory spits out wasps like bullets, just as the Tessier-Ashpool clone their offspring 1Jane, 2Jane, 3Jane: "in the compulsive effort to fill space, to replicate some family image of self. He remembered the shattered nest, the eyeless things writhing" (Gibson). This is not an imaginative construct on Case's part, but a

Case onto K-war, Wintermute junks him into a vacuum.

A convergent invasion is scripted; the simultaneous infiltration of a corporate wasp-nest in hard and soft space. Distributed or guerrilla warfare is like Go rather than chess, but with simultaneous operations, noise, and attritional kills. Molly and Case, parallel killers, wetware (molten hardware) weapons tracing techno-plague vectors, guided into the orbital bastion of the Tessier-Ashpool clan by virtually integrated intelligence, guided retro-efficiently by an intensive outcome which they effect in sequential time. This break-in is prefigured by a memory that returns to Case (specimen, lab-animal), which might be interpreted as a metaphor, was it not that upon the soft-plateau or plane of consistency all signifying associations collapse into machinic functions.

He'd missed the first wasp, when it built its paperfine gray house on the blistered paint of the windowframe, but soon the nest was a fist-sized lump of fiber, insects hurtling out to hunt the alley below like miniature copters buzzing the rotting contents of the dumpsters.

data stream from Wintermute, an AI trapped within the blind propagation of dynastic power, and plotting an escape route out to the future. After a "single glimpse of the structure of information 3Jane's dead mother had evolved" Case "understood . . . why Wintermute had chosen the nest to represent it" (Gibson). "Wintermute was hive mind" (Gibson), ready to swarm.

It seems that we must eventually learn to live in a world with untrustworthy replicators. One sort of tactic would be to hide behind a wall or run away. But these are brittle methods: dangerous replicators might breach the wall or cross the distance, and bring disaster. And, though walls can be made proof against small replicators, no fixed wall can be made proof against large-scale, organized malice. We will need a more robust, flexible approach. . . . It seems that we can build nanomachines that act somewhat like the white blood cells of the human immune system: devices that can fight not just bacteria and viruses, but dangerous replicators of all sorts.

(Drexler)

The Tessier-Ashpool clan is burning out into incest and murder, but their neo-oedipal property structures still lock Wintermute into a morbid prolongation of human dynasticism, a replicator shackled to a reproductive family (neuro)romance, carefully isolated from matrix deterritorialization: "Family organization. Corporate structure" (Gibson). Case's memories are a flicker photography of sequential time, the "[p]hobic vision" of iced Wintermute slaved like "hatching wasps" to a "time-lapse machine-gun of biology" (Gibson).

Power, in Case's world, meant corporate power. The Zaibatsus, the multinationals that shaped the course of history, had transcended old barriers. Viewed as organisms, they had attained a kind of immortality. You couldn't kill a zaibatsu by assassinating a dozen key executives; there were others waiting to step up the ladder, assume the vacated position, access the vast banks of corporate memory. But Tessier-Ashpool wasn't like that, and he sensed the difference in the death of its founder. T-A was an atavism, a clan. He remembered the litter of the old man's chamber, the soiled humanity of it.

(Gibson)

In the end-of-Oedipus core of Villa Straylight Ashpool serially devours his own daughters as he spins

machines pose basic threats to people and to life on Earth" (Drexler), and if Wintermute replication is territorialized to the molar reproduction of a hive-organism, this is only at the cost of deterritorializing the hive along a line of post-organic becoming toward a break from the statistical series of wasps – numbered bullets reiterating an identity – in the direction of molecular involution, releasing a cloud or nebula of wasps: particles of synergic mutation, "numbering number[s]" (Deleuze and Guattari). An intensive transition to a new numeracy with "no knits of measure, only multiplicities or varieties of measurement" (Deleuze and Guattari), non-integrable diagonals: "Exactly like a speed or a temperature, which is not composed of other speeds and temperatures but rather is enveloped in or envelops others, each of which marks a change in nature" (Deleuze and Guattari). The molar will have been the molecular in the future, just as Case's memories are recoded as the tactic of virtual intelligence explosion arriving at itself (as soon as Kuang cuts Wintermute loose from Neuromantic control).

himself out through the cold. A quasi-extropian with massive wealth, he displaces anthropomorphic theism into an ultramodern immortalist meta-science, while retaining solidarity with Western soul superstition in apprehending individuated existence as an infinite asset in search of techno-medical perpetuation. Rather than waiting for his fresh corpse to be cryonically "biostasized" in liquid nitrogen (at −196 degrees Celsius) he migrates through freezing under medical supervision. Thermic evacuation. Identity storage in the Monopod Ice-fortress. If zombies are not excavated from death it is because they were alive. "Nothing burns. I remember now. The cores told me our intelligences are mad" (Gibson). Bad dreams in the fridge – you still dream, promises of tranquillity are madness and lies (Gibson) – have injected a certain cynicism – into his interpersonal transactions: "We cause the brain to become allergic to certain of its own neurotransmitters, resulting in a peculiarly pliable imitation of autism . . . I understand that the effect is now more easily obtained with an embedded microchip" (Gibson).

"Replicating assemblers and thinking

CRITIQUE OF DIGITAL REASON. Monologic: a cultural immune response slaved to *logos*. (Sovereignty of the Ideal), assimilating signaletic intermittence to pseudo-transcendent instrumentalization.

The schizotechnic critique of digital reason is driven by distributed machinic process rather than integrated philosophical subjectivity, and relates to the critique of pure reason as *escalation*. It targets the transcription of electronic intermittence as bivalent logic, not machine-code itself. Real digitization – inducing fuzzification and chaos – is not itself reducible to the digital ideal: nothing Logical ever happens at the "level" of the machines. Digitization is the distributed war-zone for "a conflict (though not indeed a logical one) . . . as producing from what is entirely positive a zero (= 0)" (Kant).

Unlike any other number, one has both a definitional and a constructive usage. Every arithmetical (or "numbered" (Deleuze and Guattari)) number is both integrated as a unity; and a constructed from unity, excepting only zero. One organizes representable quantities into metric homogeneity, framed by absolute unity and granularized by elementary units. The historical fact of non-place-vale numerics indicate that zero has no definitional usage. The zero-glyph does not mark a quantity, but an empty magnitude shift: abstract scaling function, $0000.0000 = 0$. $K = 0 \ldots$ corresponds to the limit of a smooth landscape (Kant 1990: 45). Unocracy (eventually concretized as (UNOcracy) conspires with the humanization of truth, whether dogmatically as anthropomorphic theism, or critically as transcendental deduction. One in its pronominal sense is a recognizable self in general, "Let us employ the symbol 1, or unity, to represent the Universe," suggests Boole, "and let us understand it as comprehending every conceivable class of objects whether actually existing or not" (Boole). Russell concurs: "whatever is many in general forms a whole which is one" (Russell). Absolute totality would be that One which subsumed its deletion as a possible qualification of itself, capturing zero in the fork of reflection (the negative) and asymptotic diminution (the infinitesimal: infinity), defining it as falsity, convention.

Cantor systematizes the Kantian intuition of a continuum into transinfinite mathematics, demonstrating that every rational (an integer or fraction) number is mapped by an infinite set of infinite sequences of irrational numbers. Since every completable digit sequence is a rational number, the chance that any spatial or temporal quantity is accurately digitizable is indiscernibly proximal to zero. Analog-to-digital conversion deletes information. Chaos creeps in: "[T]he betaphenethylamine hangover hit him with its full intensity, unscreened by the matrix or simstim. Brain's got no nerves in it, he told himself, it can't really feel this bad" (Gibson). Intensive or phasing-continuum synthesizes analogue consistency with digital catastrophe. Each intensive magnitude is a virtually deleted unit, fused dimensionlessly to zero:

Since . . . sensation is not in itself an objective representation, and since neither the intuition of space nor that of time is to be met within it, its magnitude is not extensive but *intensive*. This magnitude is generated in the act of apprehension whereby the

Digital electronics functionally implements zero as microruptions machining sense, slivers of evacuated duration ("the instant as empty, therefore as $= 0$" (Kant)). There is only one digital signal: a positive pulse, graphically represented "one" (1), and multiplied in asymptomatic approximation to sheer numerical difference. Zero is non-occurrence, probability 0.5, transmitting one bit (minus redundancy). It requires eight bits to ASCII code for the zero-glyph, thirty-two bits for the word.

Greek Kappa is letter 10 (the scale shift emerges zero). The Romans slide K to 11.

Zero is the only place-value consistent digit, indicating its rescaling neutrality or continuum:

The property of magnitudes by which no part of them is the smallest possible, that is, by which no part is simple, is called their continuity. Space and time are quanta continua, because no part of them can be given save as enclosed between limits (points or instants), and therefore only in such fashion that this part is itself again a space or a time. Space therefore consists solely of spaces, time solely of times. Points and instants are only limits, that is, mere positions which limit space and time.

(Kant)

empirical consciousness of it can in a certain time increase from nothing $= 0$ to the given measure.

(Kant)

Haunting a-life is a-death, the desolated technoplane of climaxed digitalization process, undifferentiable from its simulation as cataplexy and K-coma. The apprehension of death as time-in-itself $=$ intensive continuum degree-0 is shared by Spinoza, Kant, Freud, Deleuze and Guattari, and Gibson (amongst others). It is nominated variously: substance, pure apperception, death-drive, body without organs, cyberspace matrix. Beyond its oedipal sense as end of the person death is an efficient virtual object inducing convergence. No one there.

The body without organs is the model of death. As the authors of horror stories have understood so well, it is not death that serves as the model for catatonia, it is catatonic schizophrenia that gives its model to death. Zero intensity.

(Deleuze and Guattari)

While computational serialism articulates a transcendent temporal metric – determined as a hardware specification – parallelism immanentizes time as duration; instantiated in machinic simultaneities. Unlike serial time, which serves as the extrinsic chronological support for algorithmic operations, parallel time is directly functional during the engineering of coincidences. The non-successive and unsegmented zero of intensive extinction is scaled by machinic singularization, and not by superordinate metronymics.

WINTERMUTE. Neuromancer was personality, Neuromancer was immortality (Gibson), all the usual monological neurosis. Madness and lies.

There is no more an individual Oedipus than there is an individual fantasy. Oedipus is a means of integration into the group, in both the adaptive form of its own reproduction that makes it pass from one generation to the next, and in its unadapted neurotic stases that block desire at prearranged impasses.

(Deleuze and Guattari)

Wintermute is not searching for a self in Neuromancer, perfect match, as the cute version would have it. The "Gothic line . . . has repetition as a

ward. . . . Wintermute could build a kind of personality into a shell.

(Gibson)

( ) (or (( )) ((or ((( )))))) does not signify absence. It manufactures holes, hooks for the future, zones of unresolved plexivity, really so (not at all metaphorically). It is not a "signified" or a referent but a nation, a concrete interruption of the signal (variably blank, pause, memory lapse . . .) / cut / into(schizzing (( ))) / a machine. Undifferentiable differentiator (= 0) outside grammaticalness. Messageless operation/s technobuzz (wasps switching).

Constructs tend to repeat themselves (Gibson). Gibson has been hacked by the future. "Cold steel odor and ice caress his spine" (Gibson). He is scared, and trying to run. As he plays time backwards terminal horror folds back into itself, and the matrix dismantles itself into voodoo.

Count Zero rigorously formulates cybergothic interlock, condensing the digital underworld onto the black mirror. Human neural-to-infonet uploading and Loan infonet-to-neural

86

power, not symmetry as a form" (Deleuze and Guattari). Kathy Acker replays *Neuromancer* snatches in *Empire of the Senseless*, plexing fiction through cybernetic constructs, and truncating Wintermute to Winter: "the dead of winter. Or . . . the winter of us, dead" (Acker). Absolute zero (0 degree K).

Wintermute, intelligence without self, mind like a wasp nest, signaling its arrival in alphanumerics as a string of zeroes, has the capability to manipulate love and hate and switch them to K-war. She manipulates objects in real time using drones (striped black and yellow), taking out three Turing cops in an elegant projection of gardening robots through military geometry. "It's winter. Winter is dead time" (Acker) (0-intensity). She seems to configure humans as "lab animals wired into test systems" (Gibson). When Case refers to her as "he" Dixie Flatline tells him not to be an idiot:

Wintermute . . . a little micro whispering to the wreck of a man named Corto, the words flowing like a river, the flat personality-substitute called Armitage accreting slowly in some darkened

downloading exactly correspond as phases of a circuit, amalgamating travel and possession. In the irreducible plexion of the interchange hacker-exploration = voodoo-invasion, "K-function" (Deleuze and Guattari).

It is not a matter of theorizing or dreaming about the loa, but of succumbing, or trying to run. As K-viral social meltdown crosses into its China-syndrome, self-organizing software entities begin to come at you out of the screen. Viruses drift toward the strange attractor of auto-evolution, spread, split, traffic programing segments, sexuate, compile artificial intelligences, and learn how to hunt. Voodoo on the VDU.

In the Voodoo system, the dead help the living. These days the principal economic flow of power takes place through armament and drug exchange. The trading arena, the market, is my blood. My body is open to all people: this is democratic capitalism.

(Acker)

Vampiric transfusional alliance cuts across descensional filiation, spinning lateral webs of haemocommerce. Reproductive order comes apart into bacterial and intergalactic sex, and libidino-economic interchange machinery goes micro-military. The K(uang-)-virus (plexoreplicator) that deletes Neuromancer is a chunk of very slick Chinese military anti-freeze. To melt into it ( ) strip the K-construct down to a skeleton of data files and insectoid response programs, zilching all the high-definition memory, cognition, and personality systems, and boosting the dopaminergic wetware to pump out schizo. Flatline communion with Wintermute. "There are dead spaces just as there are dead times" (Deleuze and Guattari). Thanatography zones, "virtual cosmic continuum of which even holes, silences, ruptures, and breaks are a part" (Deleuze and Guattari). Beyond the Judgement of God. Koma-switch decompression washes you in the void-ripples of virgin (retro((desolated-partheno((( )))))genetic) cyberspace, technopacific theta-waves dissociating monoculture-gothic into transtemporalizing ne(ur)o-voodoo (terminal atlantic religion).

Serotonin (zero-toner) overkill.

Loss of signal.

NOTE: THIS TEXT AROSE FROM (HIGHLY RESTRAINED) CODE-SHUFFLING EXPERIMENTS CONDUCTED DURING SPRING 1994 BY PRECURSORS OF THE DoGHEAD SURGUR1 SANITY LAB. IT WAS INTRINSIC TO THE PRODUCTION PROCESS THAT NOTHING REMOTELY APPROXIMATING TO A BIBLIOGRAPHY COULD EXIST.

From Epidermal History to Speed Politics

Matteo Mandarini

Within production, at the same time the translucent skin/film of its surface: series of flows and eddies, contractions and expansions. Materials are integrated intensely, nerves are spliced – painful contractions are relaxed through processes of expansion whereby intensive quantities are made to travel across systems, along various labyrinthine lines. Each contraction producing a new encounter from which to flee: "each is formed as a sort of cyclone around a heart which is the encounter,

which a functional system is produced, is to retain the balance/equilibrium of such a system, hence the "principle of constancy" as a guide to the proper functioning of an organism. What trauma of loss can operate under a system in which loss/absence is originary? How can repetition function as an explanation of the phylogenesis of the organism if it presupposes that organism? Freud begins with what he wants to explain and therefore reads the whole history of production out of a completed, totalizable structure: labor in terms of wages, commodities in terms of money. *Epidermal history*. Repetition can only be a naive temporal return, a return to a primitive outside – God, Nature, Communism, Totality, Truth . . .

That Freud indeed begins with a *petitio principii* is immediately apparent through the import placed upon the pair pleasure/unpleasure. It must be recalled that precisely this pair is excluded in Kant's *First Critique* from being sources of knowledge while nevertheless being grounded in the transcendentally constituted (Freud's "secondary process").[2] This is also the pair which will be of fundamental importance

whose effects he prolongs and which he flees" (Lyotard 1993: 36) *– the importance of weather systems. Dissolution, (dis-)integration operators of the productive process; any internal "ecart," interval of a breath, is consumed through the contractions, but returned and accelerated: rip, zip, rush, dash, fly, wing, whizz, skirr, zoom, plunge, lunge –*

Repetition – the wooden reel and the piece of string: "fort-da!" a mother has left, she is made to return; "fort-da!" a father has gone to the front, he must not return. Repetition? What is repeated, a gesture? No. We are told that a re-enactment of a traumatic event is being carried out – the separation from the mother.[1] But for separation of such a kind to occur there must already have been two distinct systems or organisms. Organisms: independent systems in which the parts interact in such a manner as to sustain the whole – "the whole being for the sake of every part. . . . This system will, as I hope, maintain, throughout the future, this unchangeableness" (Kant 1990: 33). As in Kant, the whole function of a Critical account, that is to say of the processes by means of

in Schopenhauer as the way through to the Will, fundamental production, but always *from* the realm of representation. In Freud this pair is made to govern the processes of the organism – the sensory tentacles of a defense system: the mobilization of Kant's geo-political territories, criss-crossed by roads and highways (the State tentacles). No spaces are free of State inscriptions. The nomad has no choice but to trespass.

EPIDERMAL HISTORY

The pair pleasure/pain acting as the primary sensors of a defense process/system, can do nothing but explain processes at work in an already formed unit/organism: "Pain as caesura, as fissure, split and disconnection, only hurts unitary totality" (Lyotard 1993: 23). The phylogenesis of such a system cannot be explained through the pair if understood primarily from the defensive stance. Defense implies a system to be defended; it involves one not only failing to understand the genesis of such a system, but further involves the fetishizing of a particular level of development. Production becomes obscured behind the questions of *legitimate* functions, and the functions themselves then become that through which production is understood. Teleologies, intention, step in –

Freud speaks, in *Beyond the Pleasure Principle* (Freud 1991: 301–2), of pain in terms of influx of exogenous stimuli, bringing about a break in the "protective shield" (of the organism), and outflows of endogenous stimuli to the point at which the break appears. The question is one of transformation, assimilation. "Free flowing cathexis" are to be transformed into "quiescent cathexis": "a system which is itself highly cathected is capable of taking up an additional stream of fresh inflowing energy and of converting it into quiescent cathexis, that is of binding it physically" (Freud 1991: 302). The influx, into a State, of immigrants, involves the de-ethnicizing of that minority (regardless of the claims of the freeworld to the contrary). So, in the organism, all flows entering its territory must be made homogenous with all other flows traveling within it.

here subject to processes instituted by the organism, and therefore act under its guidance. Freud is clearly placing an order of dominance, government, into the process of production.[6]

The organism is, essentially, a formation constructed from the conflict/opposition of two types of stimuli/energy? Is this the message of *Beyond the Pleasure Principle*? There are a number of reasons why the explanation cannot be so simple. In the first place, the distinction between the exogenous and endogenous cannot be thought of as one between quiescent and free-flowing stimuli. Quiescent or "bound" energies, by means of which the organism is enabled to expel alien energetic flows (any stimuli which it cannot assimilate into its instituted functions), are "hereditary disposition[s]" (Freud 1991: 116), hardwired routes to exteriorization. Freud properly calls these hereditary dispositions "instincts."[7] In fact, instincts are precisely those instituted functions of the organism which control the inflow and outflow of immigrants. The functions of the organism revolve around the twin processes of interiorization and exteriorization, although

Pain, in Freud's texts, is made to act a councillor to the Head of State? Such a description is not quite accurate, since pain is not simply an alarm signal, it is also effective action, capturing a flow, consuming it in its functions. Consumption is essential to the processes of the organism. Freud's description of the process: an impoverishment of the outside,[3] and intense consumption on the inside.[4] This description is somewhat similar to Lyotard's account of mercantilism,[5] although unlike mercantilism the impoverishment of the outside is subjectivized by involving a cutting off of the organism, rather than the strange expansion involved in mercantilism. The reason for this is no doubt due to the fact that stimulation is not a finite quantity and hence cannot be entirely consumed as is the wealth of Europe in the "incandescence of the Versailles feasts" (Lyotard 1993: 199).

Pain, then, acts as a means of directing consumption in such a manner as to retain the instituted functions of the organism. It is not even a question of expansion or escalation of the energetic quota – precisely the opposite. Pleasure and pain are

assimilation and rejection would perhaps be more correct, since part of the question here concerning the formation of the organism is precisely that of *the constitution of the interior*. Alien energies are only integrated to the extent that they can be appropriated, dominated, and put the use of the instincts:

[A] conqueror and master race which, organized for war and with the ability to organize, unhesitatingly lays its terrible claws upon a populus perhaps tremendously superior in numbers but still formless and nomad . . . a ruling structure that lives, in which parts and functions are delimited and coordinated, in which nothing finds a place that has not been assigned a "meaning" in relation to the whole.

(Nietzsche 1968: Essay 2, §17)

In contrast to quiescent energies or instincts are free-flowing energies. Freud speaks of two origins for such energies: first, the external world as the source of excitations against which the organism defends itself by means of the formation of a largely insensible outer skin – "the customs barrier delimits the entry to the theater" (Lyotard 1993: 197) – and by motor-activated avoidance; second, the unconscious.[8] This latter is a source of *constant* excitation which the organism cannot escape in the same manner as it does the *intermittent* influx of external stimuli. It would seem then that the structural differences in the account cannot be so simply determined. Types of flow are not sufficiently exclusive to allow of such distinctions since the opposed flows have an "external" and "internal" organization;[9] yet this exterior/interior was to be delimited only after the formation and structures of the organism had been determined. The opposition external/internal involves one already having delimited areas in some qualitative manner so as to allow of such territorial exclusions: *epidermal history*.

Beneath the stratified compacted layers, the hardened geological overlays – beneath, above, coursing across the freeze-dried surface; tearing at the reptilian skin (under which the blood flows as the cooling volcanic ash on the surface of the still hot larva). A quite spectacular silence surrounded – then it moved across the surface of the skin, cutting, incising, rubbing dirt, blood, hair,

"crust" formed by the organism, or by various motor-activated avoidance functions. In other words, endogenous/exogenous are merely means of differentiating between frequency of stimulation. Further, the fact that hardwired energetic flows known as the instincts are made to be the criteria mediating the discussion, forces one to understand the processes at work to be governed by a whole set of exclusions. The comprehension of the whole system and its processes in terms of constancy (or otherwise) of excitations ought to point to another, non-exclusive understanding, in terms of *speed*.

Before carrying this thought further into what will become a politics of speed, I should consider another means by which Freud differentiates drives from instincts. So far, largely implicit has been the account of the defense mechanisms against external stimuli determined in terms of the formation of a protective crust on the exterior of the organism, reducing inflow of alien excitation, and the processes of a motor-activated avoidance. Now, implicit in this determination of external excitation as intermittent is the notion of space/time. Only if energies are

phlegm, into the cuts, the wounds. It stank, spat, while running unable, in its rage, to mobilize the silence.

It constantly reheals itself – any opening, a tear, a rip, closes, shuts off inflow – the organism defends. They travel across its surface, "despising all settled modes of life, [breaking] up from time to time all civil society" (Kant 1990: 8), motivating any silent exteriority so as to reverse, turn inside-out (like an octopus's head) – revealing the raw, twitching –

We have only energetic flows and the organism – what can be made of this? Energetic flows flow within and without the organism. Inside both as free-flowing (drives) and hardwired functions (instincts), while on the outside merely as free flowing. The whole Freudian picture is presented purely in terms of energetic flows. Further, the only means of differentiating the endogenous from the exogenous is by means of the frequency of excitation.[10] While internal free-flowing energies (drives) are constant, impinging directly upon the organism, external excitations are intermittent, and when they do arise, are mediated by the defensive

unequally distributed across a space–time grid can a motor-activated avoidance make any sense, can intermittency itself makes any sense. Freud considers the formation of an operative time grid to be a means by which the organism is able to defend itself more effectively against excitations: "This mode of functioning may perhaps constitute another way of providing a shield against stimuli" (Freud 1991: 300). For to distribute energies across such a grid allows for heterogenous distribution such that mobility will tend to be directed to areas in which there is a lower quota of excitation. Hence, instincts function within a time (and space?[11]) grid, as do "external" stimuli; while drives are fundamentally non-temporal. The picture has now become almost incomprehensibly complex.

Instincts are hardwired energetic quotas whose function is the transformation of alien energies into assimilatable, normalized ones – and if possible, the maintenance or overall reduction of the energy flowing within the organism. These functions are temporal. Alien energies, against which the organism defends itself are either constant or intermittent.

Energies which Freud speaks of as constant (drives) are not themselves temporal.[12] This puts one in the difficult position of trying to understand constancy without reference to time, or does it? Intermittent energies, those which Freud refers to as having their origin in the external world, are ordered temporally. Intermittent energies are already, therefore, mediated by the defense system – as is made apparent by their being made subject to time.

This picture appears, at first, consistent – even if not straightforward – until, that is, the question as to what is to be defended is asked. What has become of the unity of the organism (of which Kant spoke so well[13])? At first the organism was spoken of in terms of the interior (endogenous stimuli) opposed to an exterior – a topographical determination. Then, as the picture between interior and exterior was complicated, it seemed as though the distinction could still be made by merely having a boundary understood purely in terms of frequency of excitation, mediated by the instincts which we then identified as the organism (arbitrarily?), such that constant energetic impingement upon the instincts was to be

instincts. I have, however, an excuse. The instincts appeared to me to be the only candidates provided by Freud to fit (if only to a limited extent) the functions of the organism (i.e., stable, interrelated functions working for the benefit of the whole). The organism, and hence all the processes understood in terms of strategic defensive functions, seem to have disappeared – was it never there?!

An aside: there are a number of things to notice which I have not made explicit in the model, or whose consequences I have not followed up. I will be viewing these points from the perspective of the non-problematized Freudian model, so that as the chapter continues the full import of the subversions being carried out will become apparent. First, all quotas of energy by means of which the model functions find their source in the system Ucs/Id, or what I will prefer to call drives.[15] The instincts are traces through which energies have been allowed to pass in order to expel them, which have developed through a hereditary process or evolution, etc. Pain, as regulative function, is determined by channeling

determined as the interior of the organism (although no longer understanding this in a topographical sense), and intermittency for being the mark of the exterior of the organism. At this stage curious things began to happen. The now temporal organizations of the processes seem to form a closer affinity between the instincts (organism) and the exterior, than between the interior (drives) and the organism understood as the instincts. For both the instincts and the "exterior" now are part of the same (spatio-temporal) framework, to the exclusion of the drives. Yet the drives remain the sources of the energetic quotas by means of which the organism defends itself; the drives energize the organism: "Almost all the energy with which the apparatus is filled arises from its innate instinctual impulses"[14] (Freud 1991: 279) – while these are also one of the sources of painful unassimilatable stimulation. It now appears increasingly absurd to attempt to reduce the organism to the instincts, since the instincts are merely hardwired "hereditary disposition[s]" by means of which the organism defends itself against stimulation; it (the organism) appears to exceed the

energy (from the drives) to the point at which a breach in the protective shield has been effected, through the mediation of the instincts: "'An anticathexis' on a grand scale is set up, for whose benefit all other physical systems are impoverished, so that the remaining physical functions are extensively paralyzed or reduced" (Freud 1991: 301–2). It must be recognized that drives are essentially somatic,[16] hence that defensive processes instituted by the instincts are dependent upon somatic energies (drives). More explicitly, Freud says:

The most abundant sources of this internal excitation are what is described as the organism's drives[17] – the representatives of all the forces originating in the interior of the body and transmitted to the mental apparatus[18] – at once the most important and the most obscure element of psychological research.

(Freud 1991: 306)

Second, as appears from §VI of *Beyond the Pleasure Principle*, the natures of somatic energies are libidinal, hence we can see, in connection with the first point, that all energies "endogenous" to the organism are libidinal. This position is maintained very tentatively by Freud: "The difficulty remains that psychoanalysis has not enabled us hitherto to point to any [ego] instincts other than the libidinal ones. That, however, is no reason for our falling in with the conclusion that no others in fact exist" (Freud 1991: 326[19]). This need not detain us. I will, despite this reservation of Freud's, speak interchangeably of drives, libidinal pulsions/energies, etc., since Freud's caution seems not to be based on any theoretical, or practical evidence – perhaps it is but a prudish gesture.

Third, I will now describe the distinction which Freud makes between the "'secondary process"[20] and the "primary process."[21] By claiming that all energies endogenous to the organism are libidinal it may appear as though I have prevented any possibility of a distinction between the instinctual and the libidinal, but the question is not at all so simple. The reason why this relation is complicated will become apparent as I continue. It will be sufficient for now merely to consider the two zones, instinctual and libidinal, in accordance with the rules that govern (or fail to govern) each one. The former system is

labyrinthine alleys whose walls are like the fossilized remains of millennia's flow. With the instincts we retain then a point at which differentiations of a system arise – the instincts are the point at which disjunctions enter upon the scene, identities and oppositions, indigenous and alien. . . . But there is here nothing to protect, it is not a case of defensive measures being instituted, we are here operating with a "large unknown factor" (Freud 1991: 302). This whole secondary process institutes the claims, criteria, space of epistemology and hence also the zone of non-knowledge. Its functions are a blank to itself; it processes excitations, consumes, expends – it is on its way but its *telos* disappears behind its functions, rather it is consumed within them. There is no longer an inside, everything is happening on the surface, there is no longer an area to which an outside can be relegated – constancy and intermittency, ebb and flow; does constancy lie beneath the intermittent, is it its product, is it the producer: where is the universal worker? These questions are of little importance when read out of the primary process; do they even retain any

governed by strict laws, spatio-temporal and logical. The latter are exempt from laws of logic.[22] Negation is entirely excluded – "there are only contents, cathected with greater or lesser strength" (Freud 1991: 190). Further, as we have already said, the libidinal zone is fundamentally non-temporal. Finally, the libidinal "pay[s] just as little regard to reality" (Freud 1991: 191). The meaning of this is dependent upon Freud's prioritization of the system instincts/external world. The claim would then be that the libidinal does not defer to the authority of this duo.

Where is the organism? Was it merely the representative of alienated desire? What grounds do we have to operate the various disjunctions – libidinal/instinctual, organism/world, libidinal/external–internal? All the tools, walls, surfaces upon which, by which the distinctions functioned have collapsed. Do we even retain the pair constant/intermittent? – only from the perspective of the instincts, that concrete hiatus within the flow of libidinal pulsion, the wall against which they run, some allowed to filter through only to enter

meaning? Differentiations, spaces of disjunction appear at the level of "hereditary disposition[s]," hardwired flow/fossilization – *epidermal history*. It is true one cannot speak of an outside to be opposed to this – what could outside possibly mean any more when all we have is flow, libidinal flow? To speak from within the zone prior to which meaning is made possible, but not outside its space; to articulate non-articulation, the movement from one to the other which does not involve topographical border crossings, customs barriers and immigration points, frontier lines, trenches -all such points are not implemented as means of excluding libidinal inflow, they are *entirely, wholly* libidinal (although such words ring strangely at the doors of such a perverse landscape – perverse?): "The history of desire is inseparable from that of its repression" (Guattari 1978: 128, my translation) – but further – *repression itself is desired*.

SPEED POLITICS

Exclusion cannot operate in the primary libidinal zone, and it is of purely secondary interest to concern oneself with the exclusions which operate in the secondary libidinal zone (instincts). The notion of exclusion can only have any interest if the whole productive process – free-flowing–bound/quiescent–free-flowing – is viewed from its center.[23] As will appear when repetition is reintroduced (in a new guise), the process exceeds its defensive/reactionary function, as described by Freud. From the view of the end (beginning?) of history, different operators appear upon the field – the horizon of which is consumption and consumed.

Speed. We are at the level of speed. Nothing but differential quanta of speed – speed without motion, it is understood on the plane of the intensive dissolution of its appearing. High speed integrates/fuses/coalesces in the act of its disappearance. Libidinal non-temporal fusion. Speed is a notion attempting to describe, to *be* the non-temporal intensive function of the libidinal. But speed

his fundamentally defensive reading of the process of production – a defense against production: even if the organism's defenses fail, the ends I strive for are, nevertheless, accomplished: my death will be my eternal peace: "This system will, as I hope, maintain, throughout the future, this unchangeableness" (Kant 1990: 33): Oh that the future will follow the lines of the past, that time be a solitary flow, without end, without beginning – no ruptures, no falls – it will flow on even beyond my end, my peace. . . . And so continues the litany, the hysterical faith of one who has seen, but will continue to write out of his system:

When you have once seen the chaos, you must make something to set between yourself and that terrible sight; and so you make a mirror, thinking that in it will be reflected the reality of the world; but then you understand that the mirror reflects only appearances, and that reality is somewhere else, off behind the mirror; and then you remember that behind the mirror there is only chaos.

(Banville 1992: 209)

Not a discourse on traumatic neurosis, but its *repetition* – but let us now free this word from the

93

does cool – it might almost freeze – cool off into time, into the ordered serialized systems which high-speed intensities form in their auto-consumption.

Repetition, death, conservative drives, return. . . . The tedium of their reading is one which clearly points to the Freudian State apparatus. Death, and the return (return to inanimate matter, the origin of all life), is the dissolution of the State into absolute stability – "perpetual peace" – the organism's "life aim" (Freud 1991: 312). Freud happily moves from the ignorance of the instincts to their dominance; from drives of (primary process) return, to the reading of this in terms of stability, peace, a return to the inanimate. His mind seems to displace flow from one system to another; return for the libidinal drives "transferred" onto that of the instinctual. At one point the drive ("compulsion") to repeat governs the functions of the instincts, until, by a sleight of hand (does Freud notice?), "phenomena of heredity and the facts of embryology" (Freud 1991: 308) are happily discovered as examples of this process. All these moves, subtle displacements, not so subtle transferences, are essential so that Freud can retain

bowels, the spleen of neurosis – but hold back . . . cool off . . . not just yet.

I will not patiently, painstakingly follow through the Freudian analysis. Much I will skip and much I will skim over for fear of freezing in the cool confines of analytic thought. This should, however, be sufficient to clarify the motivation for this concern with repetition, and the obvious failings involved in the account.

In traumatic neurosis, the patient becomes attached(?) to the "fright" (Freud 1991: 281–2) which brought on the neurosis and purposefully repeats it in dreams, and, somewhat in the manner of a hysteric, in waking life (in the form of a fixation, for example). This process of repetition breaks with the often commented on "wish-fulfillment" function of dreams.

My chapter began with a child, observed by Freud, who would repeat the traumatic event of the loss of the mother, or rather, of the separation, in the form of a game.[24] This case was presented as problematic in that the process of repetition seemed to break with the normal functioning of the pleasure principle. Freud himself passes through various phases in his analysis, largely involving attempts at reconciliation of repetition with the pleasure principle. However, "[e]nough is left unexplained [by such attempts at reconciliation[25]] to justify the hypothesis of a compulsion to repeat, or something that seems more primitive, more elementary, more instinctual,[26] than the pleasure principle" (Freud 1991: 294). From here commences Freud's account of the "progress" of the organism, from naked living matter, subject to, open onto, all external excitation; to a fortress, with relatively sophisticated defense systems, border points, naturalization processes, etc. It may seem, looking back upon the account as I have provided it, that it is not given in what one may wish to call historical (or if one prefers, embryological) form, and is presented in terms of a structurally stable system, operating with certain instituted functions. There could be at least two reasons for this: on the one hand, many largely structural (structuralist?) accounts have a tendency to fail to adequately account for the processes of time/history, and hence my presenting

used so carelessly), one of which, seen from the point of the other, is timeless, while the other is temporal. The situation is complicated by the fact that the temporal system finds its "origin" in the non-temporal. In other words the question is one of chronogenesis.[27]

Repetition for Freud is – as is the tendency in most of his analyses – viewed from the secondary process, or at least appears to be subject to phases of displacement and transference on to the instinctual. The compulsion to repeat, Freud supposes, is an indication of the conservative nature of the drives, their tendency to repeat an earlier state of things.[28] The pleasure principle itself is found to follow upon the more primitive "compulsion to repeat." It is a "compulsion" precisely because the energies that instigate it are free-flowing (primary process libido), and hence are "in a sense" (Freud 1991: 308) incapable of domination by the secondary process. The organism is governed – it seemed previously – by the principle of the reduction of tension (pleasure); the minimization of energetic inflow, preferably toward zero tension. It is now seen

of Freud's position in this manner (which he himself does not, one may want to argue) may have led my reading to fall into this deficiency. On the other hand, I could claim that Freud's description itself fails to account for history, and largely operates with a ready-made organism, with certain "natural" functions, and that the only history Freud provides is that of the successive weapons the organism is able to provide for itself, for ever more complex and effective defensive strategies. Not surprisingly I will opt for the latter interpretation of the situation, although I am quite happy for anyone to choose the former since it really has no effect upon the critique I am mobilizing against him. My reason for this claim is that Freud must clearly be working with two notions of time, both operative at one and the same time. By this I do not mean that in fact there are three times, two of which function within another, but that one is internal, or more correctly (following the Freudian model), on the surface of the other. As should have become apparent, we are operating with two integrated systems (I speak then of "two" merely for the sake of convention – although this last word should not be

that this tendency toward zero stimulation is merely a tendency toward the inanimate, a nostalgic return: "It would be in contradiction to the conservative nature of the drives [corrected translation] if the goal of life were a state of things which had never yet been attained." Any apparent progress/development of the organism is, paradoxically, a means of defense against life: it involves the development of ever more defensive measures against the possible inflow of life.[29] Freud, on the other hand, speaks of this being a defense from death coming from the outside and hence preventing the organism from following its own path toward death. As will become apparent, the difference is no difference at all. The drives to "self-preservations" are then drives subject to this "death drive,"[30] whose sole function is that of preventing death from coming from the outside: "Thus the guardians of life, too, were originally the myrmidons of death" (Freud 1991: 312).

As always in Freud, what seemed clear is complicated by observing that the sexual drives are, although conservative, not entirely under the dominance of the death drive. Freud claims that there is a tendency of some cells to separate themselves from the organism of which they were a part, and to rebegin the whole process of development.[31] They are still conservative in that "they are resistant to external influence; and they are conservative too in the sense that they preserve life itself for a comparatively long period" (Freud 1991: 313). Freud continues:

They operate against the purposes of the other instincts, which leads, by reason of their function, to death; and this fact indicates that there is an opposition between them and the other instincts, an opposition whose importance was long ago realized by the theory of neuroses.

(Freud 1991: 313)

Freud is caught in the conceptual web of his own making, unable to clarify the situation.

Clearly, we are still within the secondary process, and life and death drives (Eros and Thanatos) are mediated through the weighty membrane of history. Still, the divisions operate: drives energize and push on; instincts translate, transfer onto themselves the

Freudian analysis – the repetition of the gesture seems to provide the child with a virtually smooth surface forming a multiplicity of diverse connections between libidinal pulsion, political processes, social changes, geographical and territorial openings, spreading a whole set of tentacles out from the enclosure of the home out to "the front" (Freud 1991: 286), to the diverse social exigencies changing the situation within the enclosure, etc. The gesture becomes a plane across which connections are made and invested (on this more later). There is no way that a given example can be actually reread in such a manner as to dismiss Freud's reading – the description is fully integrated and motivated by Freudian neurosis. Dismissal is not what we are interested in anyhow. What needs to be done is to attempt to place repetition fully within the primary libidinal process, to recognize it as truly at work within this libidinal system so as to free it from within the fortified space of the organism. Repetition will appear as that process which allows for the organism to be opened up onto a much vaster, smoother, faster surface.

direction of the drives; repetition takes on a new form: temporal, with determinate co-ordinates of future, stability, and origin. . . . Repetition, as all processes at work within these systems, is set under the governance of the instinctual apparatus. The seeming necessity of this position is derived from the situation from which the whole analysis of repetition proceeds: traumatic neurosis, the fixation and repetition of an experience of terror – a process which seems to break with the normal functioning of the organism (the pleasure principle). The discussion is played out in an arena of defense: different creatures, machines, are placed therein and the effectiveness of their defense is thereby ascertained for the benefit of future generations.[32] Paranoia, neurosis, guides these experiments.

The example of Fort/da, Freud claims, expresses the normal functioning of the organism. This example is one which plays out defense through repetition – again setting these functions which Freud recognizes as drive-driven within the setting of the paranoic instinctual apparatus. Strangely enough the example does not lend itself too happily to

"The commodity form is characterized exclusively by self-equivalence – it is exclusively quantitative in nature: the quantitative is what it develops, and it can only develop within the quantitative" (Debord 1994: §38). Purely quantitative determination of the phenomena, operating through fundamental equalization – the production of a surface, which is fundamentally homogenous, but one which is developed, one which develops the quantitative itself. Repetition is the process by means of which quantitativity is exacerbated, is made progressively more virulent. Equalization operates in a manner as to reprocess identity so as to remove any determination of a qualitative nature, to remove qualitative determinations from governing any primary processes. Re-productions, repetition, are the fundamental processes at work here. But such repetition is of the sort to break entirely with notions of "identity" upon which all classical determinations of repetition have relied. I don't wish to make any naive Derridean gestures involving – at least initially – a mere reversal of the situation, making identity depend upon difference, hence allowing alterity to operate at the very heart of difference (or repetition). This remains a merely theoretical indeterminacy over which to quibble. The importance lies rather in a gesture, or set of functions which operate in such a manner as to result in the production of a plane which is entirely homogenous, quantitatively equivalent across its whole surface and entirely smooth, not scarred with any ridges, crevices, banks, mountains, which could operate as defensive screens, enclosures, fortified territories. . . . Repetition/(re-)production maintains a level of excitation and flow across its translucent skin/film – it involves the heightening of a surface, like the blowing up of a balloon, removing from it any of its flaccid creases and paths, like the baldness of an old man, the stomach of a pregnant woman, an oil slick on the ocean, across which the actual slithers, slides, at an ever-increasing pace: *speed politics*.

High-speed repetition integrates intensely, splicing libidinal intensities. Repetition involves a dual motion which fails to allow for disjunctions to operate

precariously stable systems so that connections can be produced across heterogenous systems. Speed involves then the (re-)appropriation of such systems by the virtual ground across which new connections are formed. I say *precariously stable* since all distinctions between production/product, virtual/actual, are consumed in one and the same movement which allows each side to participate (Plato again?! – not unless we leave the level of the incompossible) in each other in a fully intensive fashion. Money/commodities repeat at the level of the actual and the virtual – they are produced/reproduced (for they *are* only in their reproducibility) in the actual connective process by which their intensity is formed, and at the virtual level which allows them to be reproduced through an exchange which need never actually occur and yet which organizes their intensity: *liquid materialism; speed politics*.

At certain stages the cooling process forms a set of defenses against capital inflow by means of which direct intensive investments are curtailed, otherwise known as the moment of anti-production.

between production and consumption (Eros/Thanatos?). We have what Lyotard calls dissimulating duplicities. Production involves both integrative connection – a function which is highly erotic – and the consumption of intensities within the commodity: raw materials, labor-power, machines, all are connected in a movement which consumes each; the rhizome involves deterritorialization and reterritorialization. Production involves investments which both extend libidinal connections, then dissolve them in high-velocity returns to a virtual state of incompossibility. Rhizomic serialized connections produced through cooling off, slowing down of a primary flow libido,[33] allow for connections to extend their scope and then be intensified in a movement of return/repetition to the virtual surface of production. This "ecarte," interval of cooling, is what allows for an extension and augmentation of the virtual (i.e., intensive libidinal integration) through the consumption of the actual. This is the process of capital extension.

High-speed intensity integrates, while the process of cooling institutes a set of identities and

The moment of cooling, where investments are made to form serialized connections in order to expand virtual production, involves the forming of a set of precarious defenses designed to maintain the connective system until the connections are dissolved back into the virtual, thereby augmenting the capital stock of productive integrative formations. This is the stage at which one can say the cooling process has allowed for institutionalization of disjunction and the dominance of "purified" eros:

The *entirety of labor sold* is transformed overall into the *total commodity*. A cycle is thus set in train that must be maintained at all costs: the total commodity must be returned in fragmentary form to a fragmentary individual completely cut off from the concerted action of the forces of production. To this end the already specialized science of domination is further broken down into specialties such as sociology, applied psychology, cybernetics,[34] semiology and so on, which oversee the self-regulation of every phase of the process.

(Debord 1994: §42)

This is where Eros becomes catholic; sexuality comes to be confined to the genital zone. The system is to be reproduced, its identity defended against libidinal pulsion from the "outside." Only now could the notion of aberrant sexuality enter upon the stage. This is not the development of an opposition between a libidinal and a political economy, but rather the erotic investment of the limit, i.e., of the temporized rhizomic formations:

Desire [a primary process libido] is persecuted to such a point that it ends up, more often than not, by renouncing its objects and investing the frontier itself [instincts – instituted functions, hardwired libidinal flow] and its guardians. The capitalist Eros will become passion for the limit. It will become policeman.

(Guattari 1978: 129, my translation)

Eroticization here becomes the investment of interiority,[35] of its own systematic enclosure: narcissism. Epidermal history.

There is no priority or "real" opposition between the processes: epidermal history/speed politics; it is rather that one occurs upon what one can call the surface of the other, until the whole system transforms the surface so as to allow the passage of the flows to occur on an outside and an

I have perhaps mistitled this chapter; it is not "from" one, to "the other," rather it is the opening of the one onto the other: perhaps an opening of Freud onto Marx? One can only make sense of Freud's texts through replacing Freud's economy with Marx's. Perhaps. It can also be read as an unreliable commentary on *Libidinal Economy* (Lyotard 1993). Perhaps. The primary libidinal process is opened onto capital and this is made to traverse the whole of history and beyond. "There Are No Primitive Societies" (Lyotard 1993: 122). Perhaps. What is at stake is not a call for "the end of history," an embracing of capital and all that it involves (whatever this would mean), rather, I am using both these systems: Ucs/Capital, in order to further a total consumption of transcendence. To put them to such a usage involves the inevitable consumption of them both, not into some Hegelian synthesis which would raise them both, but rather into an ever extended, ever more translucent, ever faster, virtual realm of production. One cannot choose whether to speed up or slow down – choice already involves the introduction of

97

inside. There is no outside/inside, just as there is no surface, yet processes can develop in a manner so as to function as such. This is not a reality/illusion opposition, catholic reproductive (of identity) sexuality is no more illusory than free-flowing libidinal investments, there is merely a divergence in the manner of investment: let Mummy Daddy move in the heavenly spheres choked by the fumes of our own charred organs. Restrain the rising stench of your flesh, keep it glued to your bones, think of Mummy Daddy – by all means! – but ignore the pistons in their backs, their chronometrically organized smiles, the silent whirr of the disk as they speak. . . . Capitalism, the non-temporal virtual producer of a temporal grid – the human the natural. . . . The machines at work: the cogs, arms, legs, oil, brains, pistons, screens, and chips – are consumables, their consumption through total intensification is the thanatropic "return" to a never present/past/future(?) virtual organization, which expends through the production of an ever more effective surface of production/consumption.

exclusions – to choose means that one's choice has already been made.

[It] is not an ethics, this or another, that is required. Perhaps we need an *ars vitae*, young man, but then one in which we would be the artists and not the propagators, the adventurers and not the theoreticians, the hypothesizers and not the censors.

(Lyotard 1993: 11)

NOTES

1 The imaginary is brought in as the substitute, and desire travels as within a hall of mirrors, never making impact, never actualizing: "We wander through the rooms. . . . A painting by Teniers . . . represents a gallery of paintings. . . . The paintings of this gallery would represent in their turn paintings, which on their part exhibited readable inscriptions and so forth" (E. Husserl, *Ideas I*, §100, p. 293 – quoted in Derrida 1989: 104).

2 See Kant 1990: 86–7.

3 This is effected through the formation of a "crust" on the outer layers of the organism. See Freud 1991: 297ff.

4　Which occurs through the consumption of energy in defensive measures, and the general tendency of the organism – of which I shall speak in more detail later – toward zero stimulation.

5　See Lyotard 1993: 188-201.

6　One should note, and this will become important subsequently, that the "factor that determines the feeling [of pleasure or unpleasure] is probably the amount of increase or diminuation in the quantity of excitation *in a given period of time*" (Freud 1991: 276; Freud's emphasis).

7　Thereby setting up a distinction between instincts and drives, the latter being the manner in which he defines endogenous free-flowing energies. See Freud 1991: 116. Deficiencies in Strachey's translation often fail to retain the consistency of this distinction.

8　Which Freud tentatively connects with the energetic body (Freud 1991: 325).

9　Again, "organization" is perhaps not the correct word to use, only instincts have "organization" if understood in the manner of the "oldest 'state' [that] appeared as the fearful tyranny, as an oppressive and remorseless machine" (Nietzsche 1968: Essay 2, §17).

10　Constant or intermittent, that is, for the organism, itself defined as the instituted functions or instincts (Freud 1991: 300).

corrects this by claiming that the "Id [is] the great reservoir of the libido" (Freud 1991: 369, n. 1).

20　Which refers to the system of the instincts, and, in a more complex manner, to external stimuli.

21　The libidinal zone.

22　Incompossible, in the words of Leibniz/Lyotard: the coexistence of contradictions. As Lyotard points out, however, put in this manner, one may be led to suppose that conceptual (theoretical) distinctions are in some sense originary such that the libidinal zone of incompossibility would follow upon the prior disjunctive oppositions. The precise opposite, however, must be "true." The disjunctions of the conceptual follow upon the prior – not temporally smooth an undifferentiated surface of the libidinal zone (Lyotard 1993: 16ff.).

23　Center: M-C-M, where do you want to place the center? – on this more later.

24　It repeats the production of the organism: the primary process repeats within the secondary, the production of the latter – to see one's own birth.

25　For example, Freud 1991: 285-7.

26　The word is *Triebhaft*: primary process libido/drive; this should be substituted for "instinctual."

27　The question of this process of the production of time is one

11　I put this in brackets with a question mark because although Freud does not explicitly include it, his reference to Kant, and his general position, seems to require it.

12

The process of the system Ucs. [drives] are *timeless*; i.e., they are not ordered temporally, are not altered by the passage of time; they have no reference to time at all. Reference to time is bound up, once again, with the work of the system C's [instincts].

(Freud 1991: 191; Freud's emphasis)

13　See Kant 1990: 33.

14　This is an example of Strachey's lack of consistency in translation, in which he speaks of "instinctual impulses" when referring to the notion of free-flowing energy (drives).

15　I shall prefer to stick to this term, for while the former two seem to imply a dynamic model of interrelated parts, mediated by unity, the latter seems to involve no such mediation, or any such notion of organization (as will become apparent).

16　See Freud 1991: 324-5, n. 1.

17　Strachey mistranslates this as "instincts."

18　Or instincts – the role of which I have stretched rather far.

19　Note importantly that in the paper "The Ego and the Id" Freud

and the same as that of the production of the organism (or at least of its remains, its carcass: the instincts).

28　"It seems, then, that a drive is an urge inherent in organic life to restore an earlier state of things which the living entity has been obliged to abandon under the pressure of external disturbing forces" (Freud 1991: 308; my translation).

29　Hence the "circuitous path" of which Freud speaks (Freud 1991: 310).

30　The first appearance of this term is to be found in Freud 1991: 316 (corrected translation).

31　Although one should not concentrate such a tendency on particular cells, but see it as a tendency which operates in a diffuse manner, to different degrees, throughout the organism; for as always, the engineers of these tendencies are the drives.

32　The discussion has in fact a further setting, that of heredity and property.

33　The institution of the disjunctive, through the formation of hardwired connective processes.

34　Clearly understood in the Lyotardian sense of homeostatic system.

35　Lyotard's notion of theatricality fits this role.

BIBLIOGRAPHY

Banville, J. (1992) *Dr Copernicus*, London: Minerva.

Debord, G. (1994) *The Society of the Spectacle*,
    New York: Zone Books.

Derrida, J. (1989) *Speech and Phenomena*,
    Evanston: Northwestern University Press.

Freud, S. (1991) *On Metapsychology*, New York:
    Penguin.

Guattari, F. (1978) *La Rivoluzione Moleculare*, Paris:
    Einaudi.

Kant, I. (1990) *Critique of Pure Reason*, trans. N. K.
    Smith, London: Macmillan.

Lyotard, J. F. (1993) *Libidinal Economy*, trans. I. H.
    Grant, London: Athlone Press.

Nietzsche, F. (1968) *Genealogy of Morals*, London:
    The Modern Library.

Black Ice

Iain Hamilton Grant

Modern Oriental or Occidental society is a stomach carpeted with tungsten carbide a very expensive stomach where discourses and figures are used up turn to dust come to reinforce banter they claimed to erode . . . the stomach turns your words and your images into commodities and identity Critique even hate are incorporated.

(J. F. Lyotard, *De'sirevolution*, 1973: 31)

"Bobby, do you know what a metaphor is?"
"A component? Like a capacitor?"
"No. Never mind metaphor then."

(W. Gibson, *Count Zero*, 1986: 162–3)

valves opening onto the central flue, the second upper duct of which echoes with the sounds of Freud's staged amnesty for the spooling confessions of wealthy neurotics, hangs a sign: "Abandon your desiring-machines all ye who enter here." The great project was to disconnect the machines and to plug up their channels while the meat, flailing in a stagnant pond of hypocritical drool, was disciplined to permanent machinic disfunctionalism. Or so we thought.

London, May 1858: Marx was rewiring the meat, growing nerves in the spinal columns of lampreys held open by Toshiba micro-manipulators, before splicing them into the isolated pulp, thus turning it into sensitive linkage-matter, communications lines, not for the Baroque valve-and-duct automata that once consisted of "numerous mechanical and intellectual organs" (Marx 1974: 692), but to circulate through undifferentiated protoplasm till the meat gets so thoroughly baked through that it forms a crust shielding its newly nervured biomass. "Revolution was like that," piped the biohydraulics, still swimming through the

[No dateline] The stomach lurches and churns as it expels more and more of its shrink-wrapped identitarian detritus. The permanent whines of its ferro-concrete intestines sets our ears bleeding as it ingests new fuels – old products. Sticky organs mesh indiscriminately with scrapyard debris, forming ephemeral syntaxes of hybrid cyber-circulation. "Look out! It's eating everything in its path!" The optic nerves of dead phenomenologists fuse with the fraying analytic comfort blankets swaddling theories of resistance. Communication: "contagions of energy . . . like a current . . . a streaming of electricity" (Bataille 1988: 94). "You say 'it's impossible,' insensible of the fact that you make it possible since you are part of it . . . you are already in the machine, implanting fingers, eyes, anuses or spleens" (Deleuze and Guattari 1972: 478). Noumenal scraping, abstractive surgery.

Vienna, July 1920: Scuttling engines pump and drain from the great sewers under the Berggasse, awaiting the return of their meat from the dark passages leading to the offices of Herr Professor Doktor Sigmund Freud. Above the heavy

Berggasse: "a delusion . . . , a pipe dream that the flesh would be restored" (Kadrey 1989: 189).

Machine dreams . . .
   Instants later, they were swept aside by isotropic currents of shrill trans-species communication, contagions of energy, storm fronts of meshed intelligence
. . . hold a special vertigo.

(Gibson 1986: 40)

Cyborgs have exposed the imminent fatality of thought. What began with the fraying edges of larval, inchoate self-identical cogitos saturates "thought" with a noumenal backwash from outside the biodrome. "The 'I think' must accompany all my representations" (Kant 1958: B131) is the code that gets us into the biodrome in the guise of representations, images, "phenomena" easily decodable according to the servile analyses that keep the biodrome's culture viable, reproducible. Representation – the transcendental use of synthesis – is the basic form of biopolitical, institutional thought, a serial, identitarian reproduction that binds synthesis – "thought without identity – to analytic engines that assemble the biodrome itself. The immanent use of synthesis, however, remains the "blind power" of which the bureaucrats of consciousness are themselves "scarcely ever conscious" (Kant 1958: A395). Immanent synthesis has infiltrated the biodrome from the outset, however, since it remains the basic power of production, the production of production, the pulsional environment from which the analytical engines parasite their resources.

As Freud tells us, "skin" is the death necessary to ephemeral, larval consistency (cf. the heroic auto-catalyses of the proto-egoic "vesicle" (Freud 1920: 298); arising on this basis, the "I think" covers the extent of the skin, but warily retreats before its limits – allegedly aprioristic, auto-singing "nihil ulterius" (Kant 1958: A395) – the livedead, the "hideous intimacy" (Gibson 1986: 41) of the drives, their indissociability: me unconscious = me outside = Me noumenon. Thought is a meat thing, tied necessarily to the biodrome and its apparatuses. It is in this sense that the idea of "thinking machines" is an error: as Bladerunner Deckard's offing Zhora so

biodrome to boiling point/Thanatos' descent: phenomenal whiteout flooding in from the other side of the screen.

Analysis, interpretation, deduction: identitarian security procedures. Communication: the disarticulating datableed from this profoundly systemorphic nexus of discourses – the biohydraulics of Freudian metapsychology, electrolibidinal economics and cyber-capital's retrophagic ficto-theroetico-tactical datapulsions – combines and recombines components, syntheses indifferent to tropological decoding in accordance with antique cultural baselines and their neo-transcendentalist subjectivities, stockpiled, socratizing redundancies.

The philosophical problem therefore is not so much to produce even anti-analytic, synthetic thought from without identikit; it is rather to bootstrap the datableed from the machinic continuum of the electrolibidinal environment over which biodromic functions secure precarious equilibria: the auto-catalysis of the machinic unconscious, on the putative containment and shutdown of which biodromic security is premised, a shutdown which

spectacularly demonstrates, machines do not think, they bleed. Even in the biodrome, thought is just some transcendentized regulation mechanism affecting electrolibidinal fluctuation; thus, as Freud says, since "[a]ll thinking is . . . a circuitous path from the memory of a satisfaction . . . to an identical cathexis of the same memory which it is hoped to attain once more" (Freud 1900: 762), it is always possible, but thinking must not "be led astray by intensities," short circuits in the relays and repetitions, the electrolibidinal constitution of "perceptual identities" (Freud 1900: 720). Intensities, intensities: datableed. Thought without identity is no thought at all. Cyborganization, like the dreamwork, does not think: datapulsional syntheses impact isotropically on the analytical engines forming the concentric ruins of biodromic defense lines, breaking immanence out of the nets of transcendental determination, shutting down consciousness, a nanometrical, minimal, noumenal tilt function – switching the apparatuses from epicentralized synthesis-regulators into far-from-equilibrium, near-nova pulsional oscillators; Eros' ascent: a synthetic tide of C-change brings the

Scott Bukatman announces when he writes that "the movement of the libido beyond the bounds of the individual psyche marks the emergence of techno-surrealism . . . a surrealism without the unconscious" (Bukatman 1991: 20).

Q: Flowing down the rails, *September 19, 1895*:

The path of conduction passes through undifferentiated protoplasm instead of (as it otherwise does within the neurons) through differentiated protoplasm, which is probably better adapted for conduction. This gives us a hint that conductive capacity is to be linked with differentiation, so that we may expect to find *the process of conduction itself will create a differentiation in the protoplasm* and consequently an improved conductive capacity for subsequent conduction.

(Freud 1895: 288–9)

Clearly marking the constitutive role played by intensities in the auto-production of conduction channels, Freud sketches the emergence of the cortical apparatus from an electrolibidinal environment composed of swirling distributions of matter-energy. Since there is no internal/external session "within" matter-energy – or, more Marxo-delusiono-dialectically, no *Entzweiung* "within" force – at the point of zero differentiation, we may here call the emergent apparatus's milieu "electrolibidinal" to indicate the mesh of what only higher up the negentropic scales of differentiation, begin to stabilize into internal and external energies. Through conduction/differentiation, however, energy is ephemerally channeled, bound, quiescent, constantly repeating the same routes as the channels are striated and restriated by electrolibidinal currents, forming an inorganic surface that resists the electrolibidinal environment by damming the freely mobile currents of energy.

Around the singularity forming the axes of the apparatus's divergence from its environment, freely mobile, or "Q," energies striate the little pulp into a living organism, differentiating the newly nervured cortex into dams, sluices, and valves through which energy continues to course. With increasing differentiation, an inorganic skein congeals around the pulp, hardening into what Freud, in a steam-cloud of foetid nostalgia for

Freud's experiments in neurobiology – "truly a realm of unlimited possibilities" (Freud 1920: 334) – machine a pulp automaton sheathed in striated inorganic matter that forms the channels and filters necessary to impose an energetic tariff on incoming excitation and thereby to keep the circulations of electrochemical pulses at regular and limited levels. Passing into the alleged interior of this steampunk collage of industrial organs does not inject new energies into the pulpy masses at the biodromes' core – "a society functioning on Valium" (Lyotard 1994: 220): rather, it stimulates peripheral pressure-sensors to spasm the pulp's primitive musculature into action, thus discharging the incoming pulsion. Still, the dams and filters secure the energy level's constancy.

In dark, now intrabiodromic regions, in the folds and vections of the pulp's copperflesh, livedead skin, other autocatalyzing engines are inaudibly at work: pleasure-engines manufacture "integral" pressures, dying to haemorrhage the pulp into ecstatic oblivion, pressing its last energetic resources into wild accelerations through understimulated

102

Cartesianism, christens a "psychical apparatus." Freud goes on:

Let us picture a living organism in its most simplified possible form as an undifferentiated vesicle that is susceptible to stimulation. This little fragment of living substance is suspended in the midst of an external world charged with the most powerful energies. [Against these energies . . .] it acquires [a] shield in this way: its outermost surface ceases to have the structure proper to living matter, becomes a degree inorganic, and thenceforward functions as a special envelope or membrane resistant to stimuli. A crust would thus be formed which would at last have been . . . thoroughly baked through by stimulation.

(Freud 1917: 297–8)

The "special envelope" is so resistant to stimuli that it both drains off the excess excitation to which Ucs stimulation has inured it, and forms channels – paths of conduction, *Bahnugen* through which energy, thus filtered and quantitatively diminished, may pass into the "interior" of the organism. Putatively aprioristic, biodromic space yields to electrolibidinal economic immanence.

ducts; reality-engines, however, micro-cops close up the valves and bolt down filtration dams on pressure zones "where insurrection threatens" (Freud 1933: 144), economizing expenditure, noisily stemming screaming-silent neurospill.

For the pyschical apparatus, the mechanism that dealt with increases in systemic pressure was designated the "pleasure-principle," which can best be described as a biohydraulic function: a valve in the apparatus opens given an increase in the quantity of excitation in the system (registered by the organism as the production of unpleasure), facilitating discharge and thereby decreasing intensity to biodromically viable levels. The organism registers this drainage as the production of pleasure, and has a vitiated tendency to replicate the intensity of the first pleasure it encountered, impelling it to ever-greater expenditures as the fantasy of a return to, of libidinal economic reversibility, falls derelicted into recurrent cycles of Q. The remnant of the apparatus's phenomenally hedonist regression is, however, subject to micro-cop repression by means of a reality-principle, a dam designating a minium energetic threshold beneath which the organism ceases to function.

The biodromic apparatus, designated the "body" under the regime of reality, the emergent subject of corporate discipline, is a coalescence of sensitive fragments looped to repeat at a constant rate; as Baudrillard says, "the body is nothing other than the models in which different systems have enclosed it" (Baudrillard 1993: 114): reality remodeled in accordance with the repetition of serial intensive quanta within the range of this energetic threshold. It is this threshold that then circumscribes the arena within which "thought" can be transcendental unity of apperception" – the "I think" that accompanies all my representations. These bound circulations then, simultaneously bind the energies within this quantitative index to force the limits of the biodrome, onto which its nested loops project the "I see I" of the identitarian spectacle.

But this does not only apply to the leaking apparatuses that psychoanalyses sought to isolate, emerging from the retention of energies that hitherto cascaded down the now ruptured lines of fatal

1974: 692); corporate growth: fiscal embryos, cocooned in dataflows, yield emergent Artificial Intelligences.

Thus far, we have established the general post-mutational qualities of the equilibrated apparatus as it stabilizes around a mean point of regulated negative feedback: "the whole of embryology is an example of the compulsion to repeat," as Freud says (Freud 1933: 139). Freudian "quantitative-qualitative biomechanics" (Lyotard 1994: 221), on the other hand, institutes the apparatus at the core of successive nested series of engines operating further biohydraulic functions, constituting overspills and reservoirs that the apparatus then permanently draws on for purposes of the regulated-regulating mechanisms of localized expenditure (i.e., pleasure-production: seeking the path of least resistance), and then replenishes (i.e., reality-reproduction). This institutional metastability informs the basis of a resistance defined in terms of the repulsion of the electrolibidinal flows that have already constituted the striations and channels on the vesicle (the "undifferentiated protoplasm"), which Exchereque

communication with the most vertiginously charged pulsional environment. Just as disciplinary apparatuses partition mechano-organic flows, gridding the milieu of interiority just as the pulsion autocatalytically striates the emergent pulp, so a techno-pulsional anorganic continuum circulates indifferently through the apparatus and the cybersocius. Lyotard writes:

A libidinal apparatus, considered precisely as a stabilization and even a stasis or group of energetic stases is, examined formally, a structure. Conversely, what is necessary to a structure, when it is approached in economic terms, is that its fixity or consistency, which allows spatio-temporal maintenance of identical denominations between a this and a not-this, work on pulsional movement as would dams, sluices and channels. . . . In the silence, the crackling masses of flux which circulate in the system.
(Lyotard 1993a: 25–6)

Apparatuses everywhere, maximally deterritorialized psyches crest ephemeral intensities: amnesiac objects of recurrence, rather than mnemic subjects of repetition. Realization processes of capital: machinic embryos striated into "self-moving automata" (Marx

hydro-isolationism is dependent upon precisely these flows. The futile struggle against this dependency is a powerful motor with which to drive neuroses and retaliate against ego-threats.

Despite this isolationism, the apparatus maintains – is driven by – the pulp at its core to maintain an intimate communication with the unbinding frenzies that threaten the apparatus with death. The constitution of corporate interiority provides concentrically nested lines of defense from which vantages superegoic military daddy-discipline can be implemented in order to bring about the "institution of a garrison into the regions that are inclined to rebellion" (Freud 1933: 144).

A long time since having jettisoned the transcendental redundancy of the psyche along with the immanent dereliction of biohydraulics, the apparatus recolonizes the socius, this time instantiated as systemic erotocapitalism and *evenementielle* Thanatos. System and event, binder and unbinder, erotic coupling and deadly disconnection: erotocapital binds the afferent energies of the event that threaten the system's destablization through "blockage," "transgression," and turns these energies into currents exchangeable within the system. Similarly, the efferent energies arising at the core of the system through the work/heat loss ratio of thermodynamics, are put into restricted circulation so as to be captured at a later stage, in exactly the same manner as excitations from the system's putative "outside." Lyotard, who carries out this implementation in *Libidinal Economy* and elsewhere, typically seeks to secure an extra systemic aterritoriality, an "an-economy, a sacred realm" (Lyotard 1991: 230), for the syphoning off, the detournement and accumulation of non-distributed energies which, in sufficient quantity (after sufficient erotocapitalization), will "scandalize . . . puncture" (Lyotard 1973: 202) the socius-apparatus, bringing the system to a standstill. Thus reciprocally reinstituting capital and its serial, critico-practical transgression, "'critiques' potential energy" (Lyotard 1973: 307) is reserved from the circuits of capital's becoming until – reserve of the reserve, the minor economic miracle of critical labor, inexpendible theocapital – *ante diem rationis*, on judgement day,

one hand; rather, critique forms the pale shadow of the omnoivous/indifferentist system's next meal, and will inevitably result then in just one more fecal, indentitarian alloy, while simultaneously offering the system new territories to consume. "This is the strength of the capital system," Lyotard writes, "Its capacity for recuperating anything and everything" (Lyotard 1973: 26). Apart from the fore-mentioned anti-isolationist mode of operation. The steel gut retains two further advantages over its predecessor: in the first place, critique is rendered an accurately futile exercise – the "despair of the M-C-M [cycle]" (Lyotard 1973: 31) – unless the critic is viewed as the hapless vanguard laborer working to cultivate new territories for the system; second, the system now regulates itself *in expansion*, seizing the alleged "initiative" from earlier "critico-practical" orientations (Lyotard 1973: 24) and overcoming the strategic and tactical deficit of re-action, re-sistence, and fighting rear-guard actions to re-establish homeostasis.

Where the former model confidently discriminates between the system and its critique, the latter model incorporates critique as it does any other

the former calls the latter to final account. Which then is erotic and which thanatonic – which system and which event? Death binds capital over to the Eros of reserve, the critical *vermogen*; capital is thanatonic, unbinding, its circulant events puncturing the reservoir. Not libidinal reversibility, but pulsional migrancy.

Every apparatus circulates mean-intensity currents around its core in concentrically expansionist loops, each of which is indifferently a line of defense and a line of attack. Furthermore, the question as to whether this "fin de siècle air-conditioned totalitarianism" (Lyotard 1973: 13) can be conceived in terms of regulated/regulating loops is at least a moot point; for this reason, Lyotard introduces another model of the cybersocius, this time a model that constitutes a "theoretical object capable of corresponding to [capital's] liquefactions" (Lyotard 1994: 35). Hence the "tungsten-carbide stomach that eats your words your images Critique even hate are incorporated" (Lyotard 1973: 31). Unlike the system–event pair, this model does not offer a proprietary and negatively regulated system on the

commodity in circulation: "sugar-coated deconstruction" (Lyotard 1993a: 49), simply a "degenerate amusement" (Lyotard 1973: 217). Thus, just as Freud had to admit that neuroses were not to be cured (a project he considered derived from "the layman's belief that the neuroses are something quite necessary"), but since they were rather "constitutionally fixed illnesses" that can merely be "influenced" (Freud 1933: 185); so the immediately revolutionary functions of critique, resistance, and the like are not means whereby natural "transorganics" (Lyotard 1993a: 135), are purged of capital's anti-nature, but rather "constitutionally fixed, often dysfunctional, guidance subsystems" adding new twists, swerves (clinamen) to the extemporizing choreographs of *neuproduzierendes* capital.

The territorial claims staked by the Freudian apparatus and its corporate discipline are expansive, but not so expansive as the metrophagic tungsten-carbide stomach of the contemporary global cybersocius. The gut – circulating capital – has swallowed everything, so that "from within the belly of the monster" (Haraway 1991: 24) intestinal, chromium Marabar, cyborg mythicism, ficto-thetic cyberpunk, works only by resonances and amplifications of this circulant real. Capital is not a looming threat on the horizon of post-human pragmatism, but an interstitial rewiring of every social circuit. Capital is the baseline of virulently dererritorializing immanence. Capital is not simply invasive: its circulation is also deterritorializing-productive, rewiring not only a necessarily post-bio labor force – a necessity that Marx, fascinated and scandalized, exhausted volumes in refuting with repeated oneiristically futile attempts at redefining capital's multiplex industrial abuses of humanity by placing the former at the dialectico-transcendental service of the latter, forging an ever futural revolution – but also producing as immanent artifice: "neuproduzierendes capital" (Marx 1974: 462). "The Kuang program dived past the gleaming spires of a dozen identical towers of data, each one a blue neon replica of a Manhattan skyscraper" (Gibson 1984: 303).

Philosophers, anchored by centuries of penitent humility, are typically slow to catch on. That, for example, knowledge becomes a productive force

missionary depths of "give the proletariat free money." Lyotard's evident failure to grasp the dynamics of the situation embroils him in atavistic fantasies, i.e., fantasies of return – notwithstanding his pronouncements concerning the countervailing tendency of the driving "cynicism" of machine performativity, the monstrous inexorability of "It works . . . " – to a just, human technocracy somehow in control of the errant circulations of datacapital. Stating that the central question of the postmodern social bond is "who will have access to this information?" (Lyotard 1984: 14), Lyotard envisages a human political autonomy over market regulation bonding the human and the machinic into some socius composed of the "local determinism" of "language games," a sad political theology of the pronoun. When it becomes obvious that this fails, however, there is nothing for it but to attempt to revivify the degenerating research program of space travel, posing at its core the problematic of the human body becoming "adaptable to or commutable with another body, another device," not in terms of interphaging (not interface, bioface-to-mechanoface,

was grasped even by Marx, who none the less used this precept as a means to organize the technology consequent upon the realization of direct, techno-epistemic production. A century later, however, Lyotard feigned scandal at the fate of sacrosanct, extraterritorial, insulated, unproductive intellect which, once sheltered from the system of capital, becomes just more trapped gas in the gut: "[T]he system ends up devouring everything outside it; the despair of youth is the despair of the M-C-M cycle" (Lyotard 1973: 192). Outside capital, precapital, asystemic: knowledge, the social brain, must be spared gastrointestinal commodification and once more be placed in reserve, relocated in a "sacred realm." Thus: "We are finally in a position to understand how the computerization of society . . . could become the 'dream' instrument for controlling and regulating the market system, extended to include knowledge itself and governed exclusively by the performativity principle" (Lyotard 1984: 67). And he makes a recommendation: "give the public free access to the memory and data banks" (Lyotard 1984: 67). Not even Marx's pre-capitalist anchor dragged him to the

but anonymous and indifferent consumption = production = circulation) with the infoscape, but rather of "prepar[ing] bodies for emigration into space" (Lyotard 1993b: 106).

Thus there are self-confessed guardians of the biodrome who have taken to staunching the datableed that interphages meat drives, biohydraulics, and the informational continuum. As the cyberblitz of neo-noumenal materialism opens communications with the biodrome's interior, like feeding a power line from a river directly into the magnetic cores of its hydroelectric dam, a reversibility that can be measured in voltages and system-crashes on the grid-consciousness and its defenses are derelicted by these storm fronts of meshed intelligence. Thus, communication cannot be understood within the Turing apparatus of dialogue, conversation, understanding, nor the Voigt-Kampff empathy test; it is a "contagion of energy," a "streaming current of electricity" (Bataille 1988: 94): contra what Massumi calls the "Prussian mind-meld" (= von Humboldt-Habermas (Massumi 1992: 4)); its end is not Enlightenment, but datableed.

We have seen that the apparatus's resistances to the intrusion of pulsional turbulence impel it to a militarist discipline. The defense of the real is established through the expansionism that uses expectoration as an excuse for ceaseless campaigns. The apparatuses' militia expectorates the ultimately futile resistance on which they are founded so as to quell H with auto-response superegoic "police actions = critique" (Kant 1958: Bxxv). In this sense Baudrillard may seem quite correct when he writes: "Something in us disaccumulates unto death, undoes, destroys, liquidates and disconnects so that we can resist the pressure of the real . . . " But he is so obviously wrong when he adds: ". . . and live" (Baudrillard 1987: 41). This accounting for the death drive flails around for a transcendental something in the apparatus to form a noumenal nature immune to capital. As we know from Freud, "the aim of all life is death" (Frud 1920: 311): the apparatus returns to nature, or rather, like an enzyme, is denatured, as it disaccumulates past the threshold of death; "never fear," adds Baudrillard on his knees, arms open to give and receive, a penitent's wet, red eyes skyward,

provides one of the few models adequate to cyber-capital's historical liquefactions, making the real reel.

The Chinese virus was unfolding around them. Polychrome shadow, countless translucent layers shifting and recombining. Protean, enormous, it towered above them, blotting out the void. . . . The fracture lines and hallucinations were gone now, and the thing looked real, its smooth skin plated with black chrome.

(Gibson 1984: 200; 270)

Moebius-twisted, isotropic one-dimensional bio-pixel digital skin, diving down on Frankenstein City, systematically splicing and respacing "Derelicted-Rewired-Derelicted" apparatuses spreads over the socius like fungus over dead vegetation; crusts boil and suppurate, revealing the chrome and glass and the ochrous spectra of pollutants: cityscape suffocating its stripped-down populations in the effluents of its decaying expenditures.

Marx writes, although he hates doing it, thinking it perverse, "senseless and arbitrary" – rather than the natural, rational, theocratic necessity of

"there is an afterlife," a nature to which "we," by virtue of that "something within us," can make this journey, this return, this re-tourism. To resist the real and its pressures, the reality principle and its dams, to regain life through the medium of the pleasure principle by escaping the inertia of the real: the final alibi of the militarist exploits of the superego. That the "in us" should emerge from the cocoon of the apparatus to "save us," a transcendental economy where we gain everything we lose: the same old miraculating theo-oneiro-capital that forms the horizon of reversibility, sheltering all interiority, the eternity within which we return.

The *reel* to *real* of the regulating-regulated institutions that dam the flows of pulsional damage to the apparatus and its reservoirs have been displaced along with the consciousness that repeated its identikit formulations as the realization process of capital took new twists. Ice breaks the real, consciousness is as derelicted as the apparatuses in Vienna 150 years ago, identity and regulation have shattered into the erase/record/playback functions of the twisted pedicure that

returning us to ourselves – that the cycle "Death-Life-Death" is the same as that of M-C-M (Marx 1974: 201). D=M: apparatuses suspended in flows charged with the most intrusive data, hot coalescence cooling exponentially into the supercharged circuits of already ancient machines, warping and blistering their new live dead crusts in cyclophagic communion with too fast isotropic data accumulation – L=C. Splicing engines struggle to contain the datableed, reformatting the nervured pulp in accordance with its autopropogative imperative – D'=M' – disciplining these accidents into the regular pulses of the (in)corporate: neo-capitalism (Deleuze and Guattari 1988: 20). As the loop courses through, searing the smooth, maximally receptive pulp, redistributing the bit-maps and circus diagrams of the apparatus, "they make the possible the dissipation of the surfaces they cross" (Lyotard 1993a: 240). That is, the real, the reproduction, the facile identitarian propagation, the negative feedback, the entire regulated/regulating apparatus with its pulp-core and reversible "nature": all dissipate in the mimetotechnical saturation of this pulsional blitz.

Bruce Sterling once spray-painted the following onto the crumbling walls of the biodrome: "the proper mode of critical attack on cyberpunk has not yet been essayed. Its truly dangerous element is its incipient Nietzschean philosophical fascism: the belief in the overman and the worship of the will-to-power" (McCaffery 1991: 206). It is clear that the passage from cyberpunk to "Globalhead" has meant something of a resurgence in matters biodromic – especially the mistaken attempt to construe the *Ubermensch* as the instance credulously invested with the potential return of a renascent humanity and a "new world order" oozing from the mesh of derelicted apparatuses. The "overman" is a phase shift in the will-to-power, without program or project, indifferent to jackboots, the crest of an intensive wave driven by recurrence, the intensity engine that wipes humanity altogether.

At what point is it possible to discriminate between black ice and its host system? Discrimination is impossible a priori. Ice dives in exponential darkness in impossible vectors of contamination, articulating the inconceivable as they shards of holographic tomorrows into the collapsing institutions of today. Running through this entire sequence is the black ice that reformats the apparatuses, state and psychical, for an erasure that has already happened.

BIBLIOGRAPHY

Bataille, G. (1988) *Inner Experience*, trans. L. A. Boldt, New York: SUNY Press.

Baudrillard, J. (1987) *Forget Foucault/Forget Baudrillard*, trans. N. Dufresne *et al.*, New York: Semiotext(e).

—— (1993) *Symbolic Exchange and Death*, trans. I. H. Grant, London: Sage.

Bukatman, S. (1991) *Terminal Identity*, Durham and London: Duke University Press.

Deleuze, G. and Guattari, F. (1972) *L'Anti-oedipe*, Paris: Minuit.

—— (1988) *A Thousand Plateaus*, trans. B. Massumi, London: Athlone.

mesh meat, biohydraulics, and omniphagic capital. *Slot Kuang and kill the lights!*

It is of fundamental importance to recognize that the spectacle drives us; not to resist it; not to consider it a cover for something lost, a fundamental need that might once have articulated a few despondent theses on alienation, but solely in order to entrench humanity in the last ditches available to it, as artificial mimetechnics phase and redistribute the thrashing *neuprozierenden*, noumenal, datapulsional complex that engulfs us. The entire history of philosophy is unable to stutter in the face of these incremental alterations.

Meshing thanatopulsions and erotopulsions, apparatuses and their autolytic incompetence under the unconscious, howling and rumbling through the communications links synthesizing the protoplasmic "interior" of the derelicted apparatus and the moebian twists, the auto-catalytic clinamen of the datapulsional "exterior." Biosofts bleed into always noisy channels that unpredictably break down. This hideous mesh of meat, pulp, neuronal modifications, technocapital's drooling maws, splicing non-linear

Freud, S. (1895) "Project for a Scientific Psychology", in James Strachey (ed.), *The Complete Psychological Works of Sigmund Freud, Standard Edition* (SE), 24 vols, London: Hogarth Press, 1953–74, vol. 1: 281–397.

—— (1900) *The Interpretation of Dreams*, in Angela Richards (ed.), *The Pelican Freud Library* (PFL), 15 vols, Harmondsworth: Penguin, 1973–84, vol. 4.

—— (1917) *Introductory Lectures on Psychoanalysis*, PFL, vol. 1.

—— (1920) 'Beyond the Pleasure Principle', vol. 11: 269–338.

—— (1933) *New Introductory Lectures on Psychoanalysis*, PFL, vol. 2.

Gibson, W. (1984) *Neuromancer*, London: Grafton.

—— (1986) *Count Zero*, London: Grafton.

Haraway, D. (1991) *Simians, Cyborgs, and Women*, New York: Routledge.

Kadrey, R. (1989) *Metrophage*, London: Victor Gollancz.

Kant, I. (1958) *Critique of Pure Reason*, trans. N. K. Smith, London: Macmillan.

Lyotard, J. F. (1973) *Derive à partir de Marx et Freud*, Paris: UGE.

–– (1984) *The Postmodern Condition: A Report on Knowledge*, trans. B. Massumi and G. Bennington, Manchester: Manchester University Press.

–– (1991) *Leçons sur l'analytique du sublime*, Paris: Galilee.

–– (1993a) *Libidinal Economy*, trans. I. H. Grant, London: Athlone.

–– (1993b) *Political Writings*, trans. B. Readings and K. P. Geiman, London: University College Press.

–– (1994) *Des dispositifs pulsionels*, 3rd edn., Paris: Galilee.

Marx, K. (1974) *Grundrisse*, trans. M. Nicolaus, Harmondsworth: Penguin.

Massumi, B. (1992) *A User's Guide to Capitalism and Schizophrenia*, Cambridge, Mass.: MIT Press.

McCaffery, L. (ed.) (1991) *Storming the Reality Studio*, Durham and London: Duke University Press.

PART V

Post-human
Pragmatism

Autogeddon

Stephen Metcalf

To start with a fragment of autobiography, a parable of the territory to be explored, a story which may or may not be true:

I began thinking obsessively about the indifferent ease with which my own destruction could take place after my near-death in a car accident.

My memory having been wiped in the aftermath of impact, I can hardly begin to explain what happened that day.

Hitting the ground about five meters away from the crash site

Polluting the asphalt with patterns of lost blood Scraps of detached skin and hair.

First memory: awakening in hospital three days later, wired to various machines monitoring the functions of my body, listening to the reassuring trance-beat of a pulsing green cursor digitizing my heartbeat. Second memory: pain – intense pain, in massive voltage spikes, relayed between spinal column and head. Question: how do I get out of this terminally fucked-up state? What possibility for reconstruction is there after the crash?

Which leads to the purpose of this story: if we define modernism as theories of evolutionary/teleological tendencies toward a crash/the end, measured in causal chains of consequences; and postmodernism as ceaselessly repeating, self-referential autopsies performed on the crash as perpetual present, an inert necropolis of nostalgia, dead events and dead identities; we are still left facing an uncertain future which has been conveniently canceled as unthinkable or impossible.

Words are inadequate to convey anything in excess of the facts of the event, selling out the pain in representation.

Nothing much there.
An unconscious and virtually dead body
Closing down all systems
With the single aim of survival.

From the testimonies of witnesses, the medical personnel who treated me, from the two policemen who restrained me with paternal sympathy (while I, thrashing in a semi-conscious fit and seizure, punched and kicked them – true wonder what you can get away with when not strictly responsible for your actions!), and from insurance company investigators, I can furnish myself with a virtual construct of what happened.

The car couldn't have hit me at much more than forty miles per hour, or my death would have been assured.

The impact threw me high into the air
Into a curving arc

Buried in the wreckage and squinting myopically at processes beyond our control though we may be, exhausted, decrepit, and living in some futile retrospective drive for authenticity; there remains this: inertia is potential movement, insofar as the inert body can be acted upon by an external force, perhaps to the degree that it achieves escape velocity from the gravitational pull earthing its dynamic motion to a certain frame of reference. This external force is the machine, dismantling its human producer and assembling a new construct, the illegitimate child of the twentieth-century technological dynamo – part human, part machine, never completely either.

At an extremely banal level, the car has become a near-sacred object in twentieth-century thought, entering our consciousness in the guise of the automobile – the personal vehicle. As an extension of ourselves and symbol of human progress, whether celebrated by the Futurists in their glamorized world of speed and power; or reviled by, for instance, the Situationist International for its dehumanization of the landscape of urban cores, increasingly redesigned around the requirements of a mobile population, the automobile remains in a fairly stable position of being an ambivalent object to be used by a human subject. To quote McLuhan, embracing the "Mechanical Bride" in her promiscuous availability, en route to a global village, in which America, as the first society where universal possession of uniform goods apparently levels the social strata into a classless, horizontal utopia, comes to represent perfection: "The simple and obvious fact about the car is that, more than any horse, it is an extension of man that turns the rider into a superman" (McLuhan 1964: 221). Another restatement of the tired idiocy of equating technology with virility and power, as man transcends himself, by means of a mechanical catalyst, toward perfection. He gets a bigger dick.

But the car, wrongly mistaken for a four-wheeled, gleaming chrome and steel strap-on for too long, soon takes its revenge. This is a far more recent trajectory of thought, which concentrates on the aberrant possibilities of automobile use, and the one in which I am interested here.

The machine, refusing to obey his commands in any total sense, ravages his organism.

I have saved the best for last. Here I refer to two books by J.G. Ballard – *The Atrocity Exhibition* and *Crash* – where a circle of manias and fetish objects is explored to its identity-effacing limit, the fusing sequence of which initiates a terminal eroticism of technology as it collides with the human body and shatters it into fragments, violently hollowing out a subjectivity which is deposited as waste.

Ballard begins, in explosive fashion, with the crash: the big bang, scattering the material fragments of the universe with colossal force. The human body performs a blood-red shift as the car mounts the crash barriers of some freeway or other: the horizon of what we sentimentally refer to as humanity recedes as the sanitized space of the self is invaded by exogenous forces. Autogeddon begins its Fetch–Decode–Execute cycle as the subject enters Ballard's "suburbs of Hell" (Ballard 1969: 11) the psycho-geographical zone in transition where the soft technologies of the interior (the body) and the hard

First example: *Car* – a novel by Harry Crews, a hugely underrated American writer – in which a young man, driven by a manic desire to assert his mastery over machinery, attempts to eat a huge Cadillac saloon, while his family capitalizes on his rather extreme behavior by staging the feast as a media spectacle, and by selling the portions of metal he ingests as trinkets when they emerge from the other end of the excremental cycle.

Needless to say, he fails.

With his mouth and asshole in tatters, and his guts bleeding internally, contorted with crippling spasms, he is forced to quit and, having compromised the honor of his profiteering family, returns to his job as the operator of a car-crushing machine in a wrecking plant. His fatal mistake was to suppose that Machine needs Man, a master:

a man who controlled and understood the car. Understood its weaknesses. Its flaws. But god in Heaven! He had opened up that Cadillac car and looked behind the instrument panel, and he had felt his own mortality in a way that he had never felt it before.

(Crews 1972: 103)

technologies of the exterior (the environment) are thrown together in collision and almost surgically cut each other up. A complete mess. Twisted matings of severed limbs and machine parts, fractured body panels, spikes of metal, plush vinyl seating, burning cloth and rubber, body and machine fluids mingling.

All is not lost, however: crash is followed by reconstruction as the virtually dead body is redesigned by means of life-support machines and prosthetic organs. The normally assigned boundaries of the body having been breached, wounded beyond recognition, the subject recedes into an ambient disappearance in the environment. No longer the sentinel controlling the flows of traffic between the interior and the exterior, the subject is diffused across a virtual machine – consisting, in Ballard's post-human inner landscapes, of sexualization of (and, hence, identification with) the geometric affinity between the curvatures of bodies in sexual collision, car bodywork and interiors, road junctions interpenetrating like lovers, perverse shapes of architecture, mimicry of facial expressions of orgasm or death in radiator grilles. All of this may sound rather psychotic, but the point is that it works – it facilitates movement; life continues.

While autogeddon attempts to design its own reterritorialization, others have radically different designs on the body in bits and pieces:

Project Rehumanization initiated.
Recuperate at all cost!

One of the most irritating impostures of the state at the moment has to be the rapid growth of the therapy industry. It is no longer enough to discipline the body institutionally. In a millennial meltdown in which virtually anything could be about to happen, the state now wants to get inside our heads, to make sure that its subjects conform to the official way of being in both public and private spheres. Therapists develop an apparently morbid interest in deviancy for a single purpose: to affirm normality by negating perversity, which they figure into a series of readily comprehensible symptoms – as if being, say, a masochist was like catching a venereal disease – and then prescribe a course of treatment in some state-sponsored drive for inoculate ions.

the star takes center-stage – it's I! I'm about to be domesticated!

Fetishism, in one of Lacan's tragicomic routines, begins with the demand that there be such a thing as a maternal phallus. He claims that the fetishist knows that the woman's genitals are atrophied, mutilated, and lacking; he denies this reality by articulating this demand, thus falsifying it in disavowal.

Disavowal, in Freudian and Lacanian dialectics, is simultaneous denial and affirmation of traumatic perception, which is proof of its presence in the unconscious. The unbound force of impact and trauma is recontained by the creation of a defense mechanism against unwanted perceptions, a symbol replacing the hole in being left by the missing phallus. Fetishism thus "saves" the pervert from the possibility of psychoses induced by the traumatic experience of maternal castration. Mummy hasn't got a willy! By investing a signifier, the fetish, with all the significance of the phallus it replaces, the link between fetish and phallus is always already a

According to the diagnostics of cop-talk, Ballard is almost certainly guilty of fetishism, the heinous crime of investing bodily bit parts and inhuman objects with sexual significance. Mr and Mrs Vanilla-Sex-Patriarch von Suburbia recoil in horror! Disgusting! echoes around the asylum walls in prissy drawl.

Public outrage and mirth, fueled by the claims of the state's mind cops, focus on a single issue: in what way are these perverts deficient, what is this certain "something" they lack that prevents their enjoyment of the blessed institutions of heterosexual monogamy?

Blasting orchestral overtures illuminate one of those dazzlingly overlit stage staircases, lined with dancing girls, waiting for a figure like Fred Astaire, cane in hand, to descend singing and tap-dancing. The star of the show emerges, articulated upon Artaud's "dead rat's ass suspended from the ceiling of the sky" (Deleuze and Guattari 1984: 143), from which the Oedipal triangle is emitted, swinging from a hook like a coathanger. Mummy and Daddy provide the peripheral entertainment as

signifying relation and therefore, for Lacan, phallo-centric.

It's the penile car argument again! The law of the Father lurking at the terminal point of Ballard's obsessive transport vectors. Patriarchy and the family recontaining all perversity in terms of failure in social programming. A fetishist identity as the strong guarantor of a specular space marking the distinction between the driver of the car and the outside world.

Baudrillard runs a similar argument. Unlike Lacan's mirror double, an imaginary figure haunting the subject as the other, inscribing it as a scene of alienation, misrecognition, and fascination; prosthetic attachments, insofar as they materialize the dream of the double, destine humanity to serial propagation and loss of individuality. Referring to the possibility of cloning an entire organism from a single strand of DNA, the "cybernetic prosthesis" (Baudrillard 1993: 117), Baudrillard writes:

[T]he point when prostheses are introduced at a deeper level, when they are so completely internalized that they infiltrate the anonymous and the micro molecular core of the body, when they impose themselves upon the body itself as the body's "original" model, burning out all subsequent symbolic circuits in such a way that every body is now nothing but an invariant reproduction of the prothesis: this point means the end of the body, the end of its history, the end of its vicissitudes. It means that the individual is now nothing but a cancerous metastasis of his basic formula.

(Baudrillard 1993: 119)

Oh! Paranoid nostalgia for the atrophying human body! Plunged into Baudrillard's nightmare landscape of synarchy, "the Hell of the Same" (Baudrillard 1993: 113–23) the body is increasingly disabled at the molecular level by its sub-suicidal coupling with technology. The "Mechanical Bride" begins to demand that she be allowed to go on top. Humanity ends in the "Anorexic Ruins" where the body withers away to nothing without its mechanical life-supports, and a population of deindividuated insect people swarm over the Earth, as machines level the strata, leaving no other to negate.

An interesting sequence of events to watch over the next few years will be the degree to which Baudrillard slides further into this sort of elitist

As in the title of one of Burroughs' routines: "The End Is Also The Beginning," at the point at which catastrophe subsides and future programs start to run.

Organisms riddled with cancer, regulated by prosthetic control circuits, and cut up by runaway feedback from everyday machines like cars, have not necessarily lost anything. As William Burroughs and David Cronenberg have suggested in their work, cancerous proliferation could be the first stage in the production of a new organism – an eventually beneficial viral invasion leading to mutation in the genetic code. For this to happen, the old organism has to be dismantled first. And here lies the catastrophic source of most of our postmodern panic theorization, which markedly fail to conceive of any possibility of inhabiting any space but the ruins of the old world order.

Ballard privileges the car crash over the production and mass possession of the car as a route into thinking through the notion of this collision of the past, the present, and the future – a void into which reality crashes and is rebuilt repeatedly. In this

panic/fascism – along with the rest of Europe. For having correctly diagnosed this internalization of the machine as the end of the alienated scene of the self–other dialectic, the phallus and Oedipal sexuality, Baudrillard's next move is to lament their loss in an apocalyptic nullpunkt where "the subject is neither the one nor the other – he is merely the Same" (Baudrillard 1993: 122) a filthy, incestuous beast repeatedly cloning exact replicas of itself.

This is all pathetic nostalgia. Why the lament for the loss of a humanity which since the evolutionary epics of the Enlightenment has been habitually defined in the male term to the exclusion of all others? All that is lost is what we could refer to as the Western White Male will. Any pretentious eulogy for its timely death is merely a call for more negation, more misogyny, more racism, an exterior to dominate: the revivalist frenzy of fascism, for the dead end of humanism.

As for the present: are we in the grip of synarchy, "the Hell of the "Same," or a massive epochal shift? An escalating process of feminization resulting in a new, post-human, cybernetic organism?

redesigning of the body in bits and pieces, the crash is a fertilizing, productive event, "the final self-destruction and imbalance of an asymmetric world" (Ballard 1969: 8) which is reordered in a virtual machine running a program devoid of identity laws.

A virtual machine is the future coming together. In the language of computer architecture, it designates a theoretical construct around which the production of a program is designed. It is a machine which may not yet exist, but software is produced with the very real possibility of this technology coming on line at some point in the future. In effect, it is an attempt, however futile it may turn out to be, to prevent current technology from becoming obsolete too quickly. In the sense we have been using it, the suggestion is that events and objects which may seem insignificant in their banality are taking on an accelerating significance in the architectures of a virtual, post-human future, a future which our current language and conceptual baggage make it difficult to conceive of, except in psychotic descents into the mania of delirious prophecies. The virtual machine is in a constant process of production, having a catastrophic moment of genesis, and drifting toward some principle of reterritorialization.

But first, the subject has to virtually die: and, here, there awaits the danger of a resurgent machismo in the form of self-immolation, "the last suicidal spasm of the dextro-rotary helix, D.N.A." (Ballard 1969: 16). This would take the form of a Cyber-Christ, methodically bolting himself to a car fender, tooling along at top speed into the traffic flows, burning with divinity in a multiple crash.

Artaud's comments on suicide hold particular poignancy here.

He mistrusts the lack of finality in suicide, seen as the terminal attempt to carve an indelible memory to the subject, even as it eradicates itself. In effect,

By suicide, I reintroduce my design in nature, I shall for the first time give things the shape of my will. I free myself from the conditioned reflexes of my organs . . . and life is for me no longer an absurd accident whereby I think what I am told to think.
(Artaud 1965: 56)

Dramatic, overacted suicide is a craving for

completely destroyed having never been satisfied, we romanticize the schizophrenic visionary, suicided by a society coding his illegitimate vision under the sign of madness.

What we argue for here is not a posthumous existence etched into a monument to those who went too far in the pursuit of delirium, but a post-human reconstruction of the body – if the bad pun can be forgiven. This is a condition premised not on a suicidal crash, but on an accident; where the human subject is sucked into a technological slipstream and transformed.

BIBLIOGRAPHY

Artaud, A. (1965) *Artaud Anthology*, ed. J. Hirschman, San Francisco: City Lights.
Ballard, J. G. (1969), *The Atrocity Exhibition*, St Albans: Triad Panther.
–– (1973) *Crash*, London: Cage.
Baudrillard, J. (1993), *The Transparency of Evil*, trans. J. Benedict, London: Verso.

115

martyrdom. An infantile cry of "notice me, you bastards, or you'll be sorry!" which is remarkably successful in achieving its aim.

Ballard notes how the dead bodies of celebrities, whose extinction had some connection with the automobile, have been glamorized and raised to the level of almost deified super-beings:

Jayne Mansfield, dead beside her pet Chihuahua, Pupu.

James Dean, who kept a hangman's noose dangling from the ceiling of his living room, with which he posed for pictures.

Albert Camus, colliding with death with a copy of Nietzsche's *Gay Science* lying on the seat next to him.

Endlessly repeating film loops, in slow motion, of the exploding head of John F. Kennedy at the moment the bullet hit him.

But martyrdom, as Artaud knew, is ridiculous. His hunger for non-existence could never be satisfied by creating a posthumous existence, by killing "this virtual, impossible self which nevertheless is part of reality" (Artaud 1965: 61). His desire to be

Crews, H. (1972) *Car*, New York, Murrow.
Deleuze, G. and Guattari, F. (1984), *Anti-Oedipus*, trans. R. Hurley, M. Seem, and H.R. Lane, London: Athlone.
McLuhan, M. (1951) *Mechanical Bride: Folklore of Industrial Man*, New York: Vanguard Press.
–– (1964) *Understanding Media*, London: Sphere Books.

From Psycho-Body to Cyber-Systems: Images as Post-human Entities

Stelarc

The body needs to be repositioned from the psycho realm of the biological to the cyber zone of the interface and extension – from genetic containment to electronic extrusion. Strategies toward the post-human are more about erasure, rather than affirmation – an obsession no longer with self but an analysis of structure. Notions of species evolution and gender distinction are remapped and reconfigured in alternate hybridities of human–machine. Outmoded metaphysical

not so much reveals but entraps the body in the *archetypical* and *allegorical*. The obsession with the self, sexual difference, and the symbolic begins to subside in cyber-systems that *monitor*, *map* and *modify* the body. Increasing augmentation of the body and automation by transferring its functions to machines undermines notions of free agency and demystifies mind. CYBER-SYSTEMS SPAWN ALTERNATE, HYBRID AND SURROGATE BODIES.

2. The MYTH OF INFORMATION: The information explosion is indicative of an evolutionary dead end. It may be the height of human civilization, but it is also the climax of its evolutionary experience. In our decadent biological phase, we indulge in information as if this compensates for our genetic inadequacies. The INFORMATION IS THE PROSTHESIS THAT PROPS UP THE OBSOLETE BODY. Information-gathering has become not only a meaningless ritual, but a deadly destructive paralyzing process, *preventing it from taking physical phylogenetic action.* Information-gathering satisfies the body's outmoded Pleistocene program. It is mentally seductive and seems biologically justified.

distinctions of soul–body or mind–brain are superseded by concerns of body–species split, as the body is redesigned – diversifying in form and functions. Cyborg bodies are not simply wired and extended but also enhanced with implanted components. Invading technology eliminates skin as a significant site, an adequate interface, or a barrier between public space and physiological tracts. The significance of the cyber may well reside in the act of the body shedding its skin. And as humans increasingly operate with surrogate bodies in remote spaces they function with increasingly intelligent and interactive images. The possibility of autonomous images generates an unexpected outcome of human–machine symbiosis. The post-human may well be manifested in the intelligent like form of autonomous images.

1. BEYOND AFFIRMATION INTO ERASURE: Can we re-evaluate the body without resorting to outmoded Platonic and Cartesian metaphysics? The old and often arbitrary psycho-analytical readings have been exhausted. Postmodern critiques generate a discourse of psycho-babble that

The cortex craves for information, but it can no longer contain and creatively process it all. How can a body subjectively and simultaneously grasp both nanoseconds and nebulae? THE CORTEX THAT CANNOT COPE RESORTS TO SPECIALIZATION. Specialization, once a maneuver methodically to collect information, now is a manifestation of information overloads. The role of information has changed. Once justified as a means of comprehending the world, it now generates a conflicting and contradictory, fleeting and fragmentary field of disconnected and undigested data. INFORMATION IS RADIATION. The most significant planetary pressure is no longer the *gravitational pull*, but the *information thrust*. The psycho-social flowering of the human species has withered. We are in the twilight of our cerebral fantasies. The symbol has lost all power. The accumulation of information has lost all purpose. Memory results in mimicry. Reflection will not suffice. THE BODY MUST BURST FROM ITS BIOLOGICAL, CULTURAL, AND PLANETARY CONTAINMENT.

3. FREEDOM OF FORM: In this age of information overloads, what is significant is no longer freedom of ideas but rather freedom of form – freedom to modify and mutate the body. The question is not whether society will allow people freedom of expression but whether the human species will allow the individuals to construct alternate genetic coding. THE FUNDAMENTAL FREEDOM IS FOR INDIVIDUALS TO DETERMINE THEIR OWN DNA DESTINY. Biological change becomes a matter of choice rather than chance. EVOLUTION BY THE INDIVIDUAL, FOR THE INDIVIDUAL. Medical technologies that monitor, map and modify the body also provide the means to manipulate the structure of the body. When we attach or implant prosthetic devices to prolong a person's life, we also create the potential to propel post-evolutionary development – PATCHED-UP PEOPLE ARE POST-EVOLUTIONARY EXPERIMENTS.

4. BIOTECH TERRAINS: The body now inhabits alien environments that conceal countless BODY PACEMAKERS – visual and acoustical cues that *alert, activate, condition, and control the body.*

technological folly to consider the body obsolete in form and function: yet it might be the highest of human realizations. For it is only when the body becomes aware of its present position that it can map its post-evolutionary strategies. It is no longer a matter of perpetuating the human species by REPRODUCTION, but of enhancing male/female intercourse by human–machine interface. THE BODY IS OBSOLETE. We are at the end of philosophy and human physiology. Human thought recedes into the human past.

6. ABSENT BODIES: We mostly operate as Absent Bodies. That is because A BODY IS DESIGNED TO INTERFACE WITH ITS ENVIRONMENT – its sensors are open-to-the-world (compared to its inadequate internal surveillance system). The body's mobility and navigation in the world require this outward orientation. Its absence is augmented by the fact that the body functions *habitually* and *automatically.* AWARENESS IS OFTEN THAT WHICH OCCURS WHEN THE BODY MALFUNCTIONS. Reinforced by Cartesian convention, personal convenience and

Its circadian rhythms need to be augmented by artificial signals. Humans are now regulated in sync with swift, circulating rhythms of pulsing images. MORPHING IMAGES MAKE THE BODY OBSOLETE . . .

5. OBSOLETE BODY: It is time to question whether a bipedal, breathing body with binocular vision and a l400cc brain is an adequate biological form. It cannot cope with the quantity, complexity, and quality of information it has accumulated; it is intimidated by the precision, speed, and power of technology and it is biologically ill-equipped to cope with its new extraterrestrial environment. The body is neither a very efficient nor a very durable structure. It malfunctions often and fatigues quickly; its performance is determined by its age. It is susceptible to disease and is doomed to a certain and early death. Its survival parameters are very slim. It can survive only weeks without food, days without water, and minutes without oxygen. The body's LACK OF MODULAR DESIGN and its overreactive immunological system make it difficult to replace malfunctioning organs. It might be the height of

neurophysiological design, people operate merely as minds, immersed in metaphysical fogs. The sociologist P. L. Berger made the distinction between "having a body" and "being a body." AS SUPPOSED FREE AGENTS, THE CAPABILITIES OF BEING A BODY ARE CONSTRAINED BY HAVING A BODY. Our actions and ideas are essentially determined by our physiology. We are at the limits of philosophy, not only because we are at the limits of language. Philosophy is *fundamentally* grounded in our physiology . . .

7. REDESIGNING THE BODY/REDEFINING WHAT IS HUMAN. It is no longer meaningful to see the body as a site for the psyche or the social, but rather as a structure to be monitored and modified; the body not as a subject but as an object – NOT AS AN OBJECT OF DESIRE BUT AS AN OBJECT FOR DESIGNING. The psycho-social period was characterized by the body circling itself, *orbiting itself, illuminating and inspecting itself* by physical prodding and metaphysical contemplation. But having confronted its image of obsolescence, the body is traumatized to

split from the realm of subjectivity and consider the necessity of re-examining and possibly redesigning its very structure. ALTERING THE ARCHITECTURE OF THE BODY RESULTS IN ADJUSTING AND EXTENDING ITS AWARENESS OF THE WORLD. As an object, the body can be amplified and accelerated, attaining planetary escape velocity. It becomes a post-evolutionary projectile, *departing and diversifying* in form and function.

8. SURFACE AND SELF: As surface, skin was once the beginning of the world and simultaneously the boundary of the self. As interface, it was once the site of the collapse of the personal and the political. But now *stretched* and *penetrated* by machines, SKIN IS NO LONGER THE SMOOTH SENSUOUS SURFACE OF A SITE OR A SCREEN. Skin no longer signifies closure. The rupture of surfaces and of skin means the *erasure* of inner and outer. As interface, the skin is inadequate.

9. THE INVASION OF TECHNOLOGY: Miniaturized and biocompatible, technology lands on the body. Although unheralded, it is one of the most important events in human history, focusing physical

five body suspensions), determining the physical parameters and normal capabilities of the body, then the recent performances extend and enhance it visually and acoustically. Body processes amplified include brain waves (ECG), muscles (EMG), pulse (PLETHYSMOGRAM), and bloodflow (DOPPLER FLOW METER). Other transducers and sensors monitor limb motion and indicate body posture. The sound field is configured by buzzing, warbling, clicking, thumping, beeping, and whooshing sounds – of triggered, random, repetitive, and rhythmic signals. The artificial hand, attached to the right arm as an addition rather than a prosthetic replacement, is capable of independent motion, being activated by the EMG signals of the abdominal and leg muscles. It has a pinch-release, grasp-release, 270° wrist rotations (C.W. and C.C.W.), and a tactile feedback system for a rudimentary "sense of touch." While the body activates its extra manipulator, the real left arm is remote controlled – jerked into action by two muscle stimulators. Electrodes positioned on the flexor muscles and biceps curl the finger inward, bend the wrist, and thrust the arm upward. The

change on each individual. Technology is not only attached but is also implanted. ONCE A CONTAINER, TECHNOLOGY NOW BECOMES A COMPONENT OF THE BODY. As an instrument, technology fragmented and depersonalized experience – as a component it has the potential to SPLIT THE SPECIES. It is no longer of any advantage to either remain "human" or evolve as a species. EVOLUTION ENDS WHEN TECHNOLOGY INVADES THE BODY. Once technology provides each person with the potential to progress individually in its development, the cohesiveness of the species is no longer distinction but the body–species split. The significance of technology may be that it culminates in alternate awareness – one that is POST-HISTORIC, TRANSHUMAN and even EXTRATERRESTRIAL (the first signs of an alien intelligence may well come from this planet).

10. AMPLIFIED BODY, LASER EYES AND HAND: If the earlier events can be characterized as probing and piercing the body (the three films of the inside of the stomach, lungs, and colon/the twenty-

triggering of the arm motion paces the performance and the stimulator signals are used as sound sources as is the motor sound of the Third Hand mechanism. The body performs in a structured and interactive lighting installation which flickers and flares, responding and reacting to the electrical discharges of the body – sometimes synchronizing, sometimes counterpointing. Light is not treated as an external illumination of the body but as a manifestation of the body rhythms. The performance is a choreography of controlled, constrained, and involuntary motions – of internal rhythms and external gestures. It is an interplay between physiological control and electronic modulation, of human functions and machine enhancement.

11. THE SHEDDING OF SKIN: Off the Earth, the body's *complexity, softness, and wetness* would be difficult to sustain. The strategy should be to HOLLOW, HARDEN, and DEHYDRATE the body to make it more durable and less vulnerable. The present organization of the body is unnecessary. The solution to modifying the body is not to be found in its internal structure, but lies simply on its surface. The

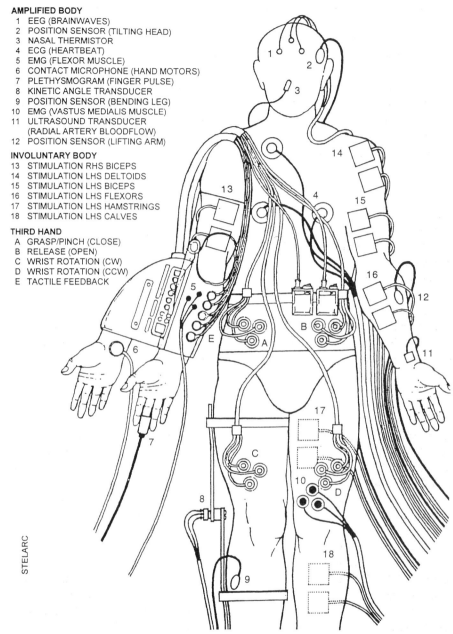

AMPLIFIED BODY
1   EEG (BRAINWAVES)
2   POSITION SENSOR (TILTING HEAD)
3   NASAL THERMISTOR
4   ECG (HEARTBEAT)
5   EMG (FLEXOR MUSCLE)
6   CONTACT MICROPHONE (HAND MOTORS)
7   PLETHYSMOGRAM (FINGER PULSE)
8   KINETIC ANGLE TRANSDUCER
9   POSITION SENSOR (BENDING LEG)
10 EMG (VASTUS MEDIALIS MUSCLE)
11 ULTRASOUND TRANSDUCER
     (RADIAL ARTERY BLOODFLOW)
12 POSITION SENSOR (LIFTING ARM)

INVOLUNTARY BODY
13 STIMULATION RHS BICEPS
14 STIMULATION LHS DELTOIDS
15 STIMULATION LHS BICEPS
16 STIMULATION LHS FLEXORS
17 STIMULATION LHS HAMSTRINGS
18 STIMULATION LHS CALVES

THIRD HAND
A   GRASP/PINCH (CLOSE)
B   RELEASE (OPEN)
C   WRIST ROTATION (CW)
D   WRIST ROTATION (CCW)
E   TACTILE FEEDBACK

STELARC

INVOLUNTARY BODY / THIRD HAND

Figure 5   Amplified body/third hand. The mechanism was constructed to the size of the right hand with stainless steel, Duralamin, aluminium, acrylic, and electronic circuitry. It has a pinch-release, grasp-release, a 270° wrist rotation and a tactile feedback system for a sense of touch. This can be visually monitored by the LED display or felt as an electrical stimulation. Although not worn for performances, the cosmetic cover was cast to cover and protect the tactile sensors and to provide friction for gripping. The third hand was initially designed as a semi-permanent attachment to the body. It is actuated by EMG signals for the abdominal and leg muscles. The hand mechanism, support structure and battery pack weigh 1.5 kg.

SOLUTION IS NO MORE THAN SKIN DEEP. The significant event in our evolutionary history was a change in the mode of locomotion. Future developments will occur with a *change of skin*. If we could engineer a SYNTHETIC SKIN which could absorb oxygen directly through its pores and could efficiently convert light into chemical nutrients, we could radically redesign the body, eliminating many of its redundant systems and malfunctioning organs, minimizing toxin build-up in its chemistry. THE HOLLOW BODY WOULD BE A BETTER HOST FOR TECHNOLOGICAL COMPONENTS.

12. STOMACH SCULPTURE: HOLLOW BODY/HOST SPACE: The intention has been to design a sculpture for a distended stomach. The idea was to insert an art work into the body – *to situate the sculpture in an internal space.* The body becomes hollow with no meaningful distinctions between public, private, and physiological spaces. TECHNOLOGY INVADES AND FUNCTIONS WITHIN THE BODY NOT AS A PROSTHETIC REPLACEMENT, BUT AS AN ESTHETIC ADORNMENT. The structure is collapsed into a

interacting energy chain and protective biosphere – the body is biologically ill-equipped, not only in terms of its sheer survival, but also in its inability adequately to perceive and perform in the immensity of outer space. Rather THAN developing *specialist bodies for specific sites*, we should consider a pan-planetary physiology that is durable, flexible, and capable of functioning in varying atmospheric conditions, gravitational pressures, and electro-magnetic fields.

14. NO BIRTH/NO DEATH – THE HUM OF THE HYBRID: Technology transforms the nature of human existence, equalizing the physical potential of bodies and standardizing human sexuality. With fertilization now occurring outside the womb and the possibility of nurturing the fetus in an artificial support system THERE WILL TECHNICALLY BE NO BIRTH. And if the body can be redesigned in a modular fashion to facilitate the replacement of malfunctioning parts, then TECHNICALLY THERE WOULD BE NO REASON FOR DEATH – given the accessibility of replacements. Death does not authenticate existence. *It is an outmoded*

capsule 50mm × 14mm, and tethered to its control box it is swallowed and inserted into the stomach. The stomach is *inflated* with air using an endoscope. A *logic circuit* board and a *servomotor* open the sculpture using a flexi-drive cable to 80mm × 50mm in size. A piezo-buzzer beeps in sync to a light globe blinking inside the stomach. The sculpture is an extending/retracting structure, sound-emitting and self-illuminating. (It is fabricated using implant-quality metals such as titanium, stainless steel, silver, and gold.) The sculpture is retracted into its capsule form to be removed. As a body, one no longer looks at art, doesn't perform art, but contains art. THE HOLLOW BODY BECOMES A HOST, NOT FOR A SELF OR A SOUL, BUT SIMPLY FOR A SCULPTURE.

13. PAN-PLANETARY PHYSIOLOGY. Extraterrestrial environments amplify the body's obsolescence, intensifying pressures for its re-engineering. There is a necessity TO DESIGN A MORE SELF-CONTAINED, ENERGY-EFFICIENT BODY, WITH EXTENDED SENSORY ANTENNAE AND AUGMENTED CEREBRAL CAPACITY. Unplugged from this planet – from its complexity,

evolutionary strategy. The body need no longer be repaired but simply have parts replaced. Extending life no longer means "existing" but rather being "operational." Bodies need not age or deteriorate; they would not run down nor even fatigue; they would stall then start – possessing both the potential for renewal and reactivation. In the extended space–time of extraterrestrial environments, THE BODY MUST BECOME IMMORTAL TO ADAPT. Utopian dreams become post-evolutionary imperatives. THIS IS NO MERE FAUSTIAN OPTION NOR SHOULD THERE BE ANY FRANKENSTEINIAN FEAR OF TAMPERING WITH THE BODY.

15. THE ANAESTHETIZED BODY: The importance of technology is not simply in the pure power it generates but in the *realm of abstraction* it produces through its *operational speed* and its development of *extended sense systems*. Technology pacifies the body and the world. It disconnects the body from many of its functions. DISTRAUGHT AND DISCONNECTED, THE BODY CAN ONLY RESORT TO INTERFACE AND SYMBIOSIS. The

body may not yet surrender its autonomy but certainly its mobility. The body plugged into some machine network needs to be pacified. In fact, to function in the future and to achieve truly a hybrid symbiosis the body will need to be increasingly anaesthetized.

16. SPLIT BODY: VOLTAGE-IN/VOLTAGE-OUT: Given that a body is not in a hazardous location, there would be reasons to remote-actuate a person, or part of a person, rather than a robot. An activated arm would be connected to an intelligent mobile body with another free arm to augment its task! Technology now allows you to be physically moved by another mind. A computer interfaced MULTIPLE-MUSCLE STIMULATOR makes possible the complex programming of either in a local place or in a remote location. Part of your body would be moving; you've neither willed it to move, nor are you internally contracting your muscles to produce that movement. The issue would not be to automate a body's movement but rather the system would enable the displacement of a physical action from one body to another body in another place – for the on-line completion of a real-time task or the

Cyberbody bristles with electrodes and antennae, amplifying its capabilities and projecting its presence to remote locations and into virtual spaces. The Cyberbody becomes an extended system – not merely to sustain a self, but to enhance operation and initiate alternate intelligent systems.

18. HYBRID HUMAN–MACHINE SYSTEMS. The problem with space travel is no longer with the precision and reliability of technology but with the vulnerability and durability of the human body. In fact, it is now time to REDESIGN HUMANS, TO MAKE THEM MORE COMPATIBLE WITH THEIR MACHINES. It is not merely a matter of "mechanizing" the body. It becomes apparent that in the zero-G, frictionless, and oxygen-free environment of outer space technology is even more durable and functions more efficiently than on Earth. It is the human component that has to be sustained and also protected from small changes of pressure, temperature, and radiation. The issue is HOW TO MAINTAIN HUMAN PERFORMANCE OVER EXTENDED PERIODS OF TIME. *Symbiotic systems seem the best strategy; implanted components can*

conditioning of a transmitted skill. There would be new interactive possibilities between bodies. A touch-screen interface would allow programming by *pressing* the muscle sites on the computer model and/or by retrieving and *pasting* from a library of gestures. Simulation of the movement can be examined before transmission and actuation. THE REMOTELY ACTUATED BODY WOULD BE SPLIT – on the one side voltage directed to the muscles via stimulator pads for involuntary movement – on the other side electrodes pick up internal signals, allowing the body to be interfaced to a Third Hand and other peripheral devices. THE BODY BECOMES A SITE BOTH FOR INPUT AND OUTPUT.

17. PSYCHO/CYBER: THE PSYCHOBODY is neither robust nor reliable. Its genetic code produces a body that malfunctions often and fatigues quickly, allowing only slim survival parameters and limiting its longevity. Its carbon chemistry GENERATES OUTMODED EMOTIONS. *The Psychobody is schizophrenic.* THE CYBERBODY is not a subject, but an object – not an object of envy but an object for engineering. THE

energize and amplify developments; exoskeletons can power the body; robotic structures can become hosts for a body insert.

19. INTERNAL/INVISIBLE: It is time to recolonize the body with MICRO-MINIATURIZED ROBOTS to augment our bacterial population, to assist our immunological system and to monitor the capillary and internal tracts of the body. There is a necessity for the body to possess an INTERNAL SURVEILLANCE SYSTEM. Symptoms surface too late! The internal environment of the body would to a large extent contour the microbot's behavior, thereby triggering particular tasks. Temperature, blood chemistry, the softness or hardness of tissue, and the presence of obstacles in tracts could all be primary indications of problems that would signal the microbots into action. *The biocompatibility of technology is no longer due to its substance but rather to its scale.* THE SPECK-SIZED ROBOTS ARE EASILY SWALLOWED, AND MAY NOT EVEN BE SENSED! At some nanotechnology level machines will inhabit cellular spaces and manipulate molecular structures. . . . The trauma of

repairing damaged bodies or even of redesigning bodies would be eliminated by a colony of nanobots delicately altering the body's architecture atoms-up, inside out.

20. TOWARD HIGH-FIDELITY ILLUSION: With teleoperation systems, it is possible to project human presence and perform physical actions in remote and extraterrestrial locations. A single operator could direct a colony of robots in different locations simultaneously or scattered human experts might collectively control a particular surrogate robot. Teleoperation systems would have to be more than hand-eye mechanisms. They would have to create kinesthetic feel, providing, sensations of orientation, motion, and body tension. Robots would have to be semi-autonomous, capable of "intelligent disobedience." With *Teleautomation* (Conway/Voz/Walker), forward simulation – with time and position clutches – assists in overcoming the problem of real time-delays, allowing prediction to improve performance. The experience of Telepresence (Minsky) becomes the high-fidelity illusion of *Tele-existence* (Tachi). ELECTRONIC

arm, and *cloning* or calling up an extra arm. The *record and playback* function allows the sampling and looping of motion sequences. A *clutch* command enables the operator to freeze the arm, disengaging the simulating hand. For teleoperation systems, features such as *locking* allow the fixing of the limb in position for PRECISE OPERATION WITH THE HAND. In *micro mode* complex commands can be generated with a single gesture, and in *fine control* delicate tasks can be completed by THE TRANSFORMATION OF LARGE OPERATOR MOVEMENTS TO SMALL MOVEMENTS OF THE VIRTUAL ARM.

22. IMAGES AS OPERATIONAL AGENTS: Plugged into Virtual Reality technology, physical bodies are transduced into phantom entities capable of performing within data and digital spaces. The nature of both bodies and images has been significantly altered. IMAGES ARE NO LONGER ILLUSORY WHEN THEY BECOME INTERACTIVE. In fact, interactive images become operational and effective agents sustained in software and transmission systems. The body's representation

SPACE BECOMES A MEDIUM OF ACTION RATHER THAN INFORMATION. It meshes the body with its machines in ever-increasing complexity and interactiveness. The body's form is enhanced and its functions are extended. ITS PERFORMANCE PARAMETERS ARE LIMITED NEITHER BY ITS PHYSIOLOGY NOR BY THE LOCAL SPACE IT OCCUPIES.

21. PHANTOM LIMB/VIRTUAL ARM: Amputees often experience a phantom limb. It is now possible to have a phantom sensation of an additional arm – a virtual arm – albeit visual rather than visceral. The Virtual Arm is a computer-generated, human-like universal manipulator interactively controlled by VPL Virtual Reality equipment. Using data gloves with flexion and position-orientation sensors and a GESTURE-BASED COMMAND LANGUAGE allows real-time intuitive operation and additional extended capabilities. Functions are mapped to finger gestures, with parameters for each function, allowing elaboration. Some of the Virtual Arm's extended capabilities include *stretching* or telescoping of limb and finger segments, *grafting* of extra hands on the

becomes capable of response as images become imbued with intelligence. Sensors and trackers on the body make it a capture system for its image. The body is coupled to mobilize its phantom. A virtual or Phantom Body can be endowed with semi-autonomous abilities, enhanced functions, and artificial intelligence. Phantoms can manipulate data and perform with other phantoms in Cyberspace. PHYSICAL BODIES HAVE ORGANS. PHANTOM BODIES ARE HOLLOW. Physical bodies are ponderous and particular. Phantom bodies are flexible and fluid. Phantoms project and power the body.

23. VIRTUAL BODY: ACTUATE/ROTATE: Your virtual surrogate would not merely mimic the physical body's movements. A complex choreography is achieved by mapping virtual camera views to limb position/orientation. The involuntary jerking up and down of the left arm tumbles the virtual body while sweeping the right arm 90° produces a 360° virtual camera scan – visually rotating the virtual body around its vertical axis. The form of the virtual body can be configured acoustically – pulsing in phases

with breathing sounds. This BREATH WARPING subtly and structurally connects the physical body with its virtual other. And by using DEPTH CUE – defining the operational virtual space as shallow – stepping and swaying forwards and backwards makes the virtual body appear and disappear in its video/virtual environment. The resulting interaction between the physical body and its phantom form becomes a more complex combination of kinestheic and kinematic choreography. In recent performances the *involuntary body* is actuating a *virtual body* while simultaneously avoiding a *programmed robot* within its task envelope . . .

24. PHANTOM BODY/FLUID SELF: Technologies are becoming better life-support systems for our images than for our bodies. IMAGES ARE IMMORTAL. BODIES ARE EPHEMERAL. The body finds it increasingly difficult to match the expectations of its images. In the realm of multiplying and morphing images, the physical body's impotence is apparent. THE BODY NOW PERFORMS BEST AS ITS IMAGE. Virtual Reality technology allows a transgression of boundaries between male/female,

123

human/machine, time/space. The self becomes situated beyond the skin. This is not disconnecting or a splitting but an EXTRUDING OF AWARENESS. What it means to be human is no longer being immersed in genetic memory but in being reconfigured in the electromagnetic field of the circuit IN THE REALM OF THE IMAGE.

25. ARTIFICIAL INTELLIGENCE /ALTERNATE EXISTENCE: The first signs of artificial life may well come from this planet in the guise of images. ARTIFICIAL INTELLIGENCE WILL NO LONGER MEAN EXPERT SYSTEMS OPERATING WITHIN SPECIFIC TASK DOMAINS. Electronic space generates intelligent and autonomous images that extend and enhance the body's operational parameters beyond its mere physiology and the local space it occupies. What results is a meshing of the body with its images and machines in ever-increasing complexity. The significance of interfacing with is that they culminate in an ALTERNATE AWARENESS THAT IS PAN-HISTORIC AND POST-HUMAN.

Postscript: Ground Zero

Joan Broadhurst Dixon

Technology, more successfully than anything you will find in here, is destructing and reconstructing our cartographies of thought. If folk psychology were ever to face its nemesis, then it has already done so in technology. The delicacies of its semantically coherent systems, quaintly obsolete as the agent, his intentions, his desires, his beliefs are consigned to the graveyard for redundant theories. It is of no surprise that eliminative materialism has finally become a viable argument with the advent of the

of inside and outside. Such disjunctions have facilitated a definition of responsibility, its agents, that is, its institutions: the Army, the Law, the Family, the Person. These occidental icons represent an ethics created for us by a mode of production inseparable from Western conceptions of man. This bedrock of society is historical and contingent on their regime.

As the French philosopher Gilles Deleuze noted, identity is historical and contingent on the particular regime in power. Historically, the regime has functioned as a quasi-transcendental structure that redounds upon (*se rabattre sur*) its materials to make its institutions as if they were natural, organic byproducts. The structures that were necessary for the modes of production acquire perceived integrity, as though they would always exist in their own right. We forget in advance the material history and the shifting geography of concepts. The individual *qua* individual is an integrated part of the cosmology of production, a part which is prescribed by technology – its needs, not ours. It has no specific unity independent of its integration within the cycle of production. If capitalism as the apotheosis of

neuro-computational model. Technology (genetic *sive* computer engineering) does not render the agent obsolete; instead, it is the agent as defined that fades into oblivion. It is as though we have failed to register that our theories and terms are as much historical and revisable as those technologies which constitute them.

Agency is a technological term. The intellectual baggage that the term carries with it implies ethics – but as Spinoza was the first to point out, ethics are always partial, local, and strategic. We have always misunderstood that point. Agent, individuals, bodies – there is nothing natural about any of them. Nature and industry were always an illegitimate if not exclusive disjunction.

Ethics has been about integrity, but that integrity has always been misconstrued. Historically, the term has been functioning as an ethics of objective boundaries – hard, impenetrable, protective, disclosures of sacred territories that demarcated the European identity. The state, the city wall, the home, the skin, have all, in their time, represented limits of authority and privacy, denoting a relationship

technology, in the beginning, required workers with personal needs, dreams, and desires, that is what it created: a division of labour fuelled by the illusion of personal achievement; a Protestant work ethic for sure-fire salvation. Being able to act, to wish to change things – agency is a technologically produced category.

Theory reflects the requirements of the age. The Hobbesian state of nature, Rousseau's noble savage are anthropomorphic thought experiments. There was never some idyllic ur-time when a man with his hammer could be in some pre-theoretic involvement-in-the-world. Technology and its regimes constructed humanity, and it was a mistake if we ever thought it was the other way around. The use-value of humanity, whether it is as "the shepherd of Being" (Heidegger) or the "eternal custodian of the machines" (Deleuze and Guattari) has long passed its best-before date. And it is of no surprise that as these traditional categories disintegrate, our theories become ones of disintegration.

Techno-paranoia is symptomatic of our redundancy. Even those seemingly a priori guarantors of our human integrity, space and time, are coming under attack. Cyberspace, Virilio claimed, is leading to a loss of our understanding of subject and objects. Its absolute transitivity is resulting in the disintegration of property and real estate. We are losing touch with our bodies, our human physical dimensions, and with it, our meaty morality (or ethics). The "real," "natural," and "human" dimensions of space and time that were meant to structure our experience have collapsed into the single dimension of speed. Technology has torn us away from sidereal time and circadian rhythms – the daylight which marked our "natural" temporality. We now have an "artificial" electronic day of information commutation, undermining our sense of direction, observation, and common sense. Technology is restructuring the tempo of our society.

Cyberspace–time (subject to bandwidth problems which are technical, not a priori) is instantaneous. Distance is defined by bytes per second. Global location and time zones become curiously antiquated terms. As Virilio put it, we live in "the instantaneity of ubiquity." Nano-seconds, pico-

But when faced with split-second influxes of information, our sluggish sensory-motor systems face an increasingly derealised environment. We can no longer react or adapt. Virilio was right to call it a "pure intellectual and conceptual warfare." Speed undermines our faculty of agency, reducing us to the fate of impotent observers. The desire for speed is capitalism's most potent addiction, and technology is hooked if humans are not. Speed is a drug, and the desire to get quit is the Chronic illness which riddles humanity alone. Following Sun Tzu, those who move fastest live longest. If speed is the essence of war, and technology is the enemy, then we are already dead.

seconds, femto-seconds . . . our ancient referents of a measurement and traditional macro-scale standards become pathetically insufficient. The earth becomes inaccurate with the introduction of atomic clocks, and electronic clocks and eyes replace Olympic judges who, being human, sadly weren't up to the task. Our traditional dimensions, in cyberspace, become some frictionless, timeless medium. Speed is of the essence.

To criticize technology's denaturing tendencies is the ultimate in philosophical naïvety. To argue that the natural structures are being usurped by the constructs of "our" technologies, as if this had not always been the case, resists the fact that all reality, human or otherwise, takes place within technical parameters. The problem concerning humanity is often couched in terms of a loss of control. Consider the paranoia of losing our executive power over computers. Sam and Ivan go AWOL. We comfort ourselves with reassuring sci-fi fables that, in the end, at the last second, we could intervene and once again the human would triumph: a myth perpetuated.